By Land and By Sea: Studies in the Folklore of Work and Leisure

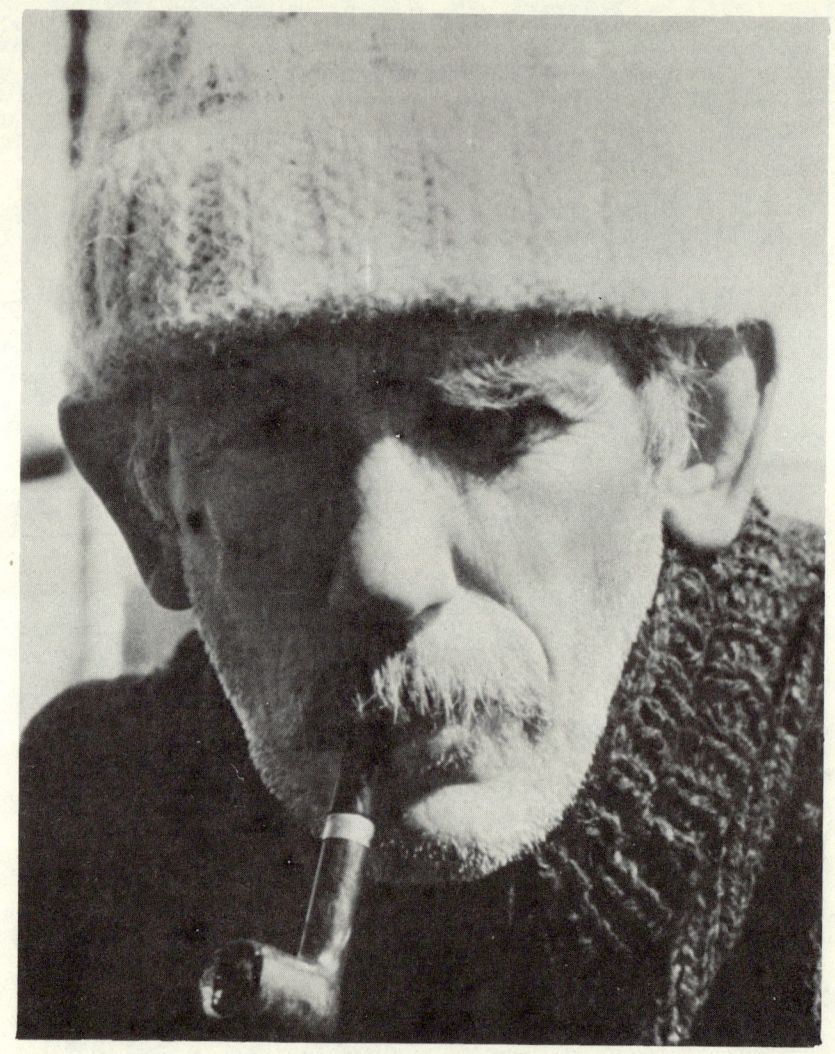

HORACE P. BECK

Jane C. Beck

By Land and By Sea: Studies in the Folklore of Work and Leisure
Honoring
Horace P. Beck
on his
Sixty-Fifth Birthday

Edited by
Roger D. Abrahams
Kenneth S. Goldstein and Wayland D. Hand
with the assistance of
Maggie Craig

LEGACY BOOKS
Hatboro, Pennsylvania
1985

Copyright © 1985 by Legacy Books

All rights reserved under International
and Pan American Copyright Conventions

LIBRARY OF CONGRESS CATALOG CARD NO: 85-80879

ISBN: 0-913714-68-2

MANUFACTURED IN THE UNITED STATES OF AMERICA

TABLE OF CONTENTS

DEDICATION vii

AFRO-AMERICAN WORKSONGS ON LAND AND SEA
Roger D. Abrahams 1

HILDA, WOMAN OF DREAMS
Jane C. Beck 10

FARM FOLKLIFE IN WOOD: JEHU F. CAMPER, DELAWARE WHITTLER
Robert D. Bethke 20

TUGBOATING ON THE CAPE FEAR RIVER: A PRELIMINARY ETHNOGRAPHIC SKETCH
Robert H. Byington 32

"FAMILY YACHT"
George Carey 46

HOBART AMORY HARE BAKER— OCCUPATION: GENTLEMAN ATHLETE
Tristram Potter Coffin 55

THE WOOD FAMILY OF PHILADELPHIA: FOUR GENERATIONS OF STONECARVING
J. Joseph Edgette 69

FOLKSONG AS A REFLECTION OF THE SHANTYBOYS' LIFE
Edith Fowke 77

FAITH AND FATE IN SEA DISASTER BALLADS OF NEWFOUNDLAND FISHERMEN
Kenneth S. Goldstein 84

SINGLEJACK / DOUBLEJACK:
CRAFT AND CELEBRATION
Archie Green 95

TOM PEPPER: THE BIGGEST LIAR
ON LAND OR SEA
Herbert Halpert and *Violetta M. Halpert* 112

THE FOLK BELIEFS AND CUSTOMS
OF SAN PEDRO'S FISHERMEN
Wayland D. Hand................................... 121

"THE MAN WHO PLUCKED THE GORBEY":
A MAINE WOODS LEGEND DEBATED IN
SLOW MOTION
Edward D. Ives 137

CRAFTING THE MODEL: MAINE LOBSTERBOAT
BUILDING AS A DESIGN TRADITION
Richard Lunt...................................... 141

METHODS OF CATCHING MARINE EELS
IN THE GILBERT ISLANDS (KIRIBATI)
Katharine Luomala................................. 167

ANY OLD PORT IN A STORM:
SEA WORDS GONE AGROUND
W. Edson Richmond 190

BELIEF PERFORMANCES ALONG
THE PACIFIC NORTHWEST COAST
Barre Toelken 201

THE GALLOPING GOURMET, OR
THE CHUCK WAGON COOK AND HIS CRAFT
John O. West..................................... 215

DEDICATION

FOLKLORISTS ARE RARELY AS COLORFUL AS THEIR INFORMANTS. Even more unusual is the phenomenon of a scholar in occupational folklore, medical doctors excepted, with actual working experience in a trade or occupation. Horace Beck is a maverick on both counts. Ruggedly handsome, straight spoken and by turns profane, with a lot of the Yankee rebel still in him, Beck might readily be taken for a sturdy seafarer from the time of our country's great sailing ships. In the drawing room and on formal occasions, however, his fine prep school education and academic polish come through, with frequent evidences of a stern New England upbringing.

In keeping with his practical training from earliest youth, Horace Beck learned most of his knowledge of seafaring from the ground up. Even as a stripling he worked on commercial fishing vessels. Doing a man's work side by side with the last of the old-time seafarers, he learned to read the sea and wind without the aid of modern navigational instruments. Even in those days many craft, actually, were without propulsive engines of any kind. In the years that followed these earliest exploits at sea he probably learned more about the life of fishermen and sailors from actual day-by-day experience on boats and around wharves and ship chandleries than he did from a lifetime of reading on maritime lore. This blend of theory and practice comes through best on the lecture platform, of course, where Beck allows his practical experience as a sailor to serve as a moderating force and even as an effective counterpoise to all of the notions of adventure and romance gained by resort to the printed page. With the sea itself as a mighty canvas and the lore and fables of countless generations as a backdrop, Beck talks wistfully, and with wit and humor, about the life and work of fishermen and mariners and on the folklore of the sea and sailors. Well into such a lecture, when with expert technical knowledge he begins to talk about the building and outfitting of old ships, or when, with jaw pointed out to sea, he discourses on marlinespike seamanship while casually casting a few hitches or tying a bowline, a carrick bend, or even a hangman's noose, Beck almost magically carries his audience back to the days of Frobisher, Marryat, Melville, and Richard Henry Dana.

The foundation for Beck's academic career was laid at the distinguished St. George's prep school at Newport, Rhode Island, where young Horace spent six eventful years, 1933-1939. A broad general education, embracing both science and letters, readied him for his collegiate training. By the time he received his A.B. degree at the University of Pennsylvania in 1943, Beck, now only twenty-three, already had a good grounding in American history and literature and had only recently discovered the burgeoning field of folklore. Coming under the tutelage of the great MacEdward Leach proved to be the crowning event of Beck's career. This famous folklorist, shored up by work in medieval literature and philology, helped to broaden and deepen Horace's grasp of literary studies and gave him a firm purchase on the tools of scholarship. Over and above this, however, came the whole new revelation of folklore and a strengthened appreciation of our country's common culture. In the interdisciplinary approach to the study of the American experience that was starting to permeate graduate education in this country, it became *de rigueur* to fit adventure and romance from the pages of Irving, Cooper, Hawthorne, Whittier, Longfellow, Melville, Poe, and many another into the full matrix of American cultural history. Adding to this impressive armamentarium of American studies, Beck began to read the classics of European and American folklore and the great books on ships and the history and folklore of the sea and sailing, among them, Falconer, Sébillot, the Bassetts, Gregor, Hadfield, Colcord, Rappoport, Morison, Cutler, Nordhoff, Anson. To these names should be added those of numerous sea captains and old salts who have written books chronicling life at sea. He not only puzzled over ship's logs, read all he could find about shipwrecks and phantom vessels, but also read extensively about privateering and piracy. Naval history, too, became a part of this ample library regimen. A stint in the Pacific on a Navy LST craft during World War II gave added meaning to Beck's reading. Whaling, likewise, laid hold of Beck's mind, and in the 1970s he plunged headlong into a study of this dwindling tradition of the sea. Once more, as we shall see later, field work went hand in hand with his library study.

By the time of his own intellectual flowering Horace Beck had already become an owner of boats and an accomplished sailor. Highlights of these early sea adventures, that were later to include voyages to many parts of the western world, were sailings with MacEdward Leach to the North Atlantic and a collecting trip on land in the Caribbean. As a special experience for his mentor, navigation with Leach was only by compass, sextant, and by the stars. The intimate friendship between Horace and Mac was built not only in the classroom, in consultation sessions, and on numerous field trips, but it grew from the trials these two faced in ordeals before the mast off the New England coast. Early testament of this saga of master and apprentice came in 1962 when Beck edited an excellent Festschrift for his mentor, *Folklore in Action: Essays for Discussion in Honor of MacEdward Leach.*

Another formative hand in Beck's development was Pennsylvania's noted anthropologist Frank Speck. Field trips with Speck gave his young protégé a good grounding in fieldwork and led to a lasting interest in the folklore of a number of Indian tribes in Eastern seaboard states. These collecting trips resulted in several articles and lesser sketches on American Indian folklore and in two book-length treatises: *The American Indian as a Seafighter in Colonial Times* (1959) and *Gluscap, The Liar* (1966). Speck's untimely death kept Beck from a deeper academic commitment to anthropology.

Leach and Speck set Horace ablaze with scholarly zeal, but even more valuable were their living tutorials in self reliance and the building of inner resources and staying power. Horace had already learned selfdependence from his father, a noted Newport eye, ear, nose and throat specialist, who insisted that his son learn hard work and manual dexterity to go along with an analytic mind and quick spirit. On the family farm at Tiverton near Newport, for example, young Beck was expected to deal with the daily problems of farm life as well as with long-range planning demanded by the change of seasons. Rapid change in weather, but particularly the harsh New England winters, steeled the young toiler of the soil for the vagaries of weather which he was later to experience many times at sea. Hard work and natural sagacity are the unfailing resources that have pulled Horace Beck through physical and spiritual crisis on more occasions than one. It was in this rural New England setting at Tiverton, too, that young Horace absorbed his first local folklore. To his mother's fine collection of Indian artifacts were added a number of local legends and popular antiquities, including accounts of buried treasure and ghost stories.

The marriage of Horace (his second) with Jane Choate in 1965 opened up a whole new life and brought inner strength and fortification. Jane Beck had also been a student of Leach. She shared Horace's world, bore him two fine children, supported his studies, and even became a sailor in her own right. In the 1970s Beck became interested in the whaling complex in Bequia, British West Indies. With the help of Jane, who stood by not only with recorder and camera but with much practical advice stemming from many years experience as a journeyman folklorist, he spent the next ten years documenting this bio-ecological system under its most primitive conditions. This preoccupation with the leviathans of the deep ultimately took the Becks to South Sea waters and the Kingdom of

Tonga in 1978. It was in Pacific waters that Horace met Albert Cook, master whaler—captain and harpooner—who, in many interviews, revealed the intimate rituals of South Pacific shore whaling. Books on this most recent phase of the Becks' work are now in the making.

The formal aspects of Beck's career are easily sketched. Conferral of the doctorate at Penn, with a dissertation on *Down-East Ballads and Songs* occurred in 1952. After serving two years as an instructor in English at his alma mater while he was still a graduate student, Beck went to Temple University in American literature and folklore for an eight-year tour of duty, 1948–1956. Then he heeded a call to Middlebury College where he taught American Literature and Folklore until his retirement in 1983. At Middlebury he was for many years curator of the Helen Hartness Flanders Collection of New England Folk Song, serving also for a time as acting head of the school's program in American literature.

Beck became a leader in New England folklore circles and belonged to various state and regional folklore societies and to the American Folklore Society, of which he became a fellow in 1968. He also belongs to the Massachusetts Marine Associates, and to other organizations on both sides of the Atlantic devoted to the history of the sea and sailing.

Horace Beck's writings range over many areas of folklore, often involving the equities of both literature and history. Less than a decade out of graduate school he proved himself a full folklore practitioner with a general book on the *Folklore of Maine* which appeared under the Lippincott imprint in 1957. (His writings on American Indian folklore have already been noted.) Beck's *magnum opus, Folklore and the Sea,* was brought out in 1973 by the Wesleyan University Press for the Marine Historical Association, Inc., and Mystic Seaport. It is a classic work that could only have been written after a lifetime of reading and devotion to the scholarship of the sea and the life of sailors. This is the book to which the neophyte and seasoned worker alike must turn for the flavor of maritime life as well as for its substance. The long bibliography in *Folklore and the Sea* opens up the field of study as no book before it in English had ever done. It is a volume that should grace the shelves of anyone interested in occupational folklore and in the cultural history of work in the English-speaking world.

Horace Beck comes as close as anyone we know to being an honest to goodness American original. Because of his almost stubborn Yankee independence, Beck is not likely to be caught up in the cant and jargon of the day, nor to be found baying with the hounds and running with the wolves. It is to him, then, a gentleman and a scholar, and yet a hardy son of the sea, and to him, a man of great heart and kidney, that we affectionately dedicate this series of essays on occupational folklore written by his students and colleagues.

AFRO-AMERICAN WORKSONGS ON LAND AND SEA

Roger D. Abrahams
University of Pennsylvania

IN ONE OF THE MORE STIRRING movie scenes in recent memory, in *Witness*, we are given a long-view shot of the members of an Amish farming community in Pennsylvania swarming across the sun-ripe fields of wheat, various carpenter's tools in hand, coming together for a barn-raising. Such events calling for labor in common provide the strongest reminders of the cooperative potential of "the world we have lost" in retreating from the small community. Perhaps only the sea shanty scenes staged by A. L. Lloyd for the movie of *Moby Dick* have more successfully captured the sheer joy erupting as energies are coordinated to get a job done, Lloyd having himself been involved in honest maritime labor as a young man.

As Horace Beck noted in his *chef d'oeuvre, Folklore and the Sea*, such shantying is still done as a way of coordinating work only throughout the West Indies, "where the wind nearly always blows and almost always from the same quarter . . . [and where there is] a great deal of labor that still requires gang effort."[1]

Here, as Beck notices, the songs are used in relation to a great many tasks, only some of which are related to the sea trades. Moreover, we can recognize their parentage primarily by their repeated lines sung in chorus: "Yankee John, Stormalong," "Johnny come down with a Hilo," "Blow the man down": in the West Indies, "their words have a strong flavor of local attitudes and environment."[2]

Songs called shanties are found in association with coordinated work activities throughout anglophonic Afro-America from Trinidad and Tobago, Providencia and Belize to the mainland United States. To be sure, as Horace and others have shown, such singing is a tradition which found its true place on the great working ships, especially those sailing the great whale-fishing grounds. But the form and the style arose in subsaharan Africa, where it is still regarded as a necessary accompaniment to any expenditure of energy, in work or in play, when the community is brought together in common endeavor.

In the great hoe gardening traditions of the African savannahs, this antiphonal song form calls people together and unites them as it gives opportunity to each voice, each body, to enter individually into the spirited intertwining of community. This great surge of voices, initiated by a voice of enlarged authority, epitomizes the special blend of invention and tradition that characterizes any large expenditure of energy throughout the Black World, on both sides of the Atlantic.

Alan Lomax describes this style with great economy: "choral and antiphonal, with the characteristic use of overlap so that at least two parts are frequently active at the same time. . . . the overall impact of the African style is multileveled, multiparted, highly integrated, multitextured, gregarious, and playful voiced. . . ."[3]

Throughout Afro-America, in both historical and contemporary records, one finds precisely this same combination of voice overlap, interlock, and 'apart-playing': that is, the establishment of vocal lines sung by individuals that weave in and out of each other, first one singer taking precedence and then another, each one underscoring an independent status by drawing on different timbres and pitch-placement, yet all entering into the ensemble effort, their voices and actions interlocked though their relationship with the master-pulse system, or what Lomax calls a "rock-steady beat." The overlapping quality emerges especially strongly in the shanty, for here, while the single voice of the shantyman instigates the singing, the others enter into the singing before the line of the leader is ended.

The shanty was taken up in the sea trades when sailors of every complexion became members of the crew of working ships, in all probability by the use of West Indians as shantymen.[4] But even a casual survey of the work songs of the slaves indicates that while specific songs were associated with special activities on board, they found other uses on other work and play occasions. Indeed, the first shanty from the international repertoire I ever heard was on land, on the West Indian Leeward Island of Nevis, where "Do, my Jolly Boys" was used as a house-moving song.[5] Similarly, Dena Epstein provides an example of the widely known "Fire Down Below" from 1851, "almost invariably sung by negroes when they have anything to do with or about a fire, whether it be working at a New Orleans fire engine or crowding wood into the furnaces of a steamboat. . . ."[6] And the song I found most often throughout the anglophonic Caribbean, used both in pulling work (such as getting boats out of water, or hauling a copper pot from one place to another) and as a game-song, was "Johnny Come Down with a Hilo":

> The poor old man he sick in bed,
> He want somebody to 'nint his head,
> Johnny come down with a hilo,
> Poor old man.

In earlier works commenting on traditional expressive activities of the slave in the West Indies, I have surveyed the nineteenth century travel reports of shantying.[7] In the United States, a great many further reports of such antiphonal work and game-songs may be found. Ironically, that the slaves sang while carrying out their tasks was seen as an indication that they had accommodated themselves to the system of forced labor—for now the apologists for slavery could argue that they were happy with their lot. Moreover, not a few observers interpreted the interactive element of the singing and working style as playful conflict, on the model of a game, describing scenes which alternate between working, singing, dancing, and contests. Here, for instance, is the popular regional novelist, James Lane Allen, on the subject:

> It was "Uncle Tom's" duty to get the others off to work in the morning. In the fields he did not drive the work, but led it . . . led the cradles and the reaping hooks, the hemp-breaking and the cornshucking. The spirit of happy music went with the workers. . . . Nothing was more common than their voluntary contests of skill and power. . . . Rival hemp-breakers of the neighborhood, meeting in the same field, would slip out long before breakfast and sometimes never stop till dinner. So it was with cradling, cornshucking or corn-cutting.[8]

But before the Civil War, such singing was used in the argument against slavery by abolitionist observers, underscoring the "plaintive sounds" of the group singing, especially as the work-crew, or "coffle gangs" went to the fields in the morning and came back in the evening.[9] And again, one of the common songs which recurs in these descriptions of coffling, is the widely found sea-shanty "Hilo":

> The songs of a slave are word pictures of every thing he sees, or hears, or feels. . . . His songs do not always indicate a happy state of mind. He resorts to them . . . to divert his thoughts from dwelling on his condition. . . .
>
> "William Rino sold Henry Silvers;
> Hilo! Hilo!

> Sold him to de Georgy trader;
> Hilo! Hilo!
> His wife she cried and children bawled,
> Hilo! Hilo!
> Sold him to de Georgy trader;
> Hilo! Hilo!"[10]

William Cullen Bryant, travelling in the American South before the Civil War, encountered just such a scene of playful work in which the singing of this same shanty was employed in connection with a cornshucking:

> [A] light-wood fire was made, and the negroes dropped in from the neighboring plantations, singing as they came. The driver of the plantation, a colored man, brought out baskets of corn in the husk, and piled it in a heap; and the negroes began to strip the husks from the ears, singing with great glee.... The songs were generally of a comic character; but one of them was set to a singularly wild and plaintive air....:
>
> > Johnny come down de hollow.
> > Oh hollow!
> > Johnny come down de hollow.
> > Oh hollow!
> > De nigger-trader got me.
> > Oh hollow!
> > De speculator bought me.
> > Oh hollow!
> > I'm sold for silver dollars.
> > Oh hollow!
> > Boys, go catch de pony.
> > Oh hollow!
> > Bring him around the corner.
> > Oh hollow!
> > I'm goin' away to Georgia.
> > Oh hollow!
> > Boys, good-by forever!
> > Oh hollow![11]

Bryant continues his description, referring to another song, "Jenny gone away," also found in the sea shanty repertoire, the "various dances, capering, prancing and drumming with heel and toe upon the floor" that came after a feast, and finally a 'fancy talk' speech given by one of the slaves.[12]

Of all the slave working and singing activities that excited both the plantocracy and the visiting observers, the one which drew the greatest attention in the United States was this cornshucking.[13] A carryover from European *harvest home* celebrations, as in the Old World, the event was a time when masters and workers came together in celebration. Here, not only did the harvest provide the occasion for a festive meal, but on this one occasion, the slaves were displayed as both compulsively—and playfully—competitive, and as singers, musicians, dancers.

> . . . the shucking frolic is considered . . . a far greater jubilee. A farmer will haul up from his field a pile of corn from ten to twenty rods long, from ten to twenty feet high. This pile consists of nothing but ears. They always break the ears from the stalk, and never cut it at the ground, as the Northern farmers do. It is so arranged that this can be on a moonlight evening. The farmer then gives a general "invite" to all the young ladies and gentlemen in the neighborhood, to come and bring their slaves; for it takes no small number to shuck such a pile of corn.
>
> The guests begin to arrive about dark, and in a short time, they can be heard in all directions, singing the plantation songs, as they come to the scene of action. When they have all arrived, the Host makes the following proposition to his company, "You can shuck the pile, or work till eleven o'clock, or divide the pile and the hands, and try a race."
>
> The last offer is generally accepted. Each party selects two of the shrewdest and best singers among the slaves, to mount the pile and sing, while all join in the chores. The singers also act the part of sentinels, to watch the opposite party—for it is part of the game for each party to throw corn on the other's pile.
>
> As soon as all things are ready, the word is given, and they fall to work in good earnest. They sing awhile, then tell stories, and joke and laugh awhile. At last they get to making all the different noises the human voice is capable of, all at the same time—each one of each partty doing his best to win the victory. One unacquainted with such scenes would think that Bedlam *had* broken loose, and all its in-mates were doing their best to thunder forth their uproarious joy.
>
> This is continued till the task is finished. They have plenty of liquor to keep up the excitement. . . . The victorious party peal forth their shouts and jests in a deafening volley, and the negroes seem fairly beside themselves. They jump, roll, and tumble about, as though "kingdom come" was already in their possession. As soon as the pile is finished, the slaves keep a sharp eye on the Host, lest he should slip out of their sight, and get to the house; for it is a rule with them cornshuckings always to tote [him] on their heads; and the moment he gives the word to proceed to the house, he expects his doom—and by dodging and running he tries to escape it. . . .[14]
>
> On arriving at the house they find that the young ladies have not been idle; for the long tables smoke and groan with the loads of poultry, pig, and all kinds of eatables, . . . As soon as the table is cleared the girls give a wink; and in a trice the room is stripped of every thing. . . . The negro fiddler then walks in; and the dance commences. After they have enjoyed their sport sufficiently, they give way to the negroes, who have already supplied themselves with torchlights, and swept the yard. The fiddler walks out, and strikes up a tune; and at it they go in a regular tear-down dance; . . .[15]

These cornshuckings seem to have rivalled Christmas as the primary festive occasions for the slaves,[16] those times when two events were the only ones in which real festive behavior on the part of the slaves was encouraged by the plantocracy, including the free roaming from plantation to plantation, feasting, drinking, and even fighting. Indeed, at least according the Barrow's extensive account, the competition which arose between the different sides in the cornshucking occasionally became bellicose.

> It is no rare occurrence for a cornshucking to terminate in a row instead of a frolic. If one side is badly beaten, there is almost sure to be some charge of fraud; . . . . a first-class row ensues, in which ears of corn fly thick and fast, and sometimes more dangerous weapons are used . . . [though] most often good humor prevails.[17]

There is little doubt that the fascination which the cornshucking held for the white observer was that it provided the opportunity to witness what must have seemed the ideal plantation work scene, with one slave sitting on top of the cornpile, improvising songs and spurring the others to do the job happily. Here, for instance, is a typical description of just such a scene, from an anonymous contributor to *The Family Magazine* in 1836, as taken from " . . . a journal kept by a gentleman who travelled through Virginia some years since."

> About eighty or a hundred men were seated around a huge heap of corn, tearing off the husk, and throwing away the denuded ears into spots where they were at once separate from the corn-pile. . . . On the summit of this pile, sat a person selected for his skill in improvisation, who gave out a line in a sort of rapid chant, at the end of which the whole party joined in a chorus. The poet seemed to have no fixed object in view, but to sing. He passed from one subject to another without regard to connexion. . . .
>
>   Oh, Jenny, gone to New-town
>   *chorus:* Oh Jenny gone away!
>   She went because she wouldn't stay,
>   Oh Jenny gone away!
>   She run'd away, an' I know why,
>   Oh, Jenny gone away!
>   For she went a'ter Jones's Bob,
>   Oh, Jenny gone away!
>   Mr. Norton, good ole man,
>   Oh, Jenny gone away!
>   Treats his niggers mighty well,
>   Oh, Jenny gone away! . . . .
>
> After running on this way for ten or fifteen minutes, any one of the company who may be so disposed, strikes in at the top of his voice with a new tune. The hint is not lost on the leader, who immediately adopts

as well as he can, his words to the air, if such it may be called, and moves on with perfect readiness in the same style, contemning both rhyme and reason. By the by, it is curious to see how they get over any difficulty about adapting their unequal lines to the tune. The latter is a bed of Procrustes.[18]

These scenic descriptions are a boon for the folklorist, for they record in such full detail a traditional event that became one of the occasions in which slave creativity was encouraged. Moreover, sufficient details are given that one can be fairly assured that the activity was not only commented upon because it featured images of "the happy slave." Moreover, Yetman includes sufficient references to accounts of cornshuckings by ex-slaves that we may be assured that it was, indeed, regarded as a significant time in their dreary rounds.[19] The cornshucking scenes, in fact, provide us with the largest single repository of song-texts that indicate that not only was improvisation countenanced and even encouraged under slavery, but that in the form of song, a good deal of commentary about slavery, working conditions, the local doings of white folks and other such subjects was to be found, songs which show that the African tradition of scandal singing was to be found in the strangest of places.[20]

Perhaps more important, materials heretofore available to folklorists to study celebrations and other festive events in American life have seemed sparse, indeed. The received attitude toward calendar customs on this side of the Atlantic is that they were actively discouraged, being regarded as Papist or pagan relics, at least until the time of national unrest when the Civil War and its aftermath created the need for national holidays, and Christmas, Harvest Home (in the form of Thanksgiving) and Midsummer's (as the Fourth of July) were resuscitated and used for the purpose of celebrating a putative past. The existence of a number of holidays celebrated in the south, which brought together slaves and masters, opens up the question from yet one more angle of how the presence of blacks provided whites with the license to engage in popular entertainments. Surely the fact that the cornshucking was both a work and a festive activity assisted in making at least this one event more permissible, even if it did encourage a certain amount of critical commentary on the system within the songs.

NOTES

[1]Horace Beck, *Folklore and the Sea*. Middletown, Conn.: Wesleyan University Press for the Marine Historical Association, Mystic Seaport, 1973, 138-39.
[2]Beck, 139.

[3] Alan Lomax, *Folksong Style and Culture*. Washington, D.C.: AAAS, 197, 94-5.
[4] Or so it is argued by Stan Hugill, in his standard work on the form, *Shanties from the Seven Seas* (London: Routledge, Kegan Paul, 1960, 8). I survey previous arguments in *Deep the Water, Shallow the Shore* (Austin: University of Texas Press, 1974), 7-10.
[5] Reported in *Deep the Water. . .* , 5.
[6] Dena Epstein, *Sinful Tunes and Spirituals*. Champaign-Urbana: University of Illinois, 1977, 176-183.
[7] See not only *Deep the Water*, chapter one, *passim* but *After Africa,* ed. John Szwed and Roger D. Abrahams (New Haven: Yale University Press, 1983), 26-9, 309-11.
[8] James Lane Allen, "Mrs. Stowe's 'Uncle Tom' at Home in Kentucky," *Century Magazine,* 34 (1887), 863. This emphasis on the contest may, in fact, have been underscored by a number of white observers, as planters were reputed to be willing to turn anything into an agonistic engagement on which they could make a wager. For an interesting account of such activities, and their toll on Southern life, see T. H. Breen, *Puritans and Adventurers: Change and Persistence in Early America* (New York: Oxford University Press, 1980), 148-62. Breen is concerned with horse-racing, and does not mention the widely held belief that the plantocrats used their strongest slaves as the "bullies" of the plantation, pitting them against those of other plantations. But there are numerous "Marster-John Tales" in the Afro-American repertoire that so depict Old Marster. See for instance, "They Both Had Dead Horses" and "Competition for Laziness" in *Afro-American Folktales,* ed. Roger D. Abrahams (New York: Pantheon, 1985), 266, 270-74, 283-84.
[9] For many references to these gangs, and their protest songs, see Epstein, *Sinful Tunes. . .* , 183.
[10] *Pictures of Slavery in Church and State*. Philadelphia: author, 1857, 197-98, quoted in Epstein, 179-80.
[11] William Cullen Bryant, *Letters of A Traveller*. New York: G. P. Putnam, 1850, 84-87.
[12] Almost always, such orations were regarded as bad imitations of white stump-speaking. For a discussion of the question, see *After Africa,* 77-95, 356-63.
[13] Epstein has brought together most of the extant reportings of the cornshucking, 178-183. To these may be added a few of the reports given below.
[14] Just how widespread this practice was is difficult to ascertain, for surely it was possible on there was a "young master" in the family. But David C. Barrow's description of the event, much referred to, contains a similar "walk around" of the host, including a picture, "A Georgia Cornshucking," *Century Magazine* 24 (1882), 876.
[15] Lewis N. Paine, *Six Years in Prison*. New York: 1851, 180-183.
[16] Richard Walser provides us with an overview of black Christmas mumming, and its present practice by whites in one region of the Carolinas, in "His Worship the John Kuner," *North Carolina Folklore* 19 (1971), 160-172. See also Epstein, *Sinful Tunes. . .* , 86, 89, 131.
[17] Barrow, "Georgia Cornshucking," 876.
[18] "Visit to a Negro Cabin in Virginia," *The Family Magazine* 3 (1836), 44. The song is, of course, the same one mentioned in Bryant, n.11 above.

[19] Norman R. Yetman, *Life Under the Peculiar Institution.* New York 1970, 62, 190, 223, 258, 267-68; in addition, Eugene D. Genovese, *Roll, Jordan, Roll* (New York: Pantheon, 1974), 733, fn.22, lists the places in which cornshucking is to be found in George Rawick's *The American Slave: A Composite Autobiography* (New York: Greenwood Press, 1972), 20 vols., which includes the material in *The Unwritten History of Slavery*, comp. and ed. Ophelia Settle Egypt, J. Masuoka, and Charles S. Johnson (Washington, D.C.: 1968). Genovese gives a quick and sharp overview in *Roll, Jordan . . .* , 315-19. In addition to these references, and those given in Epstein, see the following entries in *Afro-American Culture and Folklore: An Annotated Bibliography*, ed. Roger D. Abrahams and John Szwed (Philadelphia: ISHI, 1978), NA 625; 675; 687; 1528; 1921; 2971; 3253.

[20] Cf. William D. Piersen, "Puttin' Down Ole Massa: African Satire in the New World," in *African Folklore in the New World,* ed. Daniel Crowley (Austin: University of Texas Press, 1977), 20-34.

HILDA, WOMAN OF DREAMS

Jane C. Beck
Ripton, Vermont

IT WAS THE SUMMER OF 1972 and we were back on Bequia, a small island a few miles south of St. Vincent in the Grenadines, to do some more fieldwork. About six miles long with some 3600 inhabitants, Bequia is an island of both coral beaches and rounded hills and ridges that slope steeply into the sea. During the winter of 1971 Horace had begun his research on the island's shore based whaling complex. He had spent a month trying to get in the boats, and finally one morning as he watched the *Dart* and the *Trio* making ready to go out, the harpooner and leader of the whalemen, Athneal Ollivierre, nodded his head and said one word, "come." The next day when we met Athneal he told Horace that he could see that "he was quick as a sprat" in the boat and that he could go with him any time. That began a long friendship and a new career for Horace. He became known as "Whaler man" as he went out day after day and was finally rewarded with the ultimate experience of a successful hunt.

But there is a lot more to Bequia whaling than the hunt. If they are lucky these men take, on the average, two whales a year, and not a bit of the whale is wasted. For at least two months during February and March and sometimes into April, they go out every day but Sunday looking for their elusive quarry. Songs, stories, sayings, food preparation, clothing and custom all reflect the importance of this occupation.

That summer Horace found himself steadily in Athneal's company—they went pigeon shooting together, crabbing, mending nets, searching for timber suitable for the building of a small boat, and all the other everyday tasks of the summer months. Much of this revolved around the food supply, and after a successful hunt or search, Hilda, Athneal's wife, would insist on sharing a portion with us. Hilda was a marvelous cook and it didn't take us long to realize that we had stumbled on to not only a real source of gastronomic delight, but also somebody who could teach me about West Indian food. The fact that she was Athneal's wife would also give us another perspective on the whaling complex. Horace suggested to me that I work with Hilda, collecting her recipes and learning what I could from her. Hilda was very receptive and as so often happens with a project of this sort—although the focus may remain, additional elements come into play.

I began to wonder about Hilda's position in Bequian society. Was her apparent status due to her husband's reputation as a leader and courageous harpooner among the whale men? In the West Indies I had noticed respect for a man was seldom transferred to his mate. Perhaps it was because of her exceptional cooking talents. Food—the giving and sharing of it—played an important role in West Indian society. David Lowenthal had written that "women seldom achieve or transmit status through personal merit."[1] Was this really the case? Gradually, over time some of the subtleties of prestige and respect in Bequia society became clearer.

In Bequia, society is stratified by both color and class. Colored creoles, rather than whites, comprise the elite, while the blacks are at the other end of the scale. There is still a strong feeling amongst the Creoles that a clear complexion and good (straight) hair is desirable. Lifestyle is also an important consideration and is based on economics and social respectability.

Both Peter Wilson and Roger Abrahams have written about the significance of respectability and reputation among the West Indian males.[2] Peter Wilson refers to respectability as " a set of moral beliefs,"[3] reputation as a "moral measurement of a person's worth derived from his conduct with other people."[4] Thus respectability "is a constellation of values by which a population may be stratified into social classes,"[5] while "reputation is a constellation of values which emphasizes social differentiation."[6]

Both Wilson and Abrahams refer to the feminine value of respectability, and the male value of reputation. These differences represent a basic point of conflict within the West Indian social structure. On the one hand, there is the family and yard where people are supposed to "live nice" together. This is the realm of order, decorum and respectability. The second is the world of the rum shop, the crossroads, and the town: the realm of licence and gregarious camaraderie. It is the world that takes the men out of the home and yard. Here a man makes his reputation, a "reputation established by dramatic performance,"[7] by exhibiting his male prowess and masculinity.

But how do these values affect status among women on Bequia? Can and do women achieve status through personal merit or is it a reflection of her mate's reputation? By using Hilda as an example, it is possible to develop some insights into such a question and also to understand her role in the whaling complex.

Both Athneal and Hilda are considered Creoles and are conscious of skin gradation. When looking at some wedding pictures a friend brought over, Hilda clicked her tongue, "Oh God! Oh God! What a jumby man," she cried, referring to the husband's blackness, "He must have a good job or lots of money for she to marry him. Maybe she pick the wrong bush"[8] (meaning she had married the wrong man). Although dogs are supposed to be colorblind, Athneal claims that his three won't let a black man in the yard.

The Ollivierres live in a substantial house which has an upstairs as well as a downstairs. Upstairs includes the sleeping quarters, four bedrooms, a bathroom with toilet and shower, and a small sitting room full of trinkets and memorabilia which is apparently seldom used. Downstairs is the real living space. A small kitchen, where Hilda does all her cooking, is off the main room which serves as dining room, ironing room, living room, sitting room combined. A second smaller room holds two deck chairs salvaged from the wrecked cruise liner *Antilles* and is where Athneal and Hilda tend to sit after a meal. Beyond the house there is an outside kitchen, shower, shed and off to one side an outhouse. The yard is kept immaculate. Three dogs and usually a couple of davy birds (sea gulls that Athneal keeps for pets) loll around the yard or fight over scraps thrown to them. A small garden is filled with plants and bushes that Hilda is fond of, and beyond in another small enclosure, Athneal grows his vegetables and fruits. A fence around the yard keeps out the world beyond. There is no question that it is judged a fine home. As Roger Abrahams points out, the more the house and yard "are sealed off from the world of the road and exhibit a cool and orderly exterior, the more highly they are valued."[9] Certainly the Ollivierres exhibit a lifestyle that is indicative of the Creole elite.

Although I was often in and out of the Ollivierre household, Hilda and I set aside a couple of afternoons a week where we would talk about her recipes and food preparation. I would usually arrive around one o'clock to find Hilda resting in her deck chair after a morning's work. Hilda is a large, comfortable woman who suffers from "pressure" (high blood pressure) and sugar (diabetes) and therefore is not always in the best of health. I would join her and for an hour or so she would give me a number of recipes, which I took down in a notebook as Hilda was uncomfortable with a tape recorder. Later, as she had the ingredients on hand, she would try to make sure I was around when she put them together. As we talked I not only learned a large number of recipes but also much more about Hilda's own life.

She had been born in Venezuela in 1929 where her father, a Bequia man, had gone to prospect for gold. He and a partner staked a claim which proved to be a valuable one. For several years he worked the mine, became prosperous (with the intention of returning to Bequia to live a life of leisure) and married a "Spanish woman from South America." "Unfortunately, I came out like my father instead of my mother," Hilda told me pointing to her skin and hair. When Hilda was four or five, her father was killed and her mother sent the child to Bequia to live with her paternal grandparents. Shortly after this, her mother also died under mysterious circumstances and Hilda remained with her grandparents, learning English and being raised as a native Bequian. Today, only her family nickname of "Mamasita" betrays her Spanish roots. Her grandmother, from whom Hilda learned to cook, placed great emphasis on bringing Hilda up "nice." She was very strict with her, not allowing young Hilda to go to the usual picnics and dances. "And I'm very glad," she told me, "If I had not been kept so strict I would not have got such a good man."

Such upbringing is the ideal in Bequia, but seldom practiced. More often than not a woman will have a child or two before she settles down into a stable relationship. Again the ideal is marriage, but there is no great stigma if a couple is not "married up." But the ideal, of course, brings respectability.

In Bequia, as in the other West Indian islands, children are valued and are seen as a woman's most important asset. A woman must have "as many children as are in her belly," for these same children are her hostages to old age. "That boy going to give you a penny bread and that girl going to give you an old dress." Along with this belief goes the attitude, "If a woman born in this world and she haven't got a child, she is no use." Hilda has no children of her own. She has had numerous miscarriages and a couple of operations but to no avail. However, once again Hilda can point to her strict upbringing, commenting to me, "So you see Athneal can say nothing—he can throw nothing in my face, because he knows I kept myself nice."

Despite the fact that she had no children of her own, there are always several children in Hilda's household. As they leave home younger children take their place. All are related to the Ollivierres, and in some cases the natural mother lives next door. Every West Indian household needs children to make it function smoothly. "Those families with the most children are regarded as fortunate, for the woman household head is able to relax more, because she only needs to supervise the activities of her children."[10]

Hilda runs a tight ship and nobody can fault her in the managing of her household. She is generous beyond necessity (a basic West Indian tenet is "you give to get") urging all who come in the gate to take a bit of tea and sweet bread or a bit of something more substantial. "Better burst your belly than let good food go bad," she warns you. The importance of sharing food cannot be underestimated in the West Indies. It is more than nourishment, "it give you strength." Numerous proverbs emphasize the importance of sharing it. "Don't throw upon the ground the bread you cannot eat." "Don't forget kindness, when you don't need charity." Hilda is always ready to share, but this is not just food, it's food prepared by the best cook on the island. One young girl, who did not live in Hilda's household but came to help Hilda and also to learn to cook, was constantly teased as her body felt the benefits of Hilda's nourishment, "Since she's gone to Hilda's she's come fat like Hilda."

Thus despite her own lack of children, Hilda manages to run a household that is above reproach and known for its generosity and good food. On holidays people flock to her door and no one is turned away without food and drink. When there is an event where food is contributed, Hilda does more than her part. She is known for her Christian ways and devotedly attends church every Sunday. Indeed, Hilda is the epitome of respectability, and because of this is relegated to the upper class of Bequian society. However, just as reputation is important in establishing status and prestige within the man's world, reputation plays a similar role among women. For women this is not the world of the rum shop or the realm of license and camaraderie; it is the world beyond the yard and, symbolically, often the world of the crossroads. The world of the crossroads is more than Abrahams suggests when he talks about it as beyond the woman's world of yard and respectability. The crossroads also represents the world of the supernatural. It is at the crossroads where one trysts the devil in West Indian belief and it is the devil who bequeaths power. Another means to the realm of the supernatural is through dreams. It is Hilda's ability to dream "true, true, true," that brings her the greatest prestige. For a woman, reputation must be kept in line with respectability if she is to assume high status. Therefore, traditionally, only a few areas might be considered acceptable—for example, the practice of bush medicine, story telling and singing, and the realm of the supernatural, provided the woman does not misuse this power.

Dream messages are imbued with significant meaning to most West Indians. Dreams are discussed at great length and are examined for symbols or special content that might indicate something to the dreamer or those close to him. Certain rituals are even carried out on the strength of dreams.[11] Dream messages from a dead relative are held in particular reverence because it is believed that those closest to one in life will also aid and warn one after they have departed this world. If a dead person gives the dreamer instructions, when he or she awakes the individual must carry out those instructions.

One particular dream established Hilda's reputation within the community in no uncertain terms. One night while asleep, Hilda saw herself walking down the road when Son (one of Hilda's household) came up and told her that Athneal wanted his clothes sent up to him right away. She went home and there were a number of cars backed up to the gate—coming and going. Then an airplane appeared above the hill and flew out over Rammy (a small island off Bequia) leaving a long trail of smoke. When Hilda awoke she knew it was a bad dream and was afraid for Athneal. He wanted to go pigeon shooting, but she said she didn't want any pigeon. He wanted to go fishing, but she told him they needed no fish that day, they could have cornmeal cakes for supper. However, nothing she could say would dissuade Athneal from fishing and he went out with his brother. They had some dynamite with them and Ocoral was standing in the bow, looking for fish with the powder in his hand. His cigarette, with which he was lighting the fuse, accidently touched the powder and the explosion blew off his hand and burned his face badly. The first Hilda knew about it, Son had come to her, as in the dream, to tell her and to say that Athneal needed some clothes. A neighbor drove back and forth from the house, taking Ocoral to the hospital and taking others down.

An informer told the authorities that Athneal and his brother had been dynamiting fish and the police came over from St. Vincent to search the Ollivierre household, looking for incriminating evidence. Athneal had an unregistered revolver and as the police appeared Hilda jammed it into the pocket of her dress, the other she filled with keys and followed the police around the house, making sure they didn't "plant something." They left empty handed and the case was dropped, but Hilda was furious at the informer wishing vocally that the same thing that happened to Ocoral would happen to him. The very day that her brother-in-law was released from the hospital, the informer was dynamiting fish down in the Tobago Cays. Something went wrong, and he too blew his hand off and was taken to the hospital in Grenada. From that instant Hilda's reputation was established. She was not a woman to be trifled with. Her courage in dealing with the police was noteworthy, but her supernatural abilities in dreaming and cursing were formidable. She was a woman of power and this raised her above the ranks of ordinary women.

Not only did she herself dream things to come, but she could interpret other's dreams. News reached Bequia that something had happened to a vessel which was captained by Athneal's nephew and owned by Athneal's brother and a partner. There was uncertainty as to whether crew and vessel had been lost, or just what had happened. During those days of wondering and worry, Athneal had a dream and when he awoke he told Hilda about it. Athneal had dreamed he was down in the Tobago Cays, turtling—but it didn't look like the Cays. He and the others were on a beach; however, the beach was not sand, rather a kind of black dirt. Another man and he were looking at all the turtle tracks, but they couldn't see where they went, and then a moke with Athneal's brother (the owner of the vessel and father of the captain) driving and another man came toward them. The moke stopped beside Athneal and the second man, whom Athneal did not know, got out with a compass. Hilda told her husband it was a good dream, because the moke had been coming toward him, and the next day Athneal tried to reassure his brother, explaining about the dream. Shortly thereafter it was learned that his brother's son and the rest of the crew had been saved although the cargo had been lost.

Another day Athneal's oldest brother, Barton, appeared. He was very disturbed by a dream he had had the night before. Two of his old uncles (both dead) had come to him. His garden was all dead because it was so dry, but the trees were green. His uncles had told him to plant no more as nothing would grow. Barton was obviously shaken by the dream, but Hilda counseled him that it was not a bad dream—that the green was a good sign.

There seem to be a number of symbols that have certain meaning when dreamed about by Bequians. It is good to dream of food or anything green. To dream of a horse, an automobile or an airplane indicates that a message is coming. However, to dream of a ship is a sign of sickness or even death, particularly if the ship is going away from one. Often individuals have their own symbols. When Hilda dreams of sheep or goats she believes they represent whales. When she dreams of a particular woman who is now dead, but while living was very poor and someone to whom Hilda had given work, Hilda is worried for it is a sign of trouble or death. Athneal believes it is a good sign when he dreams of a white child.

With this importance placed on dreams and their interpretation, it is not surprising to find that dreams are considered extremely significant in regard to whaling. Other individuals will come to the whale men with their dreams in reference to catching a whale. If somebody has had a good dream the whale men will make a real effort to go out even if the wind is blowing hard or conditions do not look propitious. After a whale has been taken and the butchering is going on, a great number of people come to take part in the activities and to buy whale meat. At this time it is common for various people to tell Athneal of their dreams concerning the whaling industry.

Most whale men, and particularly Athneal, look to Hilda and her dreams for confirmation that they will be successful and perhaps to learn the number of whales they might take in a season. If Hilda tells her husband that he will be lucky that day, he walks with a light step because it usually comes to pass. Early one morning Hilda dreamed that Athneal's mother (who had been dead for over twenty years) handed her four eggs, telling her that they were for her husband. When she awoke, Hilda cooked Athneal four eggs for breakfast, after explaining to him why he wasn't receiving his usual two. Both knew it was a good dream and Hilda told Athneal, "I think you will be lucky today." Sure enough, he harpooned a cow and calf that same day, bringing the total catch for the season to four.

Over the years it has been common for Hilda to dream a good dream just prior to the harpooning of a whale. Before Athneal's first success as harpooner in 1960, Hilda had dreamed that Athneal's brother Louis was making rigging netting. This is another example of a personal dream symbol. Any time Hilda dreams of Louis working, she knows it is a good dream. (Louis is not fond of hard work.) Another year on her birthday Hilda dreamed she was standing in a field of green corn. She was cutting it with her cutlass for the children. When she awoke, she told her husband, "That is a very good dream. I think you will strike something today." Sure enough, he was successful. A more obvious dream was of Hilda and Athneal walking down near Adams, where Hilda's grandfather lived. They saw a ragged old man who spoke to them and as Hilda bent closer to hear what he was saying she felt water falling on her. She looked up and saw a monkey in a tree, "spouting water, spouting water —way up in the air." Again it proved a good dream and next day Athneal harpooned a whale.

But all Hilda's dreams about the whaling are not good and her accuracy is so well known throughout the community that when she has a bad dream, people beware. One night she dreamed that she had gone down to her aunt's to visit and on the way saw an old and a young iguana on a tree. The first was large and brown, the second, small and green. She threw a stone and hit the old one in the center of the back, but she didn't kill it. She took a stick and mashed it, but still she couldn't kill it. The creature fell off the tree and Hilda grabbed it, but could not seem to finish it off. She cut off its mouth, still to no avail. At that moment she saw Orville (the harpooner of the *Trio*, Athneal was the harpooner of the *Dart*) washing himself on a step. She called to him to come with his knife and cut off the iguana's head, but he paid her no heed and continued with his washing. When she awoke she knew it was a bad sign and all that day she watched the sea, and sure enough she saw the whalemen returning in disgust, early in the day. Athneal's harpoon had pulled out because a tourist had removed the toggle pin and Orville had not come to his aid.

A more serious dream occurred in April 1980. Hilda had fallen back asleep after Athneal had gone whaling. She saw the house filled with people—people coming and going—and when she awoke she knew it was a bad dream. She wanted to send a message to Athneal that he must be careful and watch out for trouble, but he had already left. All day she worried and couldn't eat—she didn't even have an appetite for her favorite pea soup. A neighbor brought her some fish, but she couldn't swallow it. The people on shore told her not to worry, that the whale men were fast to a calf. Then, they lost it, and Hilda was sure something was wrong. When the whale boat came into La Pompe instead of Friendship Bay she knew something had happened. Athneal was carried from the boat and then limped up to the house. He had ironed the calf and the cow had bumped the boat, throwing Athneal over backwards and knocking him out. When he came to, the pin in the bow that holds down the whale line had broken and the line was caught around his thigh and knee, cutting a wide swath to the bone. When the helmsman realized what was happening he loosened the line from the loggerhead, but not before Athneal had sustained a considerable injury. When Hilda saw his leg she passed out, but afterwards she said the house was just as it had been in her dream.

Hilda's reputation is widely established. There are some people who would prefer that she never dreamed of them, she is believed to possess such uncanny abilities. Her gift of dreaming and interpreting her own dreams and those of others invests her with power. The fact that she has been known to successfully curse someone is a sign that she is extremely powerful. However, she has not misused her power, and therefore she has stayed within the bounds of her respectability. The individual who practices obeah (a kind of West Indian witchcraft or sorcery which is broadly considered to be the practice of a supernatural craft) for his or her own personal gain is both despised and feared by the society[12] and is considered anything but respectable. If Hilda had been known to curse an individual who had not justly deserved her wrath, she would be seen in a different light. As a result her power is both respected and feared.

It is seldom that a woman's status is affected by anything other than her degree of respectability and most women are ranked in West Indian society according to their place on society's scale of respectability. As Lowenthal says, women seldom achieve status through personal merit because there are few ways a woman can enhance her reputation in accordance with the code of respectability. Unlike men, in order for women to achieve status, respectability and reputation cannot be at odds. Reputation for women as well as for men is based on power. Hilda has gained that through her ability to dream; however, she uses her power for the benefit of good—first for her husband and family, then for the world outside the home: the whale men and the community at large. If she has a good dream during the whaling season, the whale men are the first to know and to act upon it. What Hilda dreams is believed to be "true, true, true." Her reputation, therefore, is in harmony with her respectability (brought about by her lifestyle which includes her cooking abilities) and places Hilda on the top status rung of her community. She is an equal mate for Athneal whose own reputation is legion with acts of courage and strength and whose respectability is beyond reproach. (His brush with the St. Vincent police and his successful evasion of arrest only enhances his image in Bequian society.)

It is a marriage of equals, where their union lifts both a head higher than those around them. Together their lifestyle bespeaks respectability. Individually, while Athneal constantly proves his power in terms of courage, skill and leadership, Hilda reinforces hers in terms imbued with the supernatural, her ability to dream. Each can say about the other, "I picked the right bush."

NOTES

[1] David Lowenthal. *West Indian Societies.* New York: Oxford University Press, 1972, p. 138.
[2] Peter J. Wilson. *Crab Antics: The Social Anthropology of English Speaking Negro Societies of the Caribbean.* New Haven: Yale Press, 1973; and Roger D. Abrahams. *The Man-of-Words in the West Indies: Performance and the Emergence of Creole Culture.* Baltimore: The Johns Hopkins University Press, 1983.
[3] Wilson, p. 226.
[4] *Ibid.*
[5] *Ibid.,* p. 227
[6] *Ibid.*
[7] Abrahams, p. 146.
[8] All quotes are from my field journal kept daily during fieldwork.
[9] Abrahams, p. 137.
[10] *Ibid.,* p. 146.
[11] Jane C. Beck. " ' Dream Messages' from the Dead." *Journal of the Folklore Institute* 10:173-186, 1973.
[12] Jane C. Beck. "The Implied Obeah Man." *Western Folklore* 35:23-33, 1976.

FARM FOLKLIFE IN WOOD:
JEHU F. CAMPER, DELAWARE WHITTLER

Robert D. Bethke
University of Delaware

IN AN ESSAY ON AMERICAN OCCUPATIONAL FOLKLORE published nearly twenty years ago, Horace Beck observed: "Unfortunately, in the United States, all types of folklore have not received the same attention, nor have the occupations themselves been uniformly studied. . . . Seafaring, lumbering, ranching, mining, and railroading have received great emphasis; others, like farming, have been largely neglected."[1] In 1983 I had occasion to interview a middle-age man who is the seventh generation of his family to farm land in rural Kent County, Delaware. Like many of his Felton neighbors, Joe Hughes raises corn, soybeans, and broiler chickens on flat expanse typical of the upper Delmarva Peninsula.[2] He farms five hundred acres. Joe spoke mostly about present-day attachment to place and endeavor. "There are a lot of farmers who are involved in family tradition," he noted. "The tradition is simply that they farm the land as they have for generations." I found, as we talked in a workshed and later hunched over the bed of his pickup truck, that Joe was inclined to reflect on continuities; his farming experiences remained immediate, everyday, and matter-of-fact. "On a farm you don't walk away from the job at five o'clock. You live at work—you're at work twenty-four hours a day. If work's to be done, you've got to do it."

Jehu Camper, age eighty-seven, lives in a brick, one-story ranch house in Harrington, Delaware, a farming community south of Felton. Jehu and Joe know each other. Jehu was also raised on a local farm, and his family roots, like Joe's, reach deeply into local farming tradition. It is in other ways that the two men are distinctive. Jehu no longer actively farms; indeed, he has engaged in several occupations throughout his life. However, more than age and vocational circumstance separate them. Whereas Joe Hughes today relates to the presentness of farming folklife, Jehu Camper has for nearly eighty years taken stock of change. They part company when it comes to perspective on their shared agricultural heritage and their medium for articulating it.

In 1933, Jehu Camper began creating whittled assemblages in wood intended to preserve, in small scale, scenes and impressions of Delaware farming folklife internalized during the generation before Joe Hughes's birth. Undaunted by loss of sight in one eye,[3] he continued his efforts until the onset of manually impairing arthritis in the early 1980s. The workshop at the back of Jehu's property is cluttered with well-used tools, remnant wood, old calenders, and sawdust long settled. The atmosphere seems a trademark of prolific whittler folk artists throughout much of North America. Though creating his things for both personal and public pleasure, Jehu has never produced objects intended to satisfy a commercial marketplace. Despite requests, he refuses to sell the assemblages, for as a collection they represent a unified vision of agricultural workplace, personal memory, and rural Delaware agrarian history. The pieces are like historical photographs in three dimensions.[4]

Whittled folk art arising out of occupational experience has ample precedent in regional America. As Joan I. Mattie has pointed out in Canada, "many folk works have been created by older people who, in their art, recapture the places in which they have lived, the way they used to do things, and the occupations they had in their younger years."[5] Other commentators have noted that changes in technology, altering equipment and workplace environment, may inspire folk art recreations of "working lives in miniature."[6] While Jehu Camper's efforts are apparently unique within Delaware, in wider context both his general subject matter and certain individual pieces bear close comparison to the output of whittlers with similar farming experience.[7] The great majority of Jehu's objects also fall squarely within a pattern summed up by Mary Hufford as "aesthetics of life review."[8] A series of tape-recorded interviews with the folk artist spanning 1980 to 1984 make clear that his production of assemblages increased substantially with age, retirement from day-to-day vocational demands, and greater leisure time. "Folk art exhibits are filled with life-review projects that comprise a kind of three-dimensional reminiscence for their makers," writes Hufford, "whereby the past bursts into tangible being."[9] Few statements better capture the spirit and substance of Camper's place in American folk art creativity and display.

To appreciate the aesthetic output in wood by an individual like Jehu Camper is thus to move beyond mere objects, and into issues of personal motivation, sensibilities, and value-laden perspectives formed over a long lifetime. To this end I devote the remainder of this abbreviated case study, drawing solely upon Jehu's own words as compiled verbatim and edited selectively from the taped interviews.[10] Obviously, Jehu created his farming-related assemblages to be seen, and there are about 125 of them in his present collection. The two examples represented in photographs pertain directly to periodic work on the family farm, as do about half of the objects: e.g., scything, shingle making, hog hauling, quilting. The rest of the collection mixes work, recreation, and humorous incident on the farm or in the surrounding communities: e.g., goat nibbling at the clothesline, moonshiners getting caught by sheriff and deputies, elderly farmer peeping at outhouse. But regardless of topic, all of the whittlings have offered Jehu Camper a tangible medium for commentary on a self-perceived fragile past. In his hands, and in his immediate presence, the "art forms become props or cues for expanded oral narratives"[11] that bridge present with past, and that combined reach out to young and old, to strangers, and to familiars like neighbor Joe Hughes. As Horace Beck reminds us in his "Epilogue" to *Folklore and the Sea,* ". . . it must be remembered that folklore is not an item but an experience."[12]

My Life

"I was born on a farm on the west side of town about a mile from Harrington, October 10 in 1897, at ten o'clock on a Sunday morning. The farm was owned by Jehu Fleming, who had the clothing store in town. And that's who I was named after. When I was six years old my parents bought the Doctor Owens farm of fifty-five acres, which is right across the road from where I now live.

My father was a truck farmer, a pretty rough way to make a living in those days. We were poor, as most people were in that neighborhood. It wasn't any disgrace to be poor, though, because all the neighbors were. On the farm I used to drive horses, mules, and wagons. Dad had a gravel pit on the land, and my job was to drive two mules and a wagon to haul sand to town. Ten loads a day in ten hours. Had to hustle right along to make a load an hour. We got fifty cents a load for it, and five dollars a day was considered a right-sizeable amount of money in those days. Many a load of sand I hauled down the road when I was a boy.

I graduated from high school in 1916. I went to Goldey Beacom College in Wilmington [DE] for one year, then came home and got married to my wife, Lillian, who graduated from the same class in high school. We started a farm for two years. That didn't produce too much so I decided to take a Civil Service examination for a rural mail carrier; I passed the examination and was appointed a mail carrier in 1918 under Woodrow Wilson. Drove the mail two years, and politics changed—so did the rural mail carriers. Then I went to work for the railroad company and did that for two years. At the end of the two years I decided it was a poor way to make a living, so I went in business with another man and started a service station. My wife ran a restaurant in there. We sold the station in 1945. Then I went into politics. In 1950 I was elected to the State House of Representatives in Dover and served two years. Next election I was elected a State Senator for four years, 1952-56. And from there on I retired. I do till a big garden of about two acres and have farms that I rent out, which I have to look after. I'm also vice-president of the People's Bank of Harrington, and vice-president of the Delaware State Fair. Those two positions keep me pretty busy. I've had a good life.

My mother and father were both almost comedians; they both had a lot of sense of humor. They were always playing some kind of joke on the neighbors or us children. I had a cousin one time who said he'd rather come to visit our place, with Mother and Dad, than to go to a circus. Something going on all the time. And I guess I inherited it from them. It's just natural for me to want to tell something funny or listen to something funny and create something funny, to follow along with it. Part of my being today is to have a sense of humor. My mailboxes attract quite a lot of attention. It's a novelty—a crazy idea—and I carried it out. I conceived the idea when I began receiving so much trash mail: just advertisements. So I got a garbage can and made a mailbox out of it and put "Trash Mail" on it. Then I came up with the idea I ought to have an "Air Mail" one, so I put that one on a post ten feet in the air. I kept adding to them as people got interested in it. They'd suggest different kinds and I'd go ahead and fix them up and put them out there. And this created a lot of interest. I often run into people I think are strangers and they'll say, 'You're not the Camper who has all the crazy mailboxes?' I'll say, 'Yeah, that's me.' I have trouble with the vandals some. In fact, they tear them down now and then and carry them off—but I keep repairing them and putting them back.[13]

My wife and I have been married for sixty-six years. We've been happy, but it's all so rush, rush, rush nowadays. Nobody is at ease anymore. Today's a rat-race. I think that I have lived through the best times that this country will ever have. I wouldn't want to face the next fifty years—I just can't see where we're going.''

My Whittling

"Wood has always been fascinating to me. Even as a boy I'd pick out different trees: dogwood, oak, pine, holly. My dad would carry me in the woods and he'd correct me if I was wrong on the different kinds. It's always been fascinating to pick out a wood after it has come from the sawmill—hardwood for making certain things, and softwood for others. Wood is one of God's greatest gifts to man.

I'm a 'whittler'—I don't consider myself a 'wood carver.' There's a difference between 'carving' and 'whittling.' Carving, you take your knife and you start with a block of wood and shape out the thing you're going to make just with a carving knife. You don't saw anything. I can't do that too much. You go around to arts-and-crafts shows, the majority of the people do mostly geese, ducks, and all kinds of wildlife. Carvings. But I never was good at it; I've tried several times but never accomplished too much. I'm not too good of an artist, and if I have something I really want to do and do it right, I try to find a picture that I can copy off. I draw that out on a piece of paper with carbon paper so it goes onto a piece of wood. Then I saw it out on a band saw and I start into working it out with a jigsaw, sander, and knife until I complete it. I do very little painting; I can't keep the brush where I want it all the time, so I just leave most of the things I make in the 'rough . . . crude.' I seldom polish anything or sand it off, and it seems to tie in with the surroundings that you put it in. The things I make represent some part of the folklore living[14] our ancestors did when they were here on earth. There is history back of it.

My father gave me a two-bladed Barlow penknife when I was eight years old. We had a half-Indian that lived with us and worked on the farm. His mother was a Nanticoke Indian and his father was a Negro.[15] He made axe handles in order to supplement his wages. During rainy days, Saturday afternoons, and Sundays he would be working on an ax handle. One day it was raining and I had my Barlow penknife out, just whittling. He said 'Boy, why don't you make something instead of just whittling?'

I said, 'Well, I don't know how to make anything.'

He said, 'Well, I'll show you.'

So the next time he came to work he brought an old orange crate that had some white pine strips on it about an inch wide. He showed me how to make a windmill.[16] I got it done and put it up on the barn, and it ran. I went into mass production of windmills. I had one on the clothesline, one on the hen house, one on the outdoor toilet. My mother said if the old cow stood still long enough she was sure I'd put one on her. I got started whittling and I never stopped. I never had an instructor or manual training when I went to school. All that I got I picked up mostly just from experience.

In traveling around the neighborhood, and working, I would observe that the things our forefathers had used to make their livelihood were being destroyed. I knew that, someday, some people would want to see those things in their original form. I collected a few things, and I still have an old scything cradle and harrow. But it was just too costly and I didn't have the money. So I conceived the idea of making replicas of most of the things out of wood so I could put a lot of them in one place. And I proceeded to do that. After I got out of school, and later on got married, I went into whittling things that were worthwhile. Most of the things are local—things that I remember. The only book that I have ever gotten any inspiration out of is *The Foxfire Book*: it gave me a history of the old folks and how they lived. I guess I have been inspired by some of that, but a lot of things have come from my memories.[17] So many people don't know what a haystack is, and many other things have gone by the wayside. People say, 'Well, I don't know how you remember that!' Well, I grew up with it—I ought to remember it! I think of something that is about to become extinct and proceed to whittle it, and it would lead to another.

If an idea presents itself, it's a challenge from then on whether you can do it or not. You start in and get part of it done, and you add, and you keep adding to it until you end up with one piece. I've started a number of things that have wound up in the stove. One of the things I always thought I was going to make but never did was a treadmill powered by a horse. I tried it a time or two but it just didn't work out to suit me, so I gave it up. Another thing was a threshing machine powered by a steam engine. I thought it was too much work. I still have in mind that wheat thresher and treadmill but there's too much water over the dam now. I'll never be able to make them—I just can't do it. Quite often I get the question asked me, 'How long did it take you to make this?' I say, 'Well, that all depends on what kind of humor my wife is in. I don't work too steady. If she was in good humor, it took longer because I spent more time in the house watching television and maybe playing gin rummy. But if she was in bad humor, I spent a lot of time in the shop and had more time to work on the object.'

For a number of years I've been superintendent of the hobby show at the Delaware State Fair, which works right in with my whittling. People come from various parts of the state to display their handicraft. I've been displaying since 1970. A lady at the Fair one year said, 'Mr. Camper, I'm interested in becoming a whittler. What would I have to do?' I said, 'The first thing you have to do is get yourself a piece of softwood and pick out some object that you have in mind to make. Picture it out and cut it to size. Then get yourself a sharp knife, and some Band-Aids, and a few cuss words. And you get started.' She never did—I guess she just couldn't find the cuss words.

I started my museum in 1975. Before then, I had all the things that I had made displayed throughout the house and in the garage. One day my wife said, '*This* has got to go. I can't keep the house straightened up with

Fig. 1. Jehu and Lillian Camper in the small "museum" outbuilding behind their house. Fall, 1984.

Credit: University of Delaware Photographic Services

all this stuff in here!' So I didn't know if I should have a bonfire to get rid of it or build a museum. I wound up building a museum. And I'm glad I did, because it's been a lot of pleasure and a lot of people have gone through there. When I first started displaying in the building, very few people were interested. They'd look at the things and turn around and go on, with very little comment. It seemed that nobody cared too much about whittlings of that type. But the Bicentennial changed all that. In 1976 people took their hoes and shovels and went to dumps and began to dig for relics. And they began to take a second look at what I had made. We were busy continuously.

I've always wanted some kid—maybe some kid in the neighborhood—to get interested enough that I could take him in the shop and try to teach him. I tried to get my neighbor to work with wood. He bought shop equipment and made several pieces, doing relief carving. He was very good but he seemed to get disinterested and gave it up. He doesn't use the equipment at all anymore. That's one of the reasons why I'm determined to have my things preserved in some museum, somewhere. I'd like to

Fig. 2. Sorghum Molasses Mill. 26¾" L × 18" W × 13" H. Undated.

Credit: University of Delaware Photographic Services

keep my collection all together, all intact, and display it in one place in the future. I don't sell any of my things, but you couldn't haul away in a truck the number of pieces I've given away. It's a right pleasant feeling to walk into the house of somebody and see something you've made sitting on the mantle or window sill. It's a good feeling.

When I was on the farm with my father, almost all the farmers in the neighborhood would grow a patch of sugar cane. In the fall of the year they'd cut the tops off and tie the stalks up in bundles, and they'd carry them to the molasses mill. They hooked the horse to what they called a 'sweep' and pulled it around and around. The sweep turned two rollers inside a cage and the juice would pass out. They'd take the juice over to the little house and boil it down to make sugar cane molasses. Most all of the farmers in the days when I grew up made sugar cane molasses. My father did. We'd carry the sugar cane to the mill and the old fellow would grind it up and make molasses. If there was four gallons of it, he'd give us three and keep one gallon for making it. It was worth about $1.25 a gallon in those days.[18]

Fig. 3. Hog Killing. 20" L × 15½" W × 8" H. 1970.

Credit: University of Delaware Photographic Services

When my father had the farm, about five families would collect together and decide on when to kill the hogs. Most everybody raised hogs, the number according to the size of the family. At hog-killing time they'd dig a trench in the ground, put wood in it, and build a fire. They'd put water in the scaldron, and when it got hot they would roll the hog until the hair come loose. In the scene I made, one man is also scraping down a hog; one is taking out entrails; and one is stirring the lard. A lady is making sausage with a sausage grinder and sausage stuffer."[19]

Most everybody, if you stop to think about it, has some way of expressing themselves. Some do it through singing, some preaching, some acting or in athletics. Whittling is the only way I could think of that I could express myself and also create something in history that would be carried on after I passed out of this world. I have often had the thought that I would like to leave something behind, besides a name on a tombstone, to remember the name of Camper. And I feel that through my objects I may be able to do it.

Postscript

No consideration of Jehu Camper and his whittlings can leave unacknowledged the prominent role of his wife, Lillian, nor her supportive words of caring tribute: "You know, there's not too many people who have the gift that Jehu has of remembering so much and doing that kind of work. For the type of work he has done, I think you have to have a regular gift. I used to tell people that if I didn't actually know how old he was, I would say he was old as Methuselah to remember all of that way back."[20]

NOTES

Horace Beck introduced me to American folklore at Middlebury College, 1963-67. His influence on my professional career and scholarship remain profound; like the personal bond, that impact defies facile acknowledgement. Passing years reconfirm that Horace's insights and teaching go well beyond the classroom.

[1] Horace P. Beck, "Where the Workers of the World Unite: The American Occupations," in *Our Living Traditions: An Introduction to American Folklore,* ed. Tristram P. Coffin (New York: Basic Books, 1968), p. 61. See also Roger Mitchell, "Occupational Folklore: The Outdoor Industries," in *Handbook of American Folklore,* ed. Richard M. Dorson (Bloomington: Indiana University Press, 1983), pp. 128-29.

[2] There are currently between three and four thousand farmers in the State of Delaware, the vast majority of them concentrated in the agricultural-dominated counties of Kent and Sussex. Unlike the situation in many states to the west, Delaware agriculture has remained quite stable over the last decade due to diversification of crops, growth of the Delmarva poultry industry, and increasing property values. For historical details, see Joanne O. Passmore et al., *Three Centuries of Delaware Agriculture* (Delaware State Grange and the Delaware American Revolution Bicentennial Commission, 1978).

[3] "Jehu had the misfortune to lose an eye from a piece of steel when changing a tire while we were in business in the early 1930s. He had 20-20 vision in his one eye. Then in the early 1950s he had a cataract operation on his only eye; after it was back in shape he still had 20-20 vision, which was wonderful." Lillian Camper, personal correspondence, 12 November 1984.

[4] Portions of this paragraph appear in slightly different form in Robert D. Bethke, "Rural Folklife in Wood and Vision," in *Delmarva Folklife: A Book of Readings,* ed. Polly Stewart (Salisbury, MD: Salisbury State College, 1983), n.p. Reference to a whittler who, like Jehu, "adamantly refuses to sell his work" is found in Suzi Jones, ed., *Webfoots and Bunchgrassers: Folk Art of the Oregon County* (Oregon Arts Commission, 1980), p. 71.

[5] Joan I. Mattie, "Folk Art in Canada," Clinton County Historical Museum exhibit catalogue (Plattsburgh, N.Y., 1981), n.p.

[6] *From the Heart: Folk Art in Canada* (Toronto: McClelland and Stewart/Canadian Centre for Folk Culture Studies of the National Museum of Man, National Museums of Canada, 1983), p. 11.

[7]See for example *From The Heart*, pp. 87-89; and "From Field and Grove: Caricatures and Miniatures," in *Passing Time and Traditions: Contemporary Iowa Folk Artists*, ed. Steven Ohrn (Ames, Iowa: The Iowa State University/The Iowa Arts Council, 1984), p. 26.

[8]Mary Hufford, "All of Life's a Stage: The Aesthetics of Life Review," in *1984 Festival of American Folklife Programs Book,* ed. Thomas Vennum (Washington, D.C.: Smithsonian Institution, 1984), pp. 32-35.

[9]Ibid., p. 33.

[10]The present essay is derived from a more comprehensive, interpretive study in-progress of Jehu's whittlings in the contexts of Delaware folklife and American folk art. I would like to thank former students Valerie Cesna, Karen Lum, Dixie Lowen, and Mark Burgh for assistance in the fieldwork; Kim R. Burdick, co-founder of the Delaware Folklife Project, who has taken special interest in the Campers and the assemblages; and Eric Crossan and Fred Mullison, University of Delaware Photographic Services.

[11]Ohrn, *Passing Time and Traditions,* p. 4.

[12]Horace Beck, *Folklore and the Sea* (Middletown, Conn.: Wesleyan University Press, 1973), p. 409.

[13]Jehu's whimsical mailboxes project a side of his personality that comes through in numerous whittlings and narratives omitted from my treatment here. The mailboxes have become a local landmark in Harrington; in effect, they are a public statement of creativity that has full-flowering in the protected assemblages.

[14]The phrase "folklore living" was apparently picked up during the Campers' participation in the Delaware State Arts Council's Artists-in-Schools Program, Sussex County, 1977.

[15]Nanticoke Indian heritage in southern Delaware and mixed-blood Indian descendants in the state are discussed in C. A. Weslager, *The Nanticoke Indians— Past and Present* (Newark, DE: University of Delaware Press, 1983). See also Robert D. Bethke, "Struggle, Pride, and Display: The Nanticoke Indians of Delaware," in *Delmarva Folklife: A Book of Readings,* n.p.

[16]Jehu customarily uses the term "windmill" for what others call a "whirligig." He has several of them in his yard, and one of two preserved indoors away from weathering depicts a woman milking a cow. For general background and examples, see Ken Fitzgerald, *Weathervanes and Whirligigs* (New York: Clarkson N. Potter, 1967).

[17]Jehu owns a copy of *The Foxfire Book,* ed. Eliot Wigginton (Garden City, N.Y.: Doubleday, 1972), but examination of it as well as other volumes in the *Foxfire* series indicates negligible borrowing. With a few exceptions his assemblages seem attributable to scenes personally experienced and reconstructed from memory, creative whimsy, and conceivably mass-media sources other than *Foxfire* as yet unidentified.

[18]Sorghum molasses mills were scattered throughout southern Delaware from the late 1800s up until the 1950s. Passmore et al., *Three Centuries of Delaware Agriculture*, pp. 29-30, discuss the crop and conclude that most mills in the state were family and community enterprises of modest scale. For comparative material on sorghum and molasses making, see for example Henry Glassie, *Pattern in the Material Folk Culture of the Eastern United States* (Philadelphia: University of Pennsylvania Press, 1968), pp. 107-8; Shanon Jackson and Tim DeBord, "'Lasses," *Foxfire* 7:4 (Winter 1973), 273-79; Carl Fleischhauer, "A

Short Essay to Accompany the Film *How to Make Sorghum Molasses"* (Morgantown, West Virginia: Office of Radio, Television, and Motion Pictures, West Virginia University, 1974); and Suzanne Stiegelbauer, "A Folk Craft as a Folk Art: An Example of Cane Syrup Production in East Texas," *Mississippi Folklore Register* 12 (1978), 118-30.

[19] For an overview of hogs and pork foodways in rural Delaware, see Passmore et al., *Three Centuries of Delaware Agriculture,* pp. 51-54. "Hog killing time was a social event for families and neighborhoods. Many hands were needed to care for the pork meat quickly—the scalding, scraping, cutting up, salting down, curing, sausage grinding, and cooking out the lard" (pp. 51-52). Hog killings continue on family farms in Delaware, though much less frequently than when Jehu was young. Videotapes documenting a hog killing and food stuffs preparation on a small farm in Sussex County are on deposit at the University of Delaware Folklore Archives, as are a series of photographs taken during the day-long event in 1977. Former student Lee Derrickson published five of his photographs in a feature article for *Delmarva News,* 6 April 1977, p. 13. Similar photographs and write-up appear in "Slaughtering Hogs," *The Foxfire Book,* pp. 189-98. The latter was obviously not an inspiration for Jehu's assemblage, dated two years earlier. A Texas account is found in E. J. Rissman, "Hog Killing & Soap Making," in *Hunters and Healers: Folklore Types and Topics,* ed. Wilson M. Hudson (Austin: Encino Press, 1971), pp. 103-5.

[20] Jehu's whittlings, as well as Lillian's role, have not gone unnoticed. Two nonacademic accounts are: "Jehu Camper: Woodcarving," in Denise Baker, comp., *Learning About Delaware Folklore; A Delaware State Arts Council Program in Sussex County* (Delaware State Arts Council, 1978), pp. 42-45; and Chung Ho Woo and Suzanne Weiss, "Jehu Camper," in *Project P.E.T.* (Delaware Department of 'Public Instruction, 1978), pp. 62-64. Feature articles in Delaware newspapers include "The Resident Whittler," *The Harrington Journal,* 26 December 1974, p. 5; "Whittling Time Away," *Sunday News Journal,* 7 February 1984, sec. F, pp. 1-2; and "Folklife Officials Salute Jehu Camper, Wife," *The Delmarva Farmer,* 7 February 1984, p. 16. The latter article reports recognition of the Campers in a certificate from the office of the then-Governor Pierre S. du Pont acknowledging their contribution to preservation and presentation of the state's folklife heritage. The award was initiated by the Delaware Folklife Project; a retrospective exhibit co-sponsored by the Project and the Delaware State Arts Council was subsequently installed in Wilmington, 5 November-7 December, 1984. In addition to a slide-tape show, and other exhibits since the late 1970s in Delaware and Maryland, the Campers were featured at the 17th annual Festival of American Folklife in Washington, D.C., summer 1984.

TUGBOATING ON THE CAPE FEAR RIVER: A PRELIMINARY ETHNOGRAPHIC SKETCH

Robert H. Byington
University of North Carolina at Wilmington

SHORTLY AFTER I BEGAN MY FIELDWORK with tugboat crews on the Cape Fear River, one of the departmental secretaries asked me why I was spending so much time on the river. So I said I was doing some research on tugboats. "What's there to research?" she replied. "All they do is chug up and down the river." So much for the remote exoteric perspective—shared, incidentally, by probably 95 percent of the residents of Wilmington, N.C. In keeping with a typical Southern focus upon the land and what happens on it as the only things worth thinking about, Wilmingtonians do not concern themselves with water-based subcultures. The few that sporadically do—in Wilmington, N.C., at least—retain an anachronistic, disdainful view of anything having to do with the river, particularly tugboat crews, as shiftless, immoral, uneducated, irredeemably lower class, and therefore beyond the social pale. That view may have been justified by the realities of river culture in the past but it is no longer accurate and probably has not been since World War II. Nevertheless, as with most work cultures seen from the inside, there is little about tugboat operations that would be considered appropriate for a picture postcard.

The shaping principle or basic work flow of harbor tugboating is the movement through relatively unstable waters of relatively massive ships which for different reasons—usually spatial constraints, but sometimes breakdown—are unable to maneuver effectively on their own. They require the assistance of the much smaller and more maneuverable tugboats which push, pull, and sometimes tow them into position. The dominant impression one invariably receives from this spectacle is the tremendous disparity in size between the tugboats—the largest of which currently on the Cape Fear is 100 feet long, with possibly a 20 foot beam, drawing 11 feet of water—and the ships, which in the relatively small river harbor of Wilmington can be as long as three football fields, as wide as a six-lane highway, as high as a thirteen-story building, and as deep as 38 feet. The enormous bulk and power of these ships are not only difficult to describe, they are almost impossible to apprehend in any cognitive sense; and yet it is precisely these awesome forces which the tiny tugs must consistently dominate.

The job requires, first of all, a proper tool, the tugboat, which is basically a floating steel container or casing for an engine and the propeller it turns. The engines are typically 16 cylinder twin diesels (frequently obtained from cannibalized locomotives) generating three to four thousand horsepower and turning propellers (or "wheels," as they call them) up to 10 feet in diameter. The tugs also have wheelhouses, galleys, staterooms for the crews, heads, etc., all comfortable and highly functional; but horsepower is the key to successful tugboating, because *without* it, all the tug's equipment and all the men's skill will not suffice to move that ship.

Nevertheless, the job also requires appropriate equipment—lines and hawsers, communication devices, etc.—and a constellation of work techniques divided among four specialists, docking pilot, tugboat captain, tugboat engineer, and tugboat deckhand (of which in a normal crew there are two). Each of their tasks involves special knowledge and a discrete set of skills which nevertheless must function in close, intricate coordination if danger and damage (which in shipping can involve enormous costs) are to be avoided. This interactionally demanding collaboration of techniques generates other modes of communication—principally custom and verbal art—which allow the student an "objective" view of tugboatmen as very different from both the exoteric stereotype in the public mind and the esoteric view they have of themselves.

I will not discuss any of these jobs in detail, but since a knowledge of work techniques is central to understanding any occupational culture, I have to touch upon them, beginning with those of the docking pilot, the "ego ideal" of all tugboaters.

In command of any "move" is the docking pilot who almost all tugboatmen aspire to become because he occupies the top position in the pecking order and gets paid the most. He needs no perceivable skills, as such, beyond the ability to climb or descend a ship's ladder and push the button on a walkie-talkie, and his "working knowledge"—what you need to know to do the work—is so purely cerebral or visceral, so internalized, that one cannot see it working; but it is possible to describe what he does and what he needs to know in order to do it.

If a ship is sailing, the tugboat carries the docking pilot to the docked ship which he boards. He ascends to the bridge and takes command from the ship's master. Then through *direct* commands to the ship's helmsman and the ship's quartermaster (who transmits orders to the engine room) and through radioed commands to the captains of the tugs, and the captain of the lineboat, if one is needed, the docking pilot has lines cast off, and, coordinating the ship's power with that of the tugs, maneuvers the ship until it is in mid-channel and pointed down the river, whereupon the river pilot assumes command for the 23 mile trip to the sea, and the docking pilot reboards the tug. If the ship is arriving, the only difference is that the docking pilot boards the ship in the middle of the river, takes command from the river pilot, and reboards the tug when the ship is securely docked.

Sounds easy, and they make it look easy, but it involves a constant computer-like analysis and control of interdependent, ever-changing variables which are awesome. There *are* constants—the docking pilot's knowledge of the capabilities of the tugs, and his knowledge of fixed factors in river navigation—but among the things the docking pilot has to learn afresh every time he docks or sails a ship are the size of the ship, its draught (water and air), its "drag" (if there is more draught aft than forward) or—the opposite—how much it is "down by the bow," the ship's power, the state of its engines, the kind of propulsion (single-screw, twin-screw, variable pitch, or what), the size and make-up of the ship's crew, the stage of the tide, the velocity of the current, the velocity and direction of the wind, and a lot more. The combination is never exactly the same, and much of this information the docking pilot cannot acquire until he arrives at the ship. Moreover he will never know it all before he begins. For example, he has to assume that all the ship's systems are working, but as that rarely proves to be the case, almost every move is an exercise in ad hoc improvisation, the tension of which is belied, traditionally, by expressionless features and a studied casualness of stance. Docking a ship, because it involves *making* contact rather than *breaking* contact, is more problematical than sailing one; and when you realize that the tolerances within which the docking pilot must position a block-long ship at the dock are at most 6 feet and can be as small as 8 inches, you can only wonder how it's done.

The docking pilots can't tell you. The process of calculation and decision is so internalized that they find it almost impossible to identify the operative factors. One time I had been after Butch LeClerc—generally acknowledged the best docking pilot in the harbor—to explain the timing of certain orders I'd heard him give a ship's helmsman, as to how he knew *when* to issue each one in succession. He tried hard to be of help but obviously found it impossible to conceive the reasons, let alone articulate them, and concluded in exasperation, "Christ, I don't know, Bob. You just give the order and hope for the best—and if things get fucked up, blame the quartermaster."

The work techniques of the captain, engineer, and deckhands on the tugboat are easier to perceive and catalog (although in each instance the propriety of certain actions at certain times will depend as much upon "feel" as the docking pilot's decisions).

The captain of a tug, although subject to the orders of a docking pilot when a ship is being moved, is, like a sea captain, undisputed master of his little vessel and makes all the decisions affecting the crew's life aboard, what they do, when they do it, and how they do it. This is not immediately apparent because the captain is also "one of the boys" and in the close confines of the tug can hardly be aloof. Also, since his authority is absolute, he is not required to assert himself, and his orders are so low-key, so conversational in tone they are barely noticeable *as* orders. His mastery is nevertheless undisputed and apparently indisputable, regardless of the affection, or lack thereof, with which he is regarded by his crew.

While he directs and monitors everything that happens on his tug, his specific task is to navigate and drive it. This he does from the wheelhouse, which is equipped with a radar scanner, a LORAN set, a depthfinder and other conventional navigational instruments in addition to the helm, throttle, and the captain's ornate chair, in which, incidentally, he rarely sits, preferring a less formal perch by a window. From this eyrie he puts the tug through the maneuvers required of her, communicating with his crew on a move through direct verbal commands and gestures.

The engineer is responsible for operating and maintaining all the tug's mechanical and electronic systems. These consist chiefly of the main engine, typically a 16 cylinder Alco twin diesel, generating 3600 horsepower, but include the pumps, generators, and all the wiring, piping, gauges, and panels of auxiliary systems as well. The engineer is the first aboard the tug on any move and cranks up the main engine and auxiliary systems about fifteen minutes before the tug leaves the dock; he is also the last to leave, shutting down the tug's systems before he locks up and disembarks. When a tug is "all hooked up," i.e., traveling at maximum speed, the noise in the engine room is literally deafening, and most engineers wear protective ear muffs as a matter of course. In the summertime the heat in the engine room can reach temperatures of 160°F, and the engineer, usually stripped to a pair of shorts and tennis shoes, has to endure them. In the wintertime, however, he is far more comfortable than the deckhands who are handling frozen lines on the deck above. Most engineers love their engines and like their work.

The deckhands handle the lines, which are used to attach the tugs to the ships being moved, and which range in size from a 3/8 inch heaving line to 4 inch hausers. The heaving line is usually made of hemp, but all the others are plastic—polypropylene, nylon, or dacron. Each of these plastics has essentially the same tensile strength—significantly more than hemp—but different special properties, such as floatability, stretchability, resistance to heat, etc. For example, nylon and polypropylene float and dacron doesn't; but dacron is not vulnerable to heat, so that most large hausers, which are the most difficult to handle, have a core of nylon or polypropylene to make them float, and an outer layer of dacron to resist the heat generated by friction between the hauser and the bitt.

A whole book could easily be devoted to the numerous discrete ways a line is "made off" at a bitt for different purposes, the ways they are physically handled to maximize efficiency and reduce the risk of injury, the ways in which they are coiled or uncoiled on the deck (e.g., a line is always carefully coiled in a clockwise direction to reduce the possibility of those perverse loops the men refer to as "assholes"), and the ways they are knotted, spliced, or fastened for this or that purpose. There is literally a volume of "working knowledge" about lines, but the nature of this article precludes that narrow a focus and the reader will just have to take my word for it that there is more to being a deckhand than appears at first, second, or even third glance.

Since there are no schools for tugboatmen, at least on the Cape Fear River, everything they need to know to do their jobs is traditionally acquired through various kinds of informal apprenticeship to predecessors in the same line of work. Typically, one of the engineers told me he had learned about engines by simply following after "ol' Ben Edge," a legendary engineer on the river, and watching what, when, and how he did something. Everyone else, from the deckhand making off a line on a bitt to the Captain scanning a radar screen, learns the same way. It's the only way. If we accept the centrality of *work technique* in the definition of occupational culture, then it's clear that on that basis alone contemporary tugboating on the Cape Fear River, with all its utilization of and adaptation to evolving maritime technology, remains for the moment as pure a traditional folk occupation as we are likely to find.

Moreover, if, as Victor Turner (Turner 1972:340) and others have suggested, a state of liminality, of being betwixt and between established patterns, is highly conducive to the creation of folk alternatives to the value systems and behaviors on either side, then the Cape Fear River tugboatmen qualify eminently as a folk occupation in this regard as well.

For one thing, they are betwixt and between the land and the sea. While they employ nautical terminology and folk speech almost necessarily in their work with boats and ships, have common nautical skills (can "hand, reef, and steer"), are familiar with navigational instruments and charts, and can plot a course with the best of them, not a one of them to my knowledge has been a deep water sailor and none has any interest in becoming one. In fact, they fear deep water and are decidedly uneasy when called upon to go "outside" (as they occasionally are). I made two trips "outside" with two different crews during which we were out of sight of land for about fourteen hours. Since we were merely delivering the boats to a shipyard in Charleston, there was nothing to do; the weather was superb, the sea was calm, and I, in my outsider's blissful ignorance of their anxieties, found both trips idyllic. But the crews never relaxed for a minute. As we passed through the breakwater into Charleston on the first trip, the engineer who had been anxiously watching its approach for fifteen minutes, breathed a great sigh of relief and said, "God, it's just like coming into an air-conditioned room." On the second trip I was with the captain in the wheelhouse as we approached Charleston, and when we rounded the sea buoy and headed in toward the harbor, he said with a satisfied smile, "Now she smells the bottom." They don't like it out there. Since about 97 percent of the deep water seamen they encounter in their work are the foreign crews of foreign flag vessels whom they regard with ethnocentric condescension, they also reject an *identity* as seamen. Although they have a large number of nautical traditions, they like to think of themselves as landsmen, difficult as that may be.

For one thing, the rhythm of their lives is determined by always erratic and unpredictable ship schedules, so that only when they are on their annual vacations can they schedule any aspect of their lives with some degree of certainty. Even those crews that are "off" (i.e., so far down in the rotation order as to make it unlikely they will be called out) are on standby and must be reachable. They cannot plan anything, cannot join in anything but impromptu social activities close to home, cannot assume civic obligations, cannot guarantee their presence at their kid's graduation ceremonies, and so on. Like seamen, therefore, they do not enjoy the stability and cannot participate in the normal activities of the land-based culture they identify with.

They occupy a liminal status in at least one other respect. With the exception of the docking pilots, all of whom completed high school, most of the tugboatment left school earlier, some of them in sixth or seventh grade, to help their fathers fish, to work on a dredge, or whatever. Most of them have lived on or near the water all their lives. They have had little formal education, therefore, and because they have always worked with their hands at one task or another, can be considered "blue collar" or working class in the common sense of that phrase. They are "woikuhs," and share almost all the traditions of white working class culture in the region, including a virulent racism.

Nevertheless, because of certain economic factors peculiar to the shipping industry (including a strong union), a deckhand, the lowest paid member of a tugboat crew, will easily make $35,000 a year with an average amount of overtime and can make a good bit more. This automatically places them in a tax bracket, on a socioeconomic level, with the white middle-class of the region whose values and life-style they do not presently share but, from all indications, would like to, and don't know how. As one of my student assistants once said, "They have white collar salaries, but blue collar mind-sets." In time the normal processes of social assimilation may gradually eliminate the liminality in which they presently exist, but for the moment they are in a phase of incipient transition from a body of traditions they have always known to a set they think they aspire to, but with which they are still decidedly uncomfortable.

This uncertainty about who they are and where they fit into things is also reflected in the ambivalence between certain genres of their expressive culture and their actual social values. They are keenly aware that to the extent there is any image of them at all in the public mind ashore, it is that of rowdy drunkards and brawlers unfit to associate with decent folks. They resent this stereotype because it could not be farther from the truth. They are model husbands and fathers to a man, several of them are deeply religious, and my impression is the majority don't drink anything harder than Dr. Pepper. They all speak with contempt (although not in his presence, to be sure) of the one captain, a holdover from the old days, who does drink a lot. While not in the least bit sanctimonious, they are as upright a bunch of straight arrows as I have ever encountered. It was months before I realized this, however, because their favorite stories are about heroic tugboatmen whose chief claim to fame lies in the herculean drinking feats attributed to them. These legendary excesses are remembered so fondly in narrative after narrative, one often capping the other, that I can only assume it is admired behavior regardless of its total absence in their own lives.

There is a similar and probably related ambivalence between the lurid macho images they project of themselves in sexual reminiscences or boasts and the almost demure nature of their actual behavior with women. It is as if they feel something, for better or worse, has gone out of tugboating, and they attempt to retain some semblance of it in the fantasies of their expressive culture.

They maintain a continuity between past and present in other behaviors as well. Although hand-held radios have greatly facilitated communication between the docking pilot on the bridge of a ship and the captains in the tugs below (which are usually out of the docking pilot's range of vision), it was not always that easy. Only a few years back, they communicated entirely by whistles, and developed rather elaborate signal systems. The docking pilot, using a police whistle for the tug on the ship's stern and the ship's whistle for the one on the ship's bow, would command them to "Push in full," or "Back down half," or whatever, with varying combinations of long and short blasts. The tugs would acknowledge with their own whistles. It worked, but caused occasional hardship. One of the tugboat captains told me that when he was decking for tugboat Captain X years ago, the Captain would refuse to open the wheelhouse windows in the winter because of the cold. This meant he couldn't hear the police whistle of the docking pilot signalling from the wing of the ship's bridge, so he always stationed one of the deckhands on the roof of the wheelhouse to hear the whistle and transmit the signal to him by pounding on the roof. That way only the deckhand got cold.

The radio has eliminated the need for all that, of course, but, curiously, while the docking pilot now transmits and the tug captains receive by radio, the tugboat captains still acknowledge with the tug's whistle, the pulling of which involves more effort than a simple "Roger" into a microphone. I asked one of the tug captains why they continued to acknowledge that way, and after thinking about it a few seconds he said (typically), "I don't know. We just do." It's merely one example of how traditional work processes and techniques in almost all occupations adapt to new, evolving conditions and thus persist over long periods of time.

Another common characteristic of contemporary work cultures, their occasional transformation and adaptation of externally derived elements from the environing popular culture to satisfy special occupational needs, is exemplified by one of the tugboatmen's neatest customs. At Christmastime, they choose lots and the crew of the tug that wins (which becomes the Christmas tug) gets to mount the company "Christmas tree" on the upper deck. The tree is a 12 foot length of steel pipe with a 4 foot crossbar welded on about 3 feet from one end (the bottom). Strings of lights are then tautly extended from the top to evenly spaced spots on the crossbar, and the whole thing is mounted over a smaller vertical pipe welded to the deck. The crew also mount big speakers on the tug and play Dolly Parton, Loretta Lynn and other country stars singing Christmas carols.

The lights on the "tree" are the blinking kind, and consequently the captain of that tug at Christmastime is known to everybody as "Cap'n Twinkles" ("Come in, Cap'n Twinkles" the docking pilots say over the radio.) The sight of that tug going up and down the river at night is unforgettable, and it's even more of an experience to be on it. For one thing the Coast Guard has prohibited the tree as a hazard to navigation and will make the crew take it down if they catch them with it lit. But the Coast Guard have only two boats to patrol 23 miles of river, and since all the other river craft are in collusion to protect the tug, the patrol boats are easy to elude. It's like being in an episode from *Smokey and the Bandit*. You hear an anonymous voice over the radio saying, "Cap'n Twinkles, CG161 (the number of the patrol boat) just passing No. 52 buoy headed your way." "Roger, thank you," Cap'n Twinkles says, and takes evasive action. The crew love this, but the part I enjoy most is the effect the Christmas Tug has on the crews of the ships we move. I went down river with the tug last Christmas to meet a ship we were going to dock, and when we tied up alongside, one of the ship's crew who was leaning over the railing exclaimed, "Lord, I've been goin' to sea for forty years, and this is the first time that Santa Claus ever met me on the river." The ship's deck crew were so delighted that they had us stand by for ten minutes so the engineers could shut down the ship's engines and come up on deck to shoot pictures. That one custom adds such a rich esthetic dimension to the tugboatmen's occupational lives that they begin anticipating it in memorate and legend weeks in advance, and relive it in the same way for a couple of months afterward.

Another custom probably unique to tugboating illustrates what is to me, at least, one of the most curious characteristic features of their culture, viz., a preoccupation with food. The custom derives from the fact that ships occasionally replenish their stores while in harbor. When they do this, they do not inventory the larder and order what they need from the ship chandler; they simply dispose of anything remotely perishable they have on hand and restock their freezers from scratch. Since modern seamen (especially those on tankers and container ships, which are what mostly come into Wilmington) eat extremely well, what they normally dispose of would grace the counters of any upper-class butcher shop ashore, and the tugboatmen are the beneficiaries of their largesse. When this occurs, the packages of steaks, rib roasts, legs of lamb, pork roasts, shellfish, poultry, whatever, are brought back to the dock, and at the first possible dinner-time (usually noon the next day), consumed at Lucullan feats held in the large, superbly equipped company galley built for precisely that purpose. The crew which receives the gift prepares the meal and everybody there, from the owner of the company to the lowliest machinist's apprentice in the shop, comes to the table. In my experience it has occurred as frequently as twice in ten days, as infrequently as once every five weeks or so, but it's always happening. The men relish it each time with the same enthusiasm as if it came but once a year. The occasion invariably generates stories of past feasts with which this or that crew is credited, and the recollections, ever more embellished (I have heard one of them three times), are competitively recounted.

If this were the only culinary event in their workaday world, the men's enthusiasm would be understandable, but it isn't. They are eating in almost equal ritual fashion all the time. Not only do the docking pilots and the owner (a feudal but benevolent overlord) continually put on pig pickin's, oyster roasts, and venison roasts to which everybody of any importance on the river (including the tugboat crews) is invited, but every crew consistently prepares large meals in its own tug galley, which is as well-equipped as any modern kitchen. All the men are capable cooks, each usually with a personal specialty, and they take the purchase, preparation, and consumption of these meals with the utmost seriousness. The meals themselves are the topics of conversations *at* the table, and whether you personally feel the sauce, spices, texture of the meat, consistency of the noodles, or whatever, justifies extensive comment, it's what you do if you want to be one of them, because it's what they do. I confess I don't understand this, yet. Although there are parallels in other occupational cultures (McCarl 1981:12), I have never associated with a group of men in any walk of life *quite* so similarly focused.

Their food customs exact a toll, of course, and that is principally manifest in what they call—if not with pride certainly without chagrin—the "Cape Fear belly." Except for the one or two blessed with extraordinarily appropriate metabolisms, they all have one, and I have come to regard it as almost a hallmark of their occupational identity.

The "Cape Fear belly" is of course a product of the tugboatmen's foodways, but it is maintained in rotund vigor by perhaps the overriding factor in their work environment, its boredom. Their contract specifies that they work a four day, thirty-two hour week, between the hours of 0800 and 1600. Since the longshoremen who load and unload the ships' cargoes work only in the day, most of the actual moves, the docking and sailing of the ships before or after cargo is handled, take place at night, when the tugboatmen are on overtime, what they refer to as "hours." This means that, normally, they spend the greater part of each work day hanging around the dock, and since even superfluous maintenance is hardly infinite, they have little with which to occupy the time except sit around and talk. They could of course go home, but that costs them too much. Not only would their regular wages be docked, but any hours they worked that night would not then be overtime. So they hang around doing nothing, sometimes all day.

In addition, the unpredictability of the shipping means that even though a tug has been ordered, and leaves "the hill" to dock or sail a ship at a given time and place, that ship for any number of reasons may not have arrived or be ready to leave when the tug gets there. Since the tug is frequently miles from "the hill" and the ship may arrive or leave the next minute or hour, it is considered uneconomical to order the tug back to "the hill" (when it might have to be dispatched again as soon as it arrives); so it ties up at the nearest dock and waits. Those waits consume far more time in any given week than the actual moves, and any one of them can range from fifteen minutes to three days. While the men wait, they have nothing to do and sometimes get testy with boredom, particularly when, as is often the case, there are important things they might have been doing at home. It is clearly the most depressing feature of their occupational routine, and since it is chronic rather than occasional, the one that most challenges the ethnographer to understand and interpret.

It is also the cultural scene in which narratives recapitulating and commenting upon almost every aspect of their occupational experience can most easily be collected. If techniques are primary, narratives are unquestionably the tugboatmen's most illuminating form of occupational communication. They occur abundantly and are almost exclusively focused on the central concerns of working tugboatmen: physical hazards, desirable (and undesirable) kinds of behavior in characteristic situations, occupational status, and the psychological stresses of the job.

These occupational personal experience stories form the basis of oral interaction in any occupational group and their content ranges from the day-to-day concerns of group members on the one hand to unusual occurrences or dramatic event or accident accounts on the other. They therefore comprise an invaluable adjunct to personal observation of the work techniques with which they are always directly or indirectly concerned. In the case of tugboating, the all-too-frequent and sometimes interminable wait downriver for an overdue ship becomes the most productive time that an ethnographer can spend with the men. It is an occasion when there is literally nothing to do, the atmosphere in the tug galley is thick with boredom, and job-generated concerns are articulated in revealing stories.

The narratives, typically, are didactic in nature and are one of the major vehicles in the tugboatmen's informal communications system through which they transmit occupational information which would not, under normal circumstances, otherwise be available to newcomers or recruits.

Among the many sub-genres of accident or near-miss stories, for example, are those dealing with the bridges across the Cape Fear River, which do not always open when they should to permit the passage of a ship, or do not open far enough. The Cape Fear Memorial Bridge which, as everyone on the river knows, was obsolete before it was built, is particularly troublesome in this regard and there are many stories about it. Half the trouble, of course, derives from the size and power of the ships themselves which need plenty of sea room to maneuver. They cannot respond to split-second timing in a river as narrow as the Cape Fear. An average-sized modern ship coming up the river on a full flood tide at, say, dead slow ahead, can require five minutes and a whole mile to stop from the moment the quartermaster is given the "Full astern" order. This means that once the pilot commits the ship to the bridge, usually from a distance of about three quarters of a mile, the bridge *has* to open—there's no place else for the ship to go—but it *doesn't* always.

A story is told of a W. R. Grace ship coming downriver under its own power on a full ebb tide. One tug, being pulled along by the ship, was tied up to its port bow. The tug had already sailed the ship at the W. R. Grace dock upriver and, as required by CG regulations, was accompanying it downriver through the bridges. As they approached the Cape Fear Memorial Bridge, the docking pilot, still in command on the ship's bridge, signalled the bridge-tender to open it. The bridge-tender tried (or one assumes he tried) but the mechanism malfunctioned and the bridge stayed closed. A full ebb tide on the Cape Fear river, with no wind behind it, makes about four knots, and the ship at "Dead Slow Ahead" probably another four or five. There was no way it could stop before it hit the bridge. Making a necessarily quick decision, the docking pilot ordered the tug at the ship's port bow to "Push in full," and shove the ship's bow into the west bank of the river. The ebb tide caught the stern of the ship and swept it down past the boats docked on the east bank of the river—missing them, some say, by inches—and in a matter of a minute or less, the ship was in mid-channel and headed upriver under its own power and out of danger. Lucky, to be sure, but lucky or no, it was an appropriate response to that emergency, and even if the boats docked along the river had been smashed, that's better than taking the bridge out. All tugboatmen, most of whom aspire to be docking pilots, know this story—as they know hundreds of others—and presumably would find it useful if ever in a similar situation.

Another cautionary tale, also involving the Cape Fear Memorial Bridge, has to do with a ship called the *Transcolorado*. A new freighter, the *Transcolorado* had three cargo booms mounted vertically (standing straight up from the deck, like masts) in a line running aft from the bow to the bridge. It was coming upriver with two tugs tied up alongside. This time the Cape Fear Memorial Bridge rose to its maximum height, and it was assumed that the ship with its cargo booms would pass under easily.

But maximum height was about a foot too low, and as the ship with its tugs passed under, each cargo boom in succession struck the lower girders of the span and was bent back toward the stern. The one farthest aft was driven into the wheelhouse of the ship and left a huge dent in it. The electric cables strung along the bottom of the span were also ripped loose and parted, showering the decks of the ship and tugs with a cascade of sparks. The men on the tugs thought the bridge was falling on them, and couldn't quite believe it seconds later when they were through the fire and sailing serenely upriver. The damage to the bridge was a little over $10,000, but that to the ship cost upwards of a half-million. The moral? The docking pilot should always ask for the "air draft"—i.e., the distance from the water to the highest point on the ship—of any vessel passing under the Cape Fear Memorial Bridge. From that time on, such a question has been a part of the docking pilots' standard operating procedures, and the importance of it is kept fresh in the traditional narrative about the *Transcolorado*.

The ships are so huge, powerful and, as compared to the tugs, so relatively uncontrollable, that the tug captains must remain constantly alert when their tugs are in contact, lest, like the Lilliputians with Gulliver, they be overwhelmed in some way. If the ship is single-screw, for example, the tug stationed at the stern has little to worry about, but if the ship is twin-screw, there is real danger that the tug will be sucked into the ship's propellers, mangled and sunk; so the utmost care has to be exercised, and there are a number of accident stories about this or that tug whose captain didn't.

When a ship is coming up or downriver in mid-channel, even at "Dead Slow Ahead" it is travelling at four to five knots, and the volume of water displaced by the moving hull has tremendous force as it moves toward the stern and the turning propeller. This means that the tug coming alongside or, for that matter, leaving it, must do so in the most carefully calculated way to avoid being swept back under the stern of the ship and smashed into fragments. It used to be that the river pilots, once they had taken command of a departing ship from the docking pilot, would speed it up, usually from "Dead Slow Ahead" to "Slow" ahead, before the tugs were sufficiently distant from the ship's hull to be free of its backwater, and scare the tug crews half to death. "They had to get to Southport [their destination at the mouth of the river]," the docking pilots remark bitterly.

Another hazard, sharply defined in story after story, is posed by parting lines. When a line or hawser parts under the great strain to which lines are constantly subjected in tugboating, it does not, like a snapped steel cable, whip sidewise, but rather, like a snapped rubberband, comes back with tremendous force in a straight line to the bitt. Since there is no way to anticipate a parting line, all the stories about injuries sustained by deck hands from parting lines have the same moral: once a line is made off, get away and stay away from the bitt until the line has to be handled again. If you have paid any attention to the tugboatmen talking shop, you would know all this before ever touching a line.

Like most occupations nationwide, tugboating on the Cape Fear River is on the brink of significant change, particularly in the way the work is organized, and the formal qualifications a man must have to do the work. As ships get larger and more automated, and the tugs that move them necessarily more powerful, formally acquired technological knowledge, and a stricter, more efficient organization of work energies are likely to replace the old-fashioned traditional modes of learning and doing that predominate today. Tension between the old and the new is already manifest in the labor-management relations of the one fully operational towing company on the river, and I expect it will intensify when contract renewal time rolls around again. Although it is unlikely the tugboatmen will view it this way at first, an ethnographer sees occupational change as merely the gradual merging of old work traditions with new ones, which should be no less fascinating to study than the old. He does not perceive change as threatening, therefore, and for the most part looks forward to it. That is one of the principal differences between the ethnographer and the workers he studies.

REFERENCES

McCarl, Robert S.
    1981 "The Meal's on Me: Moving Into, Up and Out of Fire Fighting Culture." *Center for Southern Folklore Magazine* 4 (Summer):12.

Turner, Victor
    1972 "Betwixt and Between: The Liminal Period in Rites de Passage." In *Reader in Comparative Religion: An Anthropological Approach.* Edited by William A. Lessa and Evon Z. Vogt. Pp. 338-347. New York: Harper and Row.

"FAMILY YACHT"

George Carey
University of Massachusetts

PERHAPS THE BEST WAY TO WRITE ABOUT A BOAT, particularly an old boat which has some history and tradition surrounding her, is to go aboard alone, sit, observe, and hope that some of the lore and the old maritime passions may filter out of that woodwork and into your own sensibilities and subsequently onto a typewritten page. I tried that approach on a foggy morning not long ago when the *Dyon* lay moored in Tenants Harbor, Maine, lay moored, I hasten to note, on the same granite rock she had graced for sixty years.

To set the record straight, *Dyon* is a 52-foot gaff-rigged sloop "designed and built," as the then current *Rudder* magazine put it, "by the Luders Marine Construction Co. for Mr. Philip L. Smith of New York and Tenants Harbor, Maine." As fate would have it, P. L. Smith would turn out to be my maternal grandfather, and as fate would further have it, the *Dyon* slipped down the ways in Stamford, Connecticut almost ten years to the day before I ever opened a blue eye on the daylight of this world. July 24, 1924 she first gathered water around her stern, and the next day, with my grandfather at the helm and Luders himself aboard to see that everything went copacetically, she set out for Tenants Harbor, the port which would become her lifelong place of hail. There she has served the Smith family for sixty years as the very essence of yacht, "one of various types of relatively small vessels, characteristically with sharp prow and graceful lines, and ordinarily used for pleasure."

At the present time *Dyon* is owned by three cousins of my generation, Philip, Stephen and Dorsey Smith, and since they have spread their seeds liberally enough to produce among them two males and two females, it appears that the *Dyon* may well sail through the reach of yet another Smith generation before the final nautical mile gets tallied up.

All these thoughts and more pressed in on me as I rowed out to the boat for my maritime seance on that foggy morning I spoke of a moment ago. I think one of the reasons I sought her out on this sodden day was that that morning she had not been visible from shore as she had been during the previous two weeks of fair weather. My house at the edge of Tenants Harbor sets at such an angle that when I awake each morning and look over the aft end of the bedstead the first thing I see, framed in a pane of glass, is the *Dyon*. There she is suffusing the thin line between my conscious and subconscious as she has done ever since I can remember. Ever since I began coming to this family compound, which my visionary grandfather created back in the 1920, and 30s, that gaff-rigged sloop has been inextricably linked with the place, inextricably linked for me and for innumerable others who have come here with what comprises summer by the Maine seacoast. Even in recent years when for various reasons the yacht did not go overboard every season, late spring frequently called forth an anxious litany:

"*Dyon* going in this summer, Steve?"

"No, not this year I'm afraid."

"Oh, sorry to hear that, " and you were too, for it meant that the vacation would be shy a very special component. The picture was not going to be quite complete.

So I sit below in the main salon and listen to the condensation drip off the huge sail cover onto the varnished cabin top and observe, hoping the ghosts will surface. Everything is the original or an accurate replica of what once was: the dark blue velvet covers and cushions, the white inlaid panelling set against the dark stained varnish work, the handsome bronze ports, three to a side, and the neat brightwork of the old fashioned skylight. There is a delightful symmetry at work down here, everything on the port side matching exactly its counterpart on the starboard side, and this subtle precision is very soothing to the eye.

I am astonished by the size of the quarter berths. In the brochures for modern yachts these would doubtless be advertised as ample for two people apiece, but we know that over the years they gave good rest to only the captain and the navigator. Between these berths the varnished companionway leads up five steep steps to the deck, for the depth of this vessel is deceptive. When you look at the curve of her lines from the water, she is far from a high-sided thing, less than three feet of freeboard, but if you go aboard and go below, down down down, you understand what old mariners meant when they spoke of a deep vessel. Giants could live aboard this yacht in easy comfort.

Not that my grandfather was a giant, not by a long shot. He stood a mere 5' 4" but in my imagination he towers well above that. And when he went to Luders with his idea for *Dyon* in 1923 he was no Johnny-come-lately to the yachting scene, In the 1890s when still a student at Harvard, his father bought him a 45 foot gaff-rigged cutter which in the style of the times carried a press of sail that would intimidate any average sailor. Once married with a family underway, he acquired secondhand a 40 foot sloop, also gaff-rigged and also called *Dyon*, which he sailed until he went off to war in 1917.

What actually inspired the old man to build the second *Dyon*, I cannot say for sure, but I suspect it was his innate love of sailing and the sea coupled with a desire to garnish his summer property with an appropriate yacht which he could use to entertain his friends. By the mid 1920s P. L. had secured sizeable landholdings on Hart's Neck along Tenants Harbor's southern shore, several miles of shore front and more than a dozen dwellings which he had built or bought from local farmers or fisherfolk. Though I was too young to experience it personally, I've always imagined this coastline compound as a sort of Gatsbian arrangement four hundred miles north of Long Island. My grandfather might approach a friend on a cold New York street corner in February and say something like "Harold, I've this place in Maine and I'd enjoy having you in one of the cottages for a couple weeks in August if you and Sally would like to come." There was no rental involved in this bargain, just the supposition that while they were there Sally and Harold would do P. L.'s bidding: play on his tennis courts, admire his formal gardens, attend his parties, and sail on his yachts.

And for those fortunate enough to be invited there was more than a handful of boats to "mess around in," though I suppose they used other terms for it at the time. P. L.'s fleet included a number of powerful speed launches with names like *Nip* and *Tuck*, three North Haven sailing dingies and three Luders 16 foot Redwing sloops. Of that fleet the *Dyon* was unquestionably the queen except during a handful of years when she was eclipsed by the *Skunk*, a 58 foot commuter that the old man had Luders build him in 1928. Powered by two 305 horsepower Sterling Dolphin engines she ate up the miles and the gas, but at twenty cents a gallon, the latter didn't matter all that much. Though the *Skunk* passed out of the family shortly after the market fell flat on its face in '29, I am happy to report a modern testament to her style and speed and durability: in the summer of 1973 she was picked up off of Matinicus Island in Maine hustling dope in the drug trade.

I am not quite so happy to report that the *Dyon* herself in her early days indulged in some nefarious dealings, if the tales of P. L.'s oldest son are to be believed. He claims that during the height of prohibition, he came to Maine with several of his Harvard cronies (one of whom later became the Chairman of the New York Stock Exchange) and behind the old man's back commandeered the *Dyon* and her crew and bore away for Canada. There they ducked into St. Andrews, loaded with contraband which they smuggled back into the states. But, according to this uncle, slipping through the government patrols offshore was not half so worrisome as getting their illicit cargo ashore in Tenants Harbor. P. L. was a rigid teetotaler and spirits in the compound were strictly forbidden.

Ignominy aside, what astonished me in reading the old logs and talking with the people who sailed with my grandfather in those heydays of Tenants Harbor yachting is how much the emphasis was on day trips. Though both the *Dyon* and the *Skunk* held commodious sleeping quarters for six or eight people apiece, the overnight cruise was the exception rather than the rule. In a log covering the *Skunk's* passages from 1928-29, I find only one instance when passengers stayed aboard and that was on a dash down the coast to Amesbury on the Merrimac River with a return the following day. More typical was an afternoon coastwise voyage which began in Tenants Harbor at 1100, made stops and shoreside forays at North Haven, Northeast Harbor (lunch), Bar Harbor, back to Long Island in Seal Bay on Vinalhaven, North Haven again with a return home by 1930 in the evening—a maritime gallop of more than 100 miles that would take the sensible cruising man in a sailing vessel a good week or more to complete.

Though the *Dyon* was not expected to cover this kind of ground, it is obvious that she too was conceived more for single day journeys than for long ocean hauls. Her cockpit, for instance, is enormous. You can spread twelve adults about in it this way and that and never for a minute feel cramped. Add to that the seeming acres of varnished surface on the cabin top where ten more can leisurely stretch out (beware the tack lest you land in the cold Gulf of Maine when the boom sweeps low coming across) and you have all the ingredients of a seafaring infraction or a well conceived drowning party. Indeed, of late years I have seen the *Dyon* sashay out the harbor with a crowd aboard which made me hope that all the coast guard personnel in Christendom were soaking up beer in an isolated pub somewhere and pray that the Almighty might keep the terrible swift sword of his meteorological wrath sheathed for the space of yet one more summer's afternoon.

Years back when the old man ran his fiefdom with steely precision there was a certain set pattern to the average *Dyon* outing. The evening before, the old crank telephone that linked the cottages together would ring and P. L.'s voice would come over the line announcing an outlook of fair weather for the morrow and the promise of a day's sail on his yacht. Be at the dock at eight-thirty sharp. If you were wise you were punctual, for the vessel embarked promptly, and should you be left standing with your picnic basket at dockside, your tardiness kindled dismay and the renewal of your free summer cottage in the compound might stand in open jeopardy.

For those who showed up on time, they could expect to find the yacht in along the wharf, Captain Pike and the steward dressed in the approved uniform at hand to help the women and children aboard, and then with a signal from the owner, the vessel would be away, bound out of the harbor for a long day—sometimes eight or ten hours, sometimes longer—coursing the lower reaches of Penobscot Bay. One cousin, now on the windward side of eighty, attributes her cataracts to those endless hours spent as a youth squinting at sunlit waters aboard the *Dyon*. And there was no respite either; P. L. did not believe in going ashore for lunch, even though he owned several offshore islands. You sat there for however many hours and you conversed and admired the scenery and the boat and ate your lunch and you damn well had a good time. If you were young you behaved. If you didn't, as my mother did not one time, you got set on a bell buoy for a few hours, as she did, to cool your heels.

In all this seafaring, P. L.'s wife, Belle, my grandmother, had little interest. She detested the water and seldom ventured out on it. When the old man was away in New York what she would do in lieu of actually going boating was to have the paid crew bring one of the yachts in along the dock and then invite her female friends aboard for lunch or high tea. This way she felt the seagoing staff earned their keep and she could have her own kind of outing without passing the entire time in mortal terror. When the old man was in residence she suffered anguish enough, however, for off he would go on those long day jaunts with all the children and a host of others, and come late afternoon Belle would pace feverishly up and down the veranda of the seaside house staring vacantly eastward for any telltale sign of that huge gaff-rigged sail.

From all reports, my grandmother did not worry without cause; the old man was a notoriously bad sailor. One of the older generation who sailed with him often told me with unvarnished candor, "I never once saw your grandfather with a chart in his hand." Another companion who had been in P. L.'s employ for many years and sailed with him alone a good deal recalled bouncing off more than one Maine rock with full way on. But as he was quick to point out, "When we hit like that, I never acted as if anything had happened, and neither did he."

My grandfather also had the reputation of driving a boat hard and never tying a reef into those 1350 square feet of Egyptian cotton. My father, then a shiny new son-in-law, remembers distinctly a terrifying beat up the Eggemoggin Reach into the teeth of a 45 knot northwester. P. L. absolutely refused to shorten down; the jib blew away and the metal spreader on the port side bent double. The mast miraculously held, but they had to hobble into the Benjamin River for repairs.

By the late 1930s the depression had eaten into P. L.'s yachting grandeur and his summer estate. Many of the boats had been sold away; black alder claimed the formal gardens and weeds grew between the tennis court lines. During World War II, the place lay absolutely fallow and Nazi submarines lurked beneath the waters that the *Dyon* and the *Skunk* had plied with such abandon a decade before. If there was ever talk in these years of actually selling the *Dyon*, I do not know of it, but in 1943 the old man died, and at the war's end, the time came to divide up the estate. The boat passed into the hands of the youngest son, Horace Webster, who, following the preppy guidelines, had been nicknamed Bubble. (We also have a Nip, a Flip, a Tripp, a Tiff and a Biff in this family compound.)

Of all the four of P. L.'s progeny, it was appropriate that the vessel fall to him. (Actually he bought it from the estate.) Unlike the others Bubble knew the water well and appreciated intensely the way of a fine yacht. What began for him in 1947 was a love affair with the *Dyon* that would endure with undiluted vigor until the day he died in the summer of 1970.

For someone who had known the vessel when she was under a paid captain's constant surveillance and the luster of care was still upon her, it must have been hard for H. W. to come to his newly acquired relic after she had sat six years unattended in Snow's Shipyard in Rockland. Daylight pierced almost every seam and she lay three full weeks swelling in her cradle while the men in the yard tried to cajole my uncle into selling the old thing for an antique. But like his father before him, H. W. was pigheaded and he hung on, and within a year he had the *Dyon* sailing once more, out on those familiar waters of lower Penobscot Bay.

Though the currents and the seascape along the Maine coast stay much the same generation in and generation out, yacht owners and yachting styles change. Now in the postwar years, the only concession that H. W. made to the grandeur of the 1920s was to take along, when he went cruising with his family and friends, the last retainer of P. L.'s estate, a Nova Scotian named Dowling who was a cross between Howard Blackburn and Leonardo da Vinci. Dowling went ostensibly as cook and deckhand, but spent most of his time working on the cranky engine, a chronic problem that had beset the yacht since her inception. (In four pages of a *Dyon* log I discovered from 1924, the engine broke down five times bringing the vessel from Connecticut to Maine.)

If H. W. never attained the yachting opulence and style of his father, he far outstripped him as a sailor. There was in Bubble, or so it seems, a stern reaction to P. L.'s cavalier attitude towards seamanship which stemmed no doubt from an incident that occurred in the thirties while tacking out of the St. George's River. Bubble, then a young medical student, had the helm. He knew implicitly that they were closing fast on Jenks Ledge and implored the old man to bring the vessel over.

"We'll tack," P. L. said, "when I say 'tack'."

Then they struck, the hideous grinding of lead on granite as the vessel shelved out on the reef. Above the rumble the old man's voice came again,

"Alright, now tack."

But it was six and one half hours later before the order could be carried out.

So H. W. became the cautious, sensible mariner his father had never been. I seldom saw him underway without a chart at hand, and in all his twenty-four years of ownership he never set the *Dyon* aground. What is more, he came to know his boat much more intimately than P. L. for he did a great deal of the maintenance himself. Family folkore has it that he is the only person to have ever taken the boat out alone, an endeavor which makes Hercules' toils in the Augean Stables seem downright frolicsome. Like all men who dote on boats as surrogate mistresses, Bubble fancied her almost to a fault and lavished on her gifts, some often tendered in a most roundabout manner. One year for Christmas his wife, Sallie, received a brand new electric bilge pump in her stocking with an unpretentious note attached: "Love and Merry Xmas; now you won't have to pump so often."

Still, in all his passion for the *Dyon*, my uncle was not a selfish man. He shared his yacht's joys with others, particularly his children, and they in turn came to respect the boat, not just as a sailing yacht, but as a family heirloom, their link with both the family past and the sea. Under their father's tutelage all three became accomplished seamen, knowledgeable in the intricacies of their vessel and sensitive to the winsome nature of the Maine coast. Only once after an early mishap did this third generation ever bring this old vessel to woe and that was not exactly their fault. Under tow in Fox Island Thoroughfare without wind and with (yet again) a balky engine, the lobsterman pulling them skinned a mark and bounced the *Dyon* off a large stone in on the North Haven Shore. His response, typical of men who have little time for yachtsmen anyway, came over his shoulder to those on board:

"Deep, ain't she."

In more recent times the *Dyon* has become even more firmly linked with the family compound at Tenants Harbor. Not only does she swing to her familiar mooring off the south shore between Memorial Day and Columbus Day, but now in winters she resides on the estate in a long shed, known locally as 'the shipyard', which P. L. built for a large vessel in 1930, but never used. Her launching each spring and her hauling each fall have become annual rites of passage which outline definitively the summer yachting season in the community.

Awhile after that foggy morning I spent aboard the *Dyon* trying to dredge up the past, I took two trips aboard the old boat in order to set some more matters in chronological line. There was an afternoon sail, late summer, then in mid-September a short cruise. It had been a while since I had done this sort of thing, as for a twenty-year stretch I had owned a Concordia and had viewed P. L.'s creation most frequently across a patch of water, invariably from astern desperately trying to keep up. For the afternoon junket we had a bright northwest day with puffs off the land in excess of twenty knots, and for a crew we were virtually undermanned: one of the owners and seventeen hands. Up forward, three Goliath cousins of the fourth generation wrestled with halyards (thank God!) while I stayed aft and worked the winchless mainsheet (my God!). H. W.'s youngest son, Steve, had the helm and orchestrated the outing with considerable aplomb considering the weight of his responsibilities.

We flew east out the harbor, out beyond the infamous bell buoy where my mother spent her unpleasant time in remission of some long forgotten seagoing sin. There we bore away to the southward, down by Hart's Ledge towards Mosquito Island in front of the familiar coastline and the cottage veranda where my grandmother had paced out her anxious vigils. I stood by the mast, looked aft, and in my mind's eye flashed an old faded black-and-white photograph P. L. had taken on what must have been a day much like this in these very same waters more than fifty years before. By the look of it the wind is fresh for there is a cant to the vessel. Captain Pike sits on the weather rail in his white skipper's hat and tan windbreaker. Bubble in his mid-teens has the helm, flanked by my mother and his other sister, both older and dressed in dark sailor suits. A huge uncle reclines in a tie on the fantail along with several other unidentifiable passengers.

The mind's eye refocuses and clears away on the present: same scenery, different cast. No paid captain in evidence now, just Steve steering the yacht with his young son Justin in his lap as the vessel bends to a twenty knot gust. They are flanked by a covey of cousins, the women revealing far more epidermis than their forebears. Long brown willowy limbs taper away to painted toes and fingers. The men recline informally in green and yellow polo shirts. But the conversation that floats off to leeward no doubt has the ring of timelessness about it: The small boating mishap of two days before, the frightful tennis performance of that morning, the equally unaccountable shenanigans at a party two nights before, the peerless Maine day and the surroundings, Matinicus out to sea, Monhegan ahead, the Camden Hills astern beneath their cumulus cover, and of course the yacht itself, this yacht, *Dyon*, which so handsomely draws all these sensibilities together. This was, I knew then, the indelible pattern of summer life.

    The cruise differed little in its impact, only now there were but three of us, Steve, myself and Maynard Bray. We loosed a bright southwest scamper up Penobscot Bay along a coastline giving way to fall, and then alone at anchor in the Barred Island we watched a long spent yellow moon rise out of the sea to the east. Below by candlelight we told the tales all yachtsmen tell, and I know my grandfather and my uncle would have laughed and nodded approvingly had they been listening in the darkness, which I knew they were. By far the most arresting yarn came from Maynard Bray. As it turned out, his professional life brought him to the study of old wooden boats, but as a young boy Maynard had simply been a kid growing up on the coast of Maine, by nature drawn to the water. During World War II when the *Dyon* lay hibernating at Snow's Shipyard in Rockland (H. W. had taken his medical degree off to war and P. L. lay dying of a creeping cancer in Tenant's Harbor), his father took him to look the place over. In one of the big sheds they stumbled across the *Dyon* biding her time. Maynard's words stick in my mind: "I looked up at her in that shed and she seemed huge to me with that big deep keel. The green bottom sides just went upwards forever till they flared out towards the water line. I remember my father. He pointed up and said, 'See that, you see that? That, my boy, is a *yacht.*'"

    Indeed.

HOBART AMORY HARE BAKER—OCCUPATION: GENTLEMAN ATHLETE

Tristram Potter Coffin
University of Pennsylvania

TODAY, ONE COULD START A FOOTBALL TRIVIA SESSION with the question, "Who was Hobey Baker?" Even on the campus of Princeton University where the hockey rink (his other sport) is named after him, the average undergraduate doesn't know or care what he did. Sportswriters, the scops of so many heroes, have forgotten him completely. Nor are the reasons hard to come by. First, Baker was a hero, not to the American public, which in the days before World War I had yet to be addicted to football, but to what is generally called "society," to that upper crust of debutantes and their beaux who attended the best schools and colleges on that portion of the Atlantic Coast which runs from Baltimore to Boston. He was a hero at a time when manly sports were slowly replacing big game hunting, and even war, as an outlet for upper class *machismo* and when Americans were developing their very own national games from British rounders and rugby. It was the time of the fictional exploits of Dink Stover and Frank Merriwell (who could make a baseball curve twice on the way to the plate) and of the real-life adventures of Teddy Roosevelt and his friends who went to faraway places few would ever see. For all the sad young men, Baker was not only real and immediate, he was "one of us," fated as his fame might be to inundation when the frontier backwashed across the Eastern Seaboard.

Furthermore, as the American public at large became addicted to college, and then professional, football, Baker's place as Saturday's hero was taken by a steady parade of highly publicized figures who have turned all football heroes into one with (to borrow Joseph Campbell's phrase) a thousand faces. No man's individuality can stand what sports publicity has done to our "gridiron greats" and no man can be remembered long when his limited heroism is repeated week after week, year after year, by the Gipper, the Galloping Ghost, Albie, Squirmin' Herman, Whizzer, Doc, Broadway Joe, the Juice, etc., etc., etc.

Nonetheless, the legend of Hobey Baker is worth a close look, not only because he was one of the very first heroes of that occupation sports, but also because he was a real gentleman (born of the purple), and not what almost all American heroes are or are meant to be: natural gentlemen—Natty Bumppos, Virginians, Abe Lincolns, Dwight Eisenhowers.

Who then was Hobey Baker? Hobart Amory Hare Baker was born in Bala-Cynwyd, Pennsylvania on what is loosely called the Philadelphia Main Line on January 15, 1892. His family was highly respectable. His father, A. Thornton Baker, an old Princeton halfback who manufactured upholstery, was a member of the right clubs like the exlusive Racquet Club and the most exclusive Fish Club. His mother, Mary Augusta Pemberton, was an ex-debutante of the same cut. An uncle was President of the Jefferson Medical College and one of the leading physicians in the city. In the family, which was originally Presbyterian but became of course Episcopalian, there was one other child, a brother Thornton, one year older than Hobey.

When Hobey was fifteen the marriage of his parents, which had been a rocky one, ended in divorce—a source of embarrassment and even humiliation in the Main Line society of that day. For a number of years before, while the marriage was in trouble, the two boys had been pretty well neglected, brought up by relatives, without a stable home, and with almost no motherly affection. As was, and is, customary at this level of society (particularly after a divorce), the prep school was given the job of training the boys, *in loco parentis*. Thornton and Hobart were packed off to the most exclusive school of all, St. Paul's in Concord, New Hampshire, when they were twelve and eleven years old. St. Paul's and then Princeton were to be Hobey's home and pillars of stability, their masters and professors his parents, for the next decade of his short life.

Children of divorced parents, and especially those who are deprived of a stable homelife, have many of the characteristics which are seen in Hobey Baker: particularly the defensiveness (which in his case took the form of reserve and shyness among strangers) and the desperate need for attention. The latter, which can display itself in rebelliousness or promiscuity, was satisfied in Hobey's case by sports, and the abnormal attention and adulation he received from his athletic ability was probably as important to him as air and water. It gave a purpose to the sort of fanatic practicing of which he was capable, and his long lonely nights skating on the pond at St. Paul's or those hours spent kicking field goals after football practice were for him an avenue to attention just as similar hours were to be an avenue out of poverty for farm and ghetto boys later in the twentieth century.

St. Paul's like its counterparts, Groton, St. Mark's, St. George's, Kent, was modelled on the British public schools, especially Eton, Harrow, and Thomas Arnold's Rugby. Its purpose, paralleling the purpose of the United States Military Academy to turn out line-officers, was to turn out gentle businessmen and their associates. In the early years of the twentieth century, this meant to produce "recruits to true manhood" who had been given a conservative training in ideas, particularly political ideas; who would embrace the tenets of the Episcopal Church; who would be fully aware of honor; who would accept discipline and the concept of rank easily; who would dress properly and, with impeccable manners, maintain appearances at all times. In short, the young would be quite like the parents who were footing the considerable bills.[1]

Today, for many, this program with its antifeminist attitudes, its emphasis on athletics and youth, its intellectual blandness and political conservatism, is anathema. America has spent much of the twentieth century undermining the tremendous influence which these Eastern Seaboard institutions have had on American life. The very schools and colleges have themselves been modified; in fact, Woodrow Wilson had already started on Princeton by the time Baker arrived there. But the fact remains: the products of these institutions have made good citizens, effective line-officers in the conduct of American affairs, and constitute one of the country's most civilized segments.

The colleges to which the products of St. Paul's and the rest would go to round off this indoctrination were led by the Big Three: Harvard, Yale, and Princeton, followed by their satellites, the other members of the present Ivy League.[2] None of them were anywhere near as large in 1910-1914 as they are today (Princeton had 1300-1400 undergraduate students when Baker was there), and although there were plenty of undergraduates with less distinguished backgrounds than Baker's, it was the men from "St. Grottlesex" who set the tone for the campus and dominated the best clubs and fraternities. The rest, the F. Scott Fitzgeralds from places like Minnesota via Newman Academy, looked up to these men and either rebelled against them or, more likely, tried to emulate them. Fitzgerald, at the start of "The Rich Boy," describes them with the famous lines: "They are different from you and me. They possess and enjoy early, and it does something to them. . . . They think, deep in their hearts, that they are better than we are. . . ." Fitzgerald never got over their superiority—a lot of his colleagues have never gotten over it either. It is quite revealing that John Davies, who has done the standard biographical work on Baker,[3] felt free to write (probably somewhat inaccurately) that the "first 'poor' people" Baker ever met were the men he found under him when he joined the 141st Squadron in the First World War. He had certainly played hockey against many he would have labelled "toughs," but it is true he didn't see those opponents on a day-to-day basis, and many of his father's generation did make it through life without ever getting to know members of the madding crowd as friends.

So it was. The upperclass undergraduates vied for superiority through fraternal, social, academic, and athletic achievement like pups in a litter of wolves, testing themselves for the time when they would have to struggle for excellence in the world of business, or perhaps law, medicine, or politics. They were guided by a semi-servile group of highly trained masters and professors, for whom shaping the man was the main task of the academician. Of course sports, derived as they are from war, gave the student his most dramatic proving ground. Sports, especially sports in which one could display self-discipline, teamwork, leadership, and courage (games like football, hockey, crew, baseball) were required of all. The games were to be played hard, to win, but within the rules, under "the code." And for those without the skill to make the varsity, there were second squads and intramural leagues. Success in athletics gave instant respect, even adulation, on the campus, and upon graduation offered a *carte blanche* in the financial world of the Eastern Seaboard cities and outposts such as Cleveland, Chicago, or St. Louis. So if there were dozens of Tom Buchanan's "seeking . . . for . . . some irrecoverable football game" whose lives had reached at twenty-one "such an acute limited excellence" that all following was to savor of "anticlimax,"[4] there were also dozens more who got through the door first because of early excellence in sports and who kept that advantage through their lives. Arthur Mizener,[5] writing in the "Introduction" to Davies' book, cites that glorious moment in 1923 when T.A.D. "Tad" Jones, the Yale coach, entered the locker room at New Haven before the Blue–Crimson football game and spoke, unashamedly, to his team: "Gentlemen, you are about to play football for Yale against Harvard. Never in your lives will you do anything so important."

The Jones anecdote is revealing, not only because it established the melodramatic nobility of the code of conduct by which a man like Baker had been trained to live (he once broke into tears when learning he had been deliberately fouled by a man he considered a gentleman), but it also establishes the respect upperclass conduct engendered in people who were not so fortunate. When we make fun of the pre-World War I gentleman today, we are apt to forget that his behaviour was a model for everybody, for his employees, his servants, his associates. If a tough Canadian hockey player didn't conduct himself the way that Baker and his like did, that man still knew Baker's way was the way, and, deep down, he admired such behaviour and might even force himself to emulate it. Certainly, the whole servant class of the day was established along similar lines: the butler being as much a "gentleman" in his own world as the master of the house.[6]

Early on, football was described as "a game for thugs played by gentlemen".[7] In Baker's era it was definitely identified in the public mind with Harvard, Yale, Princeton and their opponents. The Eastern papers paid modest or no attention to Western teams, and the bulk of the All-Americans came from what is now the Ivy League. Moreover, the game was more than just a focal point for campus life. It was the focal point toward which one gravitated in later years. Woodrow Wilson, when Governor of New Jersey, attended a number of Princeton practices and was even present on the day he was elected President of the United States. The Yale-Harvard or the Yale-Princeton football game was an event of "high society", almost a festival, annually attended by alumni who had played or watched the game when they were young. Trains left New York and Boston loaded with thousands of people, and the ladies dressed for these events and the associated parties and balls as if they were Britishers at Ascot. Only the wallflowers were left out. Even today, seventy years after the war began an end to this society's ascendancy, there are many sophisticates to whom football means the Ivy League and little more, who will travel fifty to two hundred miles to see a nationally-scorned Harvard take on an equally ineffective Yale. For such people, a trip back to the stadium and campus is a trip back to the past, to a world that no longer exists, but that can be seen as real for few hours—especially if one's seats are far enough from the field so the non-Nordic background of most of the players goes unnoticed.

Today the gentleman athlete is an endangered breed, clinging perilously on the verge of extinction like the whooping crane, the red wolf, and the Tennessee darter. Supposedly such amateurs are "in it" for the sport. Like the jockey who has a "Mr." before his name on the hunt club entry board or the "paddle player" who practices for the national championships after work and on week-ends, the gentleman athlete tries to pursue excellence as "a thing apart" from his business and home life. To be sure, in our world, where young hopefuls devote almost all their waking hours to perfecting their school figures or dropshot or curveball, amateurism has come to mean second-rate. And with bigger earnings to be made in professional sports than in most businesses, the amateur who is competitive is rare indeed.

In truly amateur sports, where no one is practicing his youth and sanity away, natural coordination counts tremendously, because the overall skill levels tend to be lower. A natural athlete like Baker, and especially one who has a lonely enough psyche to spend hours on his kicking or puck-handling and conditioning, can easily dominate his fellows who are, as a group, dilettantes. And if a few rivals do have similar natural ability and similar practice habits, there is always that cushion of weaker players to capitalize on. To be a great athlete when surrounded by opponents of similar coordination and professional training is quite a different thing from being a great athlete when even a small percentage of the opposition is weak.

Another major difference between the gentlemanly sports of Baker's world and those of the modern professionals is the code under which winners and losers played. The East Coast of pre-World War I America was oriented to British sportsmanship (playing fairly for the thrill of the competition) rather than to the frontier American "win-at-all-costs" approach. In a today of Billy Martins, Bobby Knights, John McEnroes, and Red Auerbachs, we give headlines to an act of sportsmanship that would have been "of course" to Baker and his peers. In fact, the athlete who plays hard, never complains, loses with grace, and congratulates his opponent must live with the fact that he is poor copy in America and lacking in color. "You mucker" or "you dirty mucker" was the insult used in Baker's day to describe chaps who would stoop to opportunisms or illegalities that our professionals would accept as colorful and normal. And the word "muck" (manure) was not a word used in the pre-World War I years in the presence of ladies.

But even beyond "the code," all games are conducted according to two sets of rules: the actual regulations as set down in the "rule book," and "the interpretation of certain rules" that is accepted by experienced players and officials. It is breaches of the interpreted rules perhaps even more than outright breaches of the rules themselves which define good and bad sportsmanship among competitors. Whereas there are many cutthroat athletes, particularly those playing for big money, who will breach anything to win; a gentleman athlete never allows himself to take advantage of the way the game should be played. In fact, he finds pride in policing himself. Still, there is room for a certain amount of gamesmanship and psychological advantage-taking under any code. It is not ungentlemanly to "psyche" an opponent or to bully him: that is, as long as it is not overdone, one can talk to an opponent in hopes of making him self-conscious or more relaxed than he should be and one can tackle or check him particularly hard to make him flinch or be wary as the contest goes on. This sort of thing has been an accepted part of competition since time began, and deucedly correct though they may be, the Bakers of the world often master such tricks as well as any professional. It is a classic mistake to underestimate the competitiveness of a Baker. A code has nothing to do with how hard, even how desperately, a person will try. To be a good loser is not, of course, to be an easy loser.

Archetypical gentleman athlete, Hobey Baker was not large: 5' 9" and about 160 pounds. But for his day he was not that small either. (A Yale-Harvard or Yale-Princeton game at the turn of the century would see many less than six feet tall, many weighing less than 200 pounds on the field.) More important he was built like a rock, with particularly powerful legs, which made him difficult to tackle or to check. He was both a 10-second sprinter and "football fast". He was the sort of athlete one notices immediately, his coordination, way of handling himself, and natural grace catching the eye of every coach and most spectators at once. Slightly bow-legged like many fast athletes, he dominated games he played. A coach once remarked about an opposing star: "He's good, but he doesn't scare you." Baker scared you, and he sent electricity through the spectators, teammates, and opponents the minute he got the football or the puck. At St. Paul's he was the hero of the school with a fame that preceded him to Princeton.[8] When he left Princeton, his superiority was intact. Voted "the best all-round athlete" as well as the "man who has done the most for Princeton", he had lived up to his advance notices.

There is little doubt that Baker, no matter when he lived, would have been an outstanding athlete. Had he been born today instead of in 1892, he might realistically have matured to just under six feet and weighed in the 180s, big enough to star at the professional level considering his compact structure, powerful legs, and high pain threshold. Nor is there reason to think he would not have responded both to better training and practice methods as well as to superior equipment and competition. That he would have become a professional athlete today is another point. There are dozens of fine potential professional athletes who rise in the strata of society where Baker rose who will not consider a career in professional sports simply because making a living with one's body is something "one just doesn't do"—or at least doesn't do for any length of time.

Moreover, both the football and the hockey of today are less suited to the talents and flair peculiar to Baker than they were in the pre-World War I era. Football in Baker's day was a defensive game, largely because the most effective offensive weapons, the flying wedge, hurdling, and pushing the ball-carrier from behind, had been outlawed to make matters less dangerous. The forward pass had not really developed. The game had become extremely conservative in the East where it was a punting and field-goal contest in which teams jockeyed up and down the field waiting for a fumble or a dropped punt which would result in a long run or good field-position for a field-goal. The ball was fatter and larger than today's ball, and it was easy to pick it up on the bounce and to drop-kick. Games were frequently decided without a touchdown being scored: three or four dozen punts and a dozen field-goal attempts were not considered unusual.

Typically, the teams alternated kicking on the first or second of the three downs with what were almost certain to be futile smashes into the line. The defenses stacked the center, and the offenses, unskilled at forward-passing and not geared to go wide, got nowhere except against pushover opposition. Punting and hoping for a fumble or making one's opponent punt and hoping for a runback were the main "ploys" in contests between Eastern teams of equal strength. Thus, the spectators awaited the punts eagerly and were never disappointed for long. The safety man was the one they watched, and he might get the ball twenty or more times in a game. If the safety man was also the drop-kicker as Baker was, the whole offense revolved around him.

Baker developed a strategy for which he became famous. He would stand a few yards back of where he estimated the punt would come down and run forward, grabbing the ball in mid-air as the defending ends converged on him. At full speed, he would tuck the ball into his stomach and cradle it there with both arms. With this technique, he sometimes made more yardage on his punt returns than both teams would gain from scrimmage in the afternoon. The fans waited for this maneuver, and the phrase "here he comes" first used for his hockey rushes would surge from the crowd. Though he made long runs with this trick, it was also dangerous and he was often viciously wracked up, many games simply hanging on whether or not he dropped the ball. With his blonde hair identifying him (the players had no numbers), with his flair for the dramatic (he refused to wear a helmet), with his plays always being the crucial plays, he dominated weekend after weekend. No one who played with him or against him or saw one of the games he was in could miss him or forget him. Sportswriter John Tunis recalls[9]

> The whole atmosphere was electric when he was playing. Everybody would just stand up when he got the puck or caught a punt. Never wore a headguard in football and I remember that great shock of blond hair—Hobey standing waiting all alone. He was the only player on the field you looked at, the only player you saw. He could dropkick from any part of the field and from any angle. Everything he did was dramatic—because he was a vivid character—had *panache*, as the French say. He did everything with a kind of showmanship that wasn't showmanship because it was natural to him. He was a kind of panther. His coordination and footwork were so wonderful that he could take chances and do things that others wouldn't dare to. He had the faculty

of the real athlete—playing his best when he had to. He would dropkick, tackle, and run with a kind of feline intelligence, grace and charm—he would make everything look so easy. Never was anybody like Baker.

He was even better at hockey than he was at football. He was the first outstanding American player. Inducted into the United States Hockey Hall of Fame in 1973, he was also the first American to make the Canadian Hall. In his final game as an undergraduate, he scored both the tying and winning goals to defeat Harvard for the national championship. After graduation, he continued to play for the fashionable St. Nicholas Skating Club in New York. Lawrence Perry, a sportswriter for the *New York Evening Post*, describes what went on when the sign HOBEY BAKER PLAYS TONIGHT went up outside St. Nick's.[10]

> ... the scene ... would resemble a night at the opera. A line of limousines would stretch from Columbus Avenue to Central Park West on 66th St. A most fashionable audience would be inside, drawn solely by Baker's appearance. Men and women went hysterical when Baker flashed down the ice on one of his brilliant runs with the puck. I have never heard such spontaneous cheering for an athlete as greeted him a hundred times a night and never expect to again.

Hobey Baker was, then, a living Frank Merriwell and a series of demilegends began to develop about him. Like most legends they seem to be based on some sort of truth, but one has to be trusting to believe them *en masse* or to believe some of them at all.

1) Although he can run the 100-yard dash in 10 seconds flat (a remarkable time for his day), he learns upon entering St. Paul that his intramural team lacks a distance runner. He volunteers and defeats the best runner in the school.

2) At 15, he is given the prize as the best athlete at St. Paul's, excelling at baseball, tennis, swimming, as well as at track, hockey, and football.

3) The first time he puts on roller skates he does all sorts of stunts on one foot.

4) He drops in on the rifle-range and shoots a score good enough to qualify him for the varsity.

5) The first time he mounts a horizontal bar he does a 360 degree turn.

6) He practices his puck-handling on dark ponds and in unlighted arenas so that he can skate without looking down. Playing, as was the custom in his day, without substitution, he dominates every offensive and defensive thrust, carrying the puck the length of the ice again and again all evening. Lester Patrick, of New York Rangers fame, sees him play and announces he is the only amateur he knows who could make the pros at once.

7) He plays polo without knowing the first thing about horsemanship.

8) On the golf course, he's under par.

9) Too light for football, he is still the greatest punt receiver, runner, and defender of his time. He can pass beautifully, though that skill was seldom called for. With the exception of Harvard's Charlie Brickley, he is the best dropkicker ever to play. And one Princeton professor assures his friends that Baker has never dropped a punt in a game.

10) He practices long after others have quit, even continuing his workouts with push-ups, tumbling, and bar-chinning in his dorm room at night and between classes.

11) He can twitch any muscle in his back upon command, juggle five balls in the air in time to a tune he whistles, and walk about the dorm on his hands. On a bet, he walks from Princeton to New York in ten hours.

12) His endurance, resistance to pain, and self-discipline are unbelievable. He wears as little equipment as he can in hockey and football (the roughest games then played) to increase his speed. No one has ever seen him breathe hard.

13) Modest and honorable to a fault, he avoids publicity, blushes when fans, professors, girls, the press recognize him or make a fuss over him, considers his athletic ability a "freak" worthy of no special pride. Once he is said to have entered the locker-room of a semi-pro hockey team to congratulate his rivals on giving him such a "wonderful evening" when in actuality they had been trying to rough up and batter senseless that "stuck-up society kid" all night long.

Nor did the stories end with the athletic field. Typical of what might be called the "secular" anecdotes is one which supposedly occurred during a summer holiday in Massachusetts when Hobey was riding around in a Simplex auto with two other youths. Seated in the jump seat of the right running board, he was thrown out when the driver had to jam on the brakes to avoid hitting another car. Catapulted into mid-air, he realized he was going to land on a fence, so he quickly rolled his body in flight, caught the wooden gate of the fence harmlessly with a shoulder, dropped to the ground, and trotted back to the car like an acrobat who had just performed a routine stunt.

His marvelous conditioning had drawbacks, however. He trained so hard and partied so little he was completely incapable of holding liquor. He is said to have gotten drunk on a single bottle of beer (a medical marvel) at the Plaza in New York and climbed out on a ledge far above the streets during a bachelor dinner. He was also not much with the ladies. His reported sexual exploits involve excitements such as teasing a stuffy British girl by telling her he was a shoe-salesman and dancing with a seven-year-old on shipboard to Europe—a treat that did send the child directly to Seventh Heaven, but probably did little for his own love-life. His technique may well have been typified by the anecdote concerning a dance in Philadelphia. Introduced to a girl who opened matters by exclaiming: "Oh, so you're the famous Hobey Baker!" he was still irritated by her adulation when he got back to Princeton. Nonetheless, as with Frank Merriwell himself and Owen Wister's The Virginian, Baker's modesty and easy confusion probably made him attractive and certainly a challenge. He had learned enough, little as that may be, to have become engaged for a short while before his death.

Baker graduated from Princeton in 1914 as the First World War began. He had entered "business" like a typical son of Nassau, working first for an insurance company and then for J. P. Morgan & Co. at One Wall Street. He appears to have been thoroughly bored by the whole thing. Remarks such as "Think of all the things I could do today if I didn't have to go to work" and "Why didn't I get some of [my brother's] brains?" common enough complaints, probably meant a bit more to the ex-hero than they would to the ordinary college graduate trying to mature." Perhaps he was searching for that "irrecoverable football game": hockey at St. Nick's where Big Three graduates tried to recapture their college days, racing about in cars, riding motorcycles, chain-smoking, an eventual break with his New York career and a return to the family business in Philly, flying lessons. Flying was the natural end to all this, and the chance to fly in combat must have been welcome indeed. That aspect of the First World War was tailor-made for the ex-athlete.

Combat flying, as it was done in 1917-1918, was the last vestige of old battle-ways in which Achilles confronted Hector, Sir Gawain faced Bercilak de Hautdesert, and Abdul Abulbul Amir fought Skavinsky Skavar 'neath some "pale, yellow moon". While the soldiers in the trenches below had their rendezvous with choking gas and keen bayonet blades, while Mata Hari spun her webs in the boudoirs of Paris, while the girl-next-door wrung her hands and waited, the knights of the air fought far above the world, their kills recorded, their names (friend or foe) famous even back home. A couple, like Eddie Rickenbacker and Baron Richthofen (whose sister married D. H. Lawrence) are still recognized today. Nowhere does the relationship of sports to war better demonstrate itself than in those ace-vs.-ace battles of World War I.

For Baker it was college all over again. The combatants were gentlemen or gentlemanly, fighting to the death under a strict code of conduct and honor. The planes were primitive, merely extensions of the reflexes, strategy, and courage of the men flying them. He couldn't stay on the ground. One day he went up five different times. "You handle your machine instinctively," he wrote, "just as you dodge instinctively when running the ball in the open field." In the same letter, he compared having his orders to return to the front delayed to a postponement of the Yale game. Nor did the idea of dying seem to bother him. It merely increased the excitement. Death in combat he felt would be "pleasant . . . quick and sure." One time he rushed off with a fellow flier who had never been in combat before in what luckily turned out to be a vain attempt to attack eight Fokkers.

His insouciance made him highly successful. He was cited for distinguished service and exceptional gallantry, awarded the *Croix de Guerre*, and made commander of the 141st Squadron, which quickly adopted the Princeton tiger as its symbol. At home the papers picked up where they had had to leave off with his sports career, even running a characteristic story that he had taken a German almost as soon as he arrived at the front. In a chapter called "The Three Musketeers" (about Quentin Roosevelt of Harvard; John Williams Overton of Yale; and Hobart Baker of Princeton) in a book called *Diogenes Discovers Us*, John T. McGovern wrote:[12]

> [Baker's] leadership and efficiency in actual combat were so noteworthy that they continually attracted the attention and approbation of the French. The official descriptive legend attached to his name by the commanding officer was: "Nerve, daring, and uncanny skill," which is not so different, after all, from the expression in the press after a Baker day in a football game or hockey match.

On December 21, 1918, however, Baker was killed, not in combat, but in a plane crash near Tours, France. It was near the end of a "last flight" after he had received orders for his discharge. He had flouted an old flier's superstition that one doesn't go up after being ordered home, and he lost. His death made headline news in New York and Philadelphia, and phrases like "possessed every qualification of a model competitor and sportsman"; "America's ideal athlete"; and "no more cruel news . . ." filled the sub-heads and the stories.

What happened is simple enough. He decided to take just one more flight in his own Spad #2 before shipping to Paris. His friends, superstitious, tried to dissuade him, to no avail although he promised there would be no acrobatics. Chance had it that another plane with a troublesome carburetor had just been re-worked and was ready for a flight test. Again against better judgment he took off in the re-worked plane, rather than his own. Of course it stalled, as it had been doing. Baker, about a quarter of a mile out, tried to return to the field, going into a dive to regain flying speed. The plane never came out of the dive, crashing within sight of many of his friends in the 141st. Pulled from the wreckage, he died in an ambulance a few minutes later. He was buried in France in the rain to the strains of "Nearer My God to Thee". Later, the body was brought back to West Laurel Hill in Bala-Cynwyd.

It is ironic that the marriage of his sometime fiancée Jean Marie "Mimi" Scott was announced in the same papers that carried the notice of his death, one even making the announcement a sub-headline. She had probably seduced him into an engagement more as an ego-trip than anything else. She was a well-known New York belle who had been on the verge of engagement to a number of suitors. Baker, who had known her before the war, met her again in France where she was doing "something for the boys" in the form of hospital work with the Red Cross. An orphan, she was rebellious, charming, very rich, and unstable. Baker thought she was "real and wholesome," just what he had been looking for, but he did comment that he didn't know "what in hell" he would marry her on. Engagement announced, she was "madly in love" with Baker on one leave, only to be engaged to another the next time he got off.

This disappointment must be added to the fact that with the war ending and his sports career behind him[13] he had little to return to. A man of no family when he was growing up, for whom practice and sports were existence, the thought of another go at Wall Street or the family business had to be depressing. Moreover, he felt he had little aptitude for the affairs of adult life and thought all his successes had been in childish games and matters. It is easy enough to see him as desperate in December, 1918, and a final legend has grown up that he purposely crashed the plane, committing suicide rather than returning to emptiness. Davies belittles the possibility in his biography, labelling it sensationalism. But the fact is that people who knew Baker don't fully dismiss the idea. Certainly, there is no question in knowledgeable people's minds, that had Baker tried to crash land the plane without returning to the field he would have had an excellent chance of making it. The Spad #2 was an easy plane to crash land, and some pilots had been in ten or twelve such mishaps and survived them all. Baker had even made one forced landing himself. That he decided against doing it this time might be laid to his natural confidence that he could do anything physical, or it may have been a split-second "It's over. Let's end it!" decision. He may well have hoped to die in combat.

In his poem "To an Athlete Dying Young", A. E. Housman wrote:

>Smart lad, to slip betimes away
>From fields where glory does not stay
>And early though the laurel grows
>It withers quicker than the rose . . .
>
>Now you will not swell the rout
>Of lads that wore their honours out,

> Runners whom renown outran
> And the name died before the man.[14]

Maybe Hobey Baker was that "smart lad". Certainly, his name had long "outlived the man". His name may well outlive his occupation too, for he has survived as the best, and as the symbol, of a breed as near extinction as the canaller or the trapper: "gentleman athlete," in it *pour le sport!*

NOTES

[1]This particular sort of American upperclass came into being after the Civil War, rooting itself in the old British colonial families with a heavy sprinkling of newly-made money. It was decimated by the democratic impact of the First and Second World Wars, although its vestiges still survive in places like the Philadelphia's Main Line, Boston's Chestnut Hill, and New York's Upper East Side.

[2]Now Brown, Columbia, Cornell, Dartmouth, and Pennsylvania. The name comes from the roman numeral IV or I-V, which referred to the original four: the Big Three and Columbia. It has nothing to do with the vine.

[3]John Davies, *The Legend of Hobey Baker* (New York: Little, Brown, & Co., 1966). This is the standard, in fact only, biographical study of Baker. This article is heavily indebted to it for detail and background information.

[4]F. Scott Fitzgerald, *The Great Gatsby* (New York: Charles Scribner's Sons, 1953), p. 6.

[5]Arthur Mizener, "Introduction" to Davies, *op. cit.,* p. xi. Mizener incorrectly attributes the statement to Walter Camp.

[6]James Barrie's play, *The Admirable Crichton*, which was famous during Baker's youth, is about a butler who is better trained to rule than his aristocratic employers.

[7]The phrase is originally British and referred to rugby: "Rugger (rugby) is a game for thugs played by gentlemen, while soccer (association football) is a game for gentlemen played by thugs".

[8]He went to Princeton after taking an extra year at St. Paul's. His father had remarried and also suffered financial reverses in the recession of 1907. His brother, Thornton, never did go to college, entering business and letting what money could be scraped up go to Hobey and his brilliant athletic future.

[9]Quoted in Davies, pp. xxi-xxii.

[10]Quoted in Davies, p. xx.

[11]Baker was not a poor student. He was conscientious: good enough, and if not brilliant, studious in an unimaginative way. His lack of imagination probably helped him athletically and as a fighter pilot. It is easy to "think too much" under pressure.

[12]John T. McGovern, *Diogenes Discovers Us* (New York: Lincoln MacVeagh-The Dial Press, 1933).

[13]Baker had had a chance to turn pro in hockey before the war and might have had the same chance again. However, he was a gentleman and gentlemen were not apt to pursue a career in pro sports in 1918.

[14]Stanzas 3 and 5.

THE WOOD FAMILY OF PHILADELPHIA: FOUR GENERATIONS OF STONECARVING

J. Joseph Edgette
Widener University

IN THE LEAD CHAPTER IN A RECENT BOOK edited by Simon J. Bronner, he puts forth the premise that material culture is actually a manifestation of ideas into physical objects by humans who bring to their craft personal, social, and cultural influences.[1] This blending of the mental, physical, personal, and social aspects related to the artifact constitutes material culture. Henry Glassie also points out that material culture does indeed have an intellectual, rational, and abstract component.[2] Further, in my own doctoral dissertation, I have indicated that gravemarkers are more than simply artifacts containing certain pertinent information about the deceased.[3] The gravemarker does provide such data; however, it also reflects attitudes shared by a given community at the time the marker was created by its maker. The attitudes conveyed may deal with issues concerning death, style, taste, religion, and the like. In addition, the carver's ability, the influences from others in his craft, community norms, societal expectations, and client needs must all be considered when dealing with the artifact.

Therefore, if one examines gravemarkers as indicative examples of material culture, consideration must be given to the carver of the object as well as to the marker itself. It is only through his inclusion that a full and variable understanding of object, craft, craftsman, purpose, and process can be realized. Folklore scholars have pointed out the importance and necessity in considering the performer as well as the performance; the informant as well as the data; the practitioner as well as the practice; so too, in material culture we must consider the craftsman as well as the object.

The present paper endeavors to present on overview of a prominent, highly respected stonecarving family who have been practicing their craft since 1855 through four successive and successful generations. The intent here is to present a brief genealogical overview of the Wood family of Philadelphia, Pennsylvania, a capsulized version of their family business in gravemarker design and carving, a terse treatment of the general stylistic differences among the four carvers, and finally a few interesting, related anecdotes associated with specific markers carved by various members of the family. Essentially the Wood family of stonecarvers represents a wonderfully complete picture of gravestone carving from the traditional state through modern technology with transitionary stages sandwiched between.

As one travels across the city line between Philadelphia and Delaware County, one enters the small area of Upper Darby Township known as Fernwood. The Fernwood Cemetery is noticed almost immediately while traveling south. Opposite the main entrance to the cemetery is situated H. C. Wood, Inc.—Cemetery Memorials. The current president, Harvard C. Wood, III is the fourth generation to run the distinguished family business.

Aaron Wood, the founder of the business, was born in 1822.[4] According to many of the early Philadelphia street directories, he lived at various places in the western part of the city and was listed as a stonecutter by occupation throughout his life. After having married Deborah C. Meister, Aaron fathered thirteen children, nine sons and four daughters.[5] Of the offspring, three of his sons were destined to join their father at the craft of stonecutting and carving. Thomas Hargreave Wood (1858-1929), J. Frank Wood (1857-1920), and Harvard C. Wood (1858-1937) eventually ran the business with Harvard ultimately becoming sole owner.

After his marriage, Harvard C. Wood became the father of two sons and a daughter. Harvard C., Jr., born in 1906, would continue the stonecutting business, thus becoming the third generation to do so.

Harvard, Jr. married Dorthea Hutchinson, who mothered Harvard C., III, John H., and Mary Emma. Born in 1943, Harvard, III would head the family enterprise twenty-four years later. Sandra Besse Sanderson became the wife of Harvard, III, and to date has presented him with two children, Laura H. and Harvard C., IV. If perchance Harvard, IV should elect to follow in the footsteps of his father and previous generation gravestone carvers, he would become the fifth consecutive generation to run the family firm.

Therefore, in terms of the Wood genealogy, as it relates directly to the family gravestone business, we have: Aaron (1822-1904), Harvard C. (1858-1937), Harvard C., Jr. (1906-   ), and Harvard C., III (1943-   ).

The history of the Wood family cemetery memorial business serves as a splendid example of stonecutting at the traditional level and the gradual change to more modern, mechanized levels. Now in its 130th year, 115 of which have been spent at the present location, the business continues to prosper and is considered to be "Philadelphia's leading designers and builders of cemetery memorials."[6] How did this family business begin, and why did it achieve the renowned reputation it has established?

Aaron Wood is reported to have been born in West Philadelphia, where he made his home throughout his life of eighty-two years. In a brief newspaper article in 1896, Mr. Wood, then 74 years of age, was described as being "one of the oldest and best-known citizens west of the Schuykill River . . . who was in the marble business for half a century."[7]

Purchasing the properties of 3339 and 3341 Market Street, the present site of Drexel University's gymnasium, Aaron began a marble yard in 1848. However, in the late 1890s a devastating fire in City Hall destroyed all records so the present firm claims origin in 1855, a date that is easily substantiated from family records. There is, however, evidence to validate the earlier date.[8] Aaron worked out of the back of the property and the side yards with some of the work actually being done in the street. Harvard, Jr. tells the story about horses stabled nearby that were frightened by the intense noise made when Aaron would cut marble. At the time the cut was made by wire drawn back and forth with sand and water.

Because of the rapid rise in housing construction in Philadelphia, Aaron responded to the demand for marble steps, window sills, and lintels for the block after block of red brick houses that were being built.[9] Much of this work can still be seen. Before the Civil War there was a great demand for Aaron's specialization; however, after the War the use of steel replaced the need for marble.

Earlier, the public occasionally asked Aaron to cut and to carve marble cemetery memorials. He did this as a favor to the well-to-do and other members of the "carriage trade." The demand for this new commodity began to grow. What began as a sideline would soon blossom into a main business enterprise.

Harvard, III related an anecdote telling of how Aaron's family never had to do without meat: in the late 1800s butchers preferred marble blocks rather than wood on which to cut meat; they would ask Aaron for blocks of marble and would give Aaron meat in place of monetary payment.

With the opening of new cemeteries in the area, the demand for cemetery memorials grew. With the establishment of Fernwood Cemetery in 1870 Aaron decided to open a branch nearby which would deal exclusively with gravemarkers. This marble yard was to be run by his sons Thomas H., J. Frank, and Harvard C. Located on Church Lane at the Pennsylvania Railroad tracks, the business prospered from the very start. The brothers became owners of the business when their father sold it to them in 1895. J. Frank sold out to his brother Harvard, and Thomas died later.[10]

In 1896 the business was moved to its present site opposite the cemetery on Baltimore Avenue. This site is actually no more than a quarter of a mile from the original. One of the reasons for the move was the building of a trolley car route which would pass in front of the cemetery. Opportunity to increase business and provide convenience was not ignored by Harvard C. Wood.

One of the dominant features of the new location was mechanization—the use of a steam engine for cutting and polishing which replaced the outmoded handcutting. The effects of the Industrial Revolution were being felt at Fernwood. The name of the business emphasized this fact: "Steam Marble and Granite Works." Steam was indicative of power during this period. According to Harvard, Jr., the Woods purchased an engine run by illuminating gas to heat the boiler to make steam. The steam in turn ran the compressor which provided air to operate the tools, drills, and other equipment.

Even the billheads and letterheads of the business reflected the mechanization. In the beginning years the stationery headings were arranged in block form. As soon as the business changed to steam, the appearance of the stationery was altered. What could be interpreted as a wheel and piston in a memorial type style graced the top of the papers.

In 1935 Harvard C. Wood, Jr. became the third generation to head the family business. A graduate of the town Scientific School of the University of Pennsylvania where he was trained as a civil engineer, he became associated with his father in the firm in 1928. With his academic training, his progressive ideas, and knowledge of memorials, he attempted to "restore memorial art to its ancient position as a spiritual and sociological factor in the evolution of civilization."[11] Moreover, he achieved this through modern mechanization.

The third generation Wood revolutionized the idea of monument showrooms. Despite advice to the contrary, he built an ultra-modern, glass-enclosed showroom.[12] In addition he designed the building for mechanized work. An electrically operated crane moved the stones, and electric cutters, polishers, and drills for handcarving were introduced.

Harvard C. Wood, III, fourth generation, became associated with his father in the family owned and operated business in 1967. Also a college graduate, Harvard—also known as "Woody"—presently at the helm, continues the family tradition and upholds the flawless reputation of the firm. He has incorporated the latest technological changes in stonecarving techniques, but at the same time he has retained expert counsel and personalization.

When examining the evolution of the physical structures of the family business, one sees an impressive, professional, and successful development through the four generations who have made the company what it is today.

Briefly, the business began out-of-doors on Market Street in Philadelphia. The first building established at Fernwood was essentially a wooden shed next to the house at the Church Lane site. When the present site was begun, provision for a showroom was included. There were a couple of wooden buildings for working. Harvard, III explained that next to the property was a flower shop having an attractive display area. The shop went out of business, and the property was put up for sale. The Woods bought the shop but not the property. The wooden building was moved to the other side of the Wood property where it served as the showroom for the memorials.[13]

In 1931 all of the wooden structures were razed, and a new building of brick, steel, and glass was put in place. With a large glass enclosed showroom in front, office space and work space behind, H. C. Wood Memorials became a "modern" structure.

By 1958 the building had undergone some slight alterations. The top was squared, having previously been ornately decorated. In 1970, Harvard, III decided to add a larger sloping roof which created a more contemporary appearance of the overall structure.

From wooden structures to glass and brick building, from essentially handcut and handcarved monuments, through steam operated equipment to the modern sandblasting methods of today, four generations of the Wood family have maintained their devotion, service, and expertise to the community of which they are an integral part.

Because of space limitations, it will not be possible to provide an in-depth analysis of the stylistic differentiations of the Wood family carvers. However, an attempt will be made to give a general overview of the styles of each of the four main generations.

As indicated previously, Aaron began cemetery memorial carving as a sideline. However, in looking at his work one can plainly see simplicity, yet at the same time conformity to the overall stylistic needs and desires of the period. The carving reflects deliberate and careful transformation from raw stone to personalized memorial. The block lettering can be raised or carved into the stone. His liberal use of motif tends to emphasize simple and freeflowing lines and floral designs. There is enough evidence present to indicate his artistic ability.

When the three brothers went into the business, they too exhibited fine craftsmanship in carving. Though similar in style to their father's, each displays variations and attention to detail somewhat different from the others. Thomas Wood's work is closer to sculpture than the others. He created numerous beautiful effigies, many of which are still in good condition. Much of what was done during Harvard's tenure is in accordance with Victorian standards. Elaborate motifs, height, complex railings, and attractively carved monuments are his main contribution.

Harvard, Jr. brings the monument into the contemporary period. Various types in terms of style exist; however, the key feature of his work tends to be in stark personalization. Many examples can be found where the uniqueness of the marker is obviously striking as well as emotionally moving. With the advent of mechanized tools, sandblasting, and the change from marble to granite as the primary material, Harvard, Jr.'s memorials are characterized by greater dimension and a stronger attention to minute detail than previous generations.

Harvard, III attempts to preserve the traditional while he at the same time makes use of the modern. With advances in technique various materials can be combined, and greater flexibility in terms of creative aspiration are afforded. Preserving the family tradition of personalization while taking into account taste, appropriateness, and respect, Harvard, III's stonecarving talents personify keen insight into the traditional and foresight into that which is yet to come. Through the merging of time periods, his work appears "modern" yet refects a love of the traditional.

In looking at the works of these four generations, one sees the limitations restricting the traditional carver who had only hammer and chisel. One then observes the gradual introduction of mechanized tools, and the various methods of carving introduced still later in the form of sandblasting and laser.

The work done by Ludwig, Forbes, the Tashjians, and others in gravestone study can serve as models for further exploration, analysis, and evaluation of the Wood carvers.[14] Since all of the family records are still extant, the potential exists for undertaking such a study.

At a meeting of the American Folkore Society, I presented a paper which attempted to marry material culture to oral tradition in terms of narratives.[15] By seeking out and examining the story "behind" the marker, the oral tradition was explored and documented. Among the thousands of markers carved by the Wood generations there are many which arouse curiosity. Certainly both of the remaining Woods are connected with curious and interesting anecdotes related directly to the markers created by them. A few sample anecdotes follow:[16]

> The "bicycle boy" monument which once stood in Fernwood Cemetery represents a 6-year-old cyclist who pedaled his way around Philadelphia and as far away as Atlantic City until he became overheated one day, fell into a horse trough, contracted pneumonia and died. This monument was created by Thomas Wood in 1896.
> The Wood firm was contracted to place a marker on Botanist John Bartram's grave by students of Bartram High School in Philadelphia in 1948.
> The Sumerset churchyard in Bermuda has a Celtic cross carved by the Woods.
> Another interesting commission was to copy the Prayer Book Cross, an original design in Golden Gate Park, San Francisco. This commemorated the first Christian service in the English tongue on the Pacific Coast and the first use of the prayerbook by the Rev. Francis Fletcher of the Church of England, chaplain to Sir Francis Drake, on June 24, 1579.
> A local man, Dr. J. Muller was a great lover of birds. Upon his grave was placed a monument in the form of a birdbath.
> A recently completed stone by Harvard, III was designed and carved for Ralph Lewis Cleeves and his wife, Grace Lynch McKee, for placement in St. David's Churchyard, of eighteenth century vintage. According to Mrs. H. Edward Rothe, who requested the stone, she felt that, because of both the cemetery and her mother and father's interest in antiques, " . . . it would be inappropriate to place a modern stone there."[17] To conform to the shape of those present in the yard, the decision was made to follow through by using the old lettering as well. The granite used was taken from Westerley, R. I., a little village having much sentiment for the family.
> Finally, in Port au Spain at the Mucarapo Cemetery there is a monument carved by Harvard, Jr. for Mr. and Mrs. Paul Whitlock and their three young children who died in an airplane crash into the Bay there in 1944 while enroute to a new mission.

The above serve as simple examples to the potential such study can lead to. The carver can add much to the understanding of the meaning and the importance of the marker. To fully appreciate the artifact, knowledge of the carver is necessary and essential.

The four generations of the Wood family, stonecarvers of Philadelphia, provide us with a complete picture of stonecarving beginning with traditional methods and craftsmanship and leading up through present times.

As Edwin Dethlefsen states in his chapter in a recent study in archaeology, gravestones tell us much about a community;[18] however, in order to fully understand what there is to tell, one would benefit greatly by studying the carvers of the stones. Such is the case here. Knowledge of the carver is essential to the full revelation, only part of which can be experienced from his work.

NOTES

[1] Simon J. Bronner, ed., *American Material Culture and Folklife a Prologue and Dialogue* (Ann Arbor, Michigan: UMI Research Press, 1985), p. 3.

[2] Henry Glassie, *Patterns in Material Culture* (Philadelphia: University of Pennsylvania Press, 1968), p. 2.

[3] J. Joseph Edgette, *Statistical Consideration of Data Revealed by Gravemarkers in Delaware County, Pennsylvania, Spanning Three Centuries* (Ph.D. Dissertation, University of Pennsylvania, 1982), p.356.

[4] Much of the information obtained for this portion of the paper was obtained through personal interviews of both Harvard C. Wood, Jr. and his son Harvard, III. In addition family records and papers were also examined.

[5] The specific dates, ages, and other vital statistics regarding the Wood family of Philadelphia were obtained by consulting both the 1849 and 1880 Census records for the County of Philadelphia, Enumeration District 485.

[6] Harvard C. Wood, Jr., "H. C. Wood, Inc.: 100th Anniversary" (Ferrwood, Pennsylvania: Anniversary brochure, 1955), p. 3.

[7] *Philadelphia Press,* September 1896, p. 5.

[8] Taped interview with Harvard C. Wood, Jr., 4 December 1984.

[9] *Upper Darby News*, September 1955, p. 16.

[10] Telephone interview with Harvard C. Wood, III, 19 January 1985.

[11] *Philadelphia Press,* p. 5.

[12] *Upper Darby News*, p. 16.

[13] Through a careful examination of photographs and personal explanations by Harvard Wood, III, this material was compiled.

[14] Alan I. Ludwig, *Graven Images: New England Stonecarving and Its Symbols—1650-1815* (Middletown, Connecticut: Wesleyan University Press, 1966), Harriette Merrifield Forbes, *Gravestones of Early New England and the Men Who Made Them: 1653-1800* (Princeton, New Jersey: Pyne Press, 1955), and Dickran and Ann Tashjian, *Memorials for Children of Change: The Art of Early New England Stonecarving* (Middletown, Connecticut: Wesleyan University Press, 1974). These three studies are among the best respected in gravestone scholarship in America.

[15] J. Joseph Edgette, "The Gravemarker as a Springboard into Oral Tradition" (paper presented at the Annual Meeting of the American Folklore Society, San Diego, California, 12 October 1984).

[16] Anecdotes were supplied by both Harvard C. Wood, Jr. and Harvard C. Wood, III during various interview sessions.

[17] Taped interview of this client in March 1985 at the Wood establishment.

[18] Edwin S. Dethlefsen, "The Cemetery and Culture and Change: Archaeological Focus and Ethnographic Perspective" in *Modern Material Culture: The Archaeology of Us* by Richard Gould, ed. (New York: Academic Press, 1981), p. 137.

FOLKSONG AS A REFLECTION OF THE SHANTYBOYS' LIFE

Edith Fowke
York University, Toronto

> They are as jolly a crew of boys as ever you would find;
> They spend the winter pleasantly a-working in the pine. (35)[1]

THE LUMBERCAMPS PLAYED A MAJOR ROLE in preserving and spreading folksongs of all kinds in Ontario, so it isn't surprising that lumbering inspired the largest group of native songs found in this part of Canada. Those songs, composed by the men in the camps, give a very complete and vivid picture of what it was like to work in the woods in the latter half of the nineteenth century. There are songs about going up to the woods, about all the different kinds of work that had to be done, about the food, and the shanties, and how the shantyboys spent their evenings and their Sundays. There are songs about the dangers they faced and how they reacted to them. There are songs about the riverdrives, and about what they did when they came out of the woods in the spring, about their relations with girls, and about how they regarded themselves and their life.

The songs tell us who the men are that go lumbering:

> There's the farmer and the sailor, likewise mechanics too,
> Takes all kinds of tradesmen to form a lumbering crew (35),

and it tells us when they go up to the camps:

> The first day of September we were all at hand
> For to go to the shanty at Sheehan's command (173),

---

[1]The figures following the song quotations indicate pages in *Lumbering Songs from the Northern Woods* by Edith Fowke (Austin: University of Texas Press, 1970).

and when they come out:

> It was early last April when the logging was done
> I went to Fort Francis to join in the fun. (171)

The first stage was getting up to the woods which, before trains or cars, was something of a challenge, and often took several days. "The New Limit Line" describes one tough trip:

> Now we left our own homes, for the woods we were bent—
> The first night in Bobcaygeon with pleasure we spent . . .
> So we left there next morning precisely at eight
> So as to reach Minden before it got late . . .
> It was on Tuesday evening we reached Gilmour's big mills
> After toiling for five days through mud and o'er hills.
> Our horses were faggin', with hunger near blind,
> When we reached the big boarding house on the New Limit Line. (54)

A more lighthearted trip took place in northern Ontario, and the places named indicate the exact route followed:

> Come all you lads that would like to hear
> How we got up to the woods last year . . .
> From Arnprior we did push out
> All with John Pratt to show us the route.
> We travelled on till we came to Renfrew,
> 'Twas there we met up with the rest of the crew . . .
> Seven jolly boys got on a spree
> And to hire a rig we did agree . . .
> For Dacre town we hoist our sails,
> And they all thought there it was the Prince of Wales. (162)

Once the crew reached the lumbering site, they often had to build the shanties and other structures needed for the camp:

> It's when we reached our journey's end our foreman he did say:
> "It's stables we have got to build, and that without delay.
> We have got to build a blacksmith shop, likewise a shanty too,
> To hold this gang of shantyboys called Poupore's jovial crew." (43)

When the shanties were built, the work began, and many songs describe the different kinds of tasks the woodsmen had to perform:

> There were two gangs of scorers, their names I do not mind.
> They ranged the mountains o'er and o'er their winter's work to find. (37)

> So deeply in the tree of pine we notch to guide its fall,
> And not a man among us but will hear the timber call;
> And when it crashes to the ground, we'll fall to with a will,
> A-trimming up the branches and a-swearing fit to kill. (41)

> The choppers and the sawyers, they lay the timber low,
> The skidders and the swampers, they haul it to and fro. (36)
>
> Our hewers they were tasty and they ground their axes fair—
> They aimed their blows so neatly I am sure they'd split a
>   hair. (38)
>
> Then up would speak our old teamster, these words to us would say,
> "You swampers, get that rail up here, one hundred logs today";
> While our rollers with their cant hooks neat the round logs
>   they do pile,
> And they do their work without complaint and always with a
>   smile. (59)
>
> Along come the teamsters just at the break of day:
> "Load up your sleds ten thousand feet, to the river haste
>   away." (35)

The working day in the camp was long, and it usually began well before daybreak:

> Four o'clock the cook got up, his horn did loudly blow,
> Saying, "Arise, arise, my bonny boys, you to the woods must
>   go." . . .
> We would start on our weary way through dales and over hills
> Till at length our work we've reached—the stars are shining
>   still. (58)

The long hours of work were broken only by brief pauses to eat, and there are frequent references to the food, some complimentary, and some not:

> Noon time rolls around, the foreman he will say:
> "Lay down your saws and axes and haste to pork and beans." (34)
>
> There's blackstrap molasses, squaw buns as hard as rock,
> Tea that's boiled in an old tin pail and smells just like our sock.
> The beans they are sour, and the porridge thick as dough—
> When we have stashed this in our craw, it's to the woods we go. (41)
>
> Our cook's name was Jack Dunigan, the best in the woods;
> His beans they are great, and his bread it is good,
> And his elegant sea pie will make quite a meal
>   For the boys that are laboring for Martin McHale. (65)

The end of the day is also chronicled:

> Arriving at the shanty, wet, tired, and with wet feet,
> We all take off our socks and boots our supper for to eat.
> At nine o'clock or thereabout into our bunks we'll crawl
> To sleep away the few short hours until the morning call. (41)

But in some camps the boys were not too tired to spend a little time relaxing before going to bed:

> And when the last log was off the sleigh, to the shanty we would go,
> And some would talk of curious things that happened long ago,
> And some would sing their favorite songs to the rest of the jolly crew,
> But of all the songs that I love best was "Bold Jack Donahue." (47)

> If you were in the shanty when they came in at night,
> To see them dance, to hear them sing, it would your heart delight.
> Some asked for patriotic songs; some for love songs did call.
> Fitzsimmons sung about the girl that wore the waterfall. (38)

Not only did the shantyboys love to sing; they were equally fond of fiddling and dancing:

> On weekdays or Sundays we all would combine:
> We'd dance or shindig on the New Limit Line.
> We'd dance till the sweat it would smear all our clothes,
> While our rough shanty slabs knocks the nails from our toes. (56)

> Now the boys from the Chapeau can dance and can sing—
> Sure they're just as happy as any emperor or king.
> We're seven fine fiddlers; there's none of us drones,
> And Michael, my brother, can rattle the bones. (63)

Sundays also were a time of relaxation, and a chance to catch up on various things:

> Oh, Sunday it do roll around and the boys they get a rest,
> While some will go out visiting dressed in their very best.
> More would sharpen and file their saws while others grind their axe,
> And more would mend and patch their shirts and hunt their lousy 'backs. (47)

Despite the hard work, long hours, and low pay, very few of the songs voice complaints. True, one proclaims bitterly:

> Our food the dogs would bark at and our beds lie on the snow—
> My God, there is no bigger hell than Michigan-I-O. (29)

However, that is not typical. There are indeed grumblings about the early rising and sometimes about the food, but on the whole there seems to have been little resentment of the bosses, and the shantyboys apparently enjoyed their life if we can judge by the frequent references to "a jovial shanty lad," "a jolly shantyboy," "a jolly raftsman O," and such lines as:

> We are a merry set of boys, so handsome, young, and fine,
> Who spend a jolly winter a-cutting down the pine. (40)

The shantyboys' fondness for drinking is legendary ("Give the shantyboys whiskey and nothing goes wrong"), but liquor was usually forbidden in the camps so they had to wait till they came out in the spring to indulge that taste:

> It's when we get to Pembroke we will fill our glasses to the brim
> And drink a health to Dick White and Tom Poupore's shanty crew. (44)

Second only to the descriptions of life in the camps are the songs describing death in the woods or on the rivers, Just as the shantyboys appear to have composed (or re-composed) a song about every camp in which they spent a winter, they very likely composed a ballad about every one of their comrades who died. The most numerous of the many tragic accidents occurred on the river drives, and the best known of all lumbering songs recounts the story of "the foreman young Monroe":

> They had not rolled off many logs when the boss to them did say:
> "I would have you to be on your guard, this jam will soon give way."
> Those words were scarcely spoken when the jam did break and go
> And carried off those six bold youths with their foreman,
>   young Monroe. (97)

A similar fate met Jimmy Judge: "He went for to break the jam and with it he went through" (105), Jimmy Whelan: "Just as he spoke the jam it broke and let poor Whelan through" (112), Charlie Williams: "Those ragged rocks and waterfalls deprived him of his breath" (132), and young Jimmy who "was drownded on McCormick's drive on the cold Black River stream" (148).

Other rivermen were drowned in various accidents: the Haggertys and young Mulvanny were "selected to guide that boat o'er the waterfall" and were "capsized by a raging billow and soon engulfed in that mighty flood" (139); Vince Leahy "lost his life in the raging boils down by that Smithtown shore" (154); and four young men who tried to row the falls on the Grand River met their fate when "Their boat ran with quick motion, and from it they went through" (136).

A hanging limb, known as a "widow-maker," accounted for Harry Dunn: "A hanging limb fell down on him and sealed his fateful doom" (122), and for an unnamed shantyboy at Whitney's camp: "A hanging limb fell down on him and squashed him to the clay" (126), while Peter Amberley was felled by a rolling log: " 'Twas loading log sleighs at the skids that I met my fatal doom" (127). An even more gruesome fate met poor Harry Bale who worked in a shingle mill and accidentally set the carriage of the saw in gear:

> It cut him through the shoulder blade and halfway down the back;
> It threw him out upon the floor as the carriage it ran back. (117)

Ballads also chronicle the aftermath of the accidents. When a riverman was drowned the raftsmen "all sailed out together this young man for to find" (105), and when they found him they marked the place:

> There are raftsmen's bones 'neath cairns of stones where the
> foam-white waters toss,
> And many a mound where the rapids sound have been marked with a
> pine or cross. (123)

It was also their custom to contribute money to the dead man's girl or family: "A liberal subscription she received from the shantyboys next day" (98).

Perhaps the ever-present danger of their lives made the shantyboys careless about providing for their old age. They traditionally spent all their money as soon as they got it: "When we make our next stake we'll blow it again" (172), so it wasn't much wonder that at the end of their lives they lamented:

> Once I was a shantyboy, oh, wasn't I a lad!
> Now the way I spent my money, oh, wasn't it too bad!
> For it's now that I regret the day while I'm working out in
> the cold—
> Save your money while you're young, my boys, you'll need it when
> you're old. (207)

The shantyboys' happy-go-lucky ways made them favorites with the girls: "I place my mind, it never shall move, it's on a jolly raftsman O" (199), but their parents took a very different view:

> It's cruel are my parents, they do me so annoy,
> And they will not let me ramble with my jolly shantyboy. (192)

However, it's not much wonder that the mothers warn their daughters not to "throw yourself away with a reckless shantyboy" (193), for the shantyboys had quite a reputation as seducers:

> He courted me on winter's nights; with him I did comply.
> Then he was away by the first of May like a roving shantyboy. (198)

Despite their bad reputation among respectable folk, the shantyboys were proud of themselves and their occupation:

> A peavey hook it is my pride, an axe I well can handle—
> To fell a tree or punch a bull get rattling Johnny Randle. (31)

> You may search the world over and equal won't find
> Than our Bobcaygeon boys on the New Limit Line. (56)

> Oh, the forests so brown at our stroke go down, and cities
> spring up where they fell,

While logs well run and work well done is the story the
    shantyboys tell. (32)

To hew and score it is his plan
And handle his broadaxe neatly O.
It's lay the line and mark the pine,
And do it most completely O. (199)

Then hold up your head, this world never dread;
Care not for a sneer or a frown.
Stare fate in the face, if your heart's in its place,
For you can't keep a shantyboy down. (209)

And they also sang poetically of their life to come, sure that they would have a secure place in heaven:

When the word comes through for a timber crew for the river
    beyond the skies,
They'll ride the slide through the Great Divide, coming clear
    into heaven's snyes.
Those old raftsmen will be happy then with the Lord to pay
    their fee
As they sing their song as they sail along on the river of eternity.
    (214)

FAITH AND FATE IN SEA DISASTER BALLADS OF NEWFOUNDLAND FISHERMEN[1]

Kenneth S. Goldstein
University of Pennsylvania

SCHOLARS AND OTHERS involved in documenting and studying the folklore of the sea, especially that of fishermen and sailors, have commented frequently on the religiosity and "superstitious" nature of those who depend upon the sea for their living or sustenance. Ecclesiastics, on the other hand, generally prefer not to associate religion and superstition as related elements in an individual's or group's belief system for fear that religion will then be seen as essentially a form of popular belief (superstition) although the latter is unauthorized and unsanctioned by the church and frequently is in direct conflict with its principles. Peter F. Anson, Scotland's leading folklorist of fishermen and fishing ways, and himself a cleric, writes in a chapter pointedly titled "Religion and Superstition":

> There are two important factors which have always played a great part in the lives of fisherfolk of the east coast of Scotland as in most other seafaring communities, i.e. religion and superstition. The two must be classed together since superstition is no more than credulity regarding the supernatural, a misdirected reverence due to ignorance, combined with an irrational fear of the unknown. The Scottish fisherfolk possess this inborn sense of the supernatural to a strong degree, but owing largely to the survival of pagan ideas among them, the want of instruction, the comparatively little hold which the Presbyterian Kirk seems to have had over their imaginations and emotions during the two centuries that followed the Reformation, however much they may have been afraid of disobeying its ordinances, we come across an amount of extraordinary superstitions, beliefs, and practices, which ruled the daily lives of the fishing communities described in these pages, until almost within living memory. Traces of them survive to-day and even young fishermen are nervous of ignoring the superstitions of their forebears. (Anson 1930:37)

The dichotomy is immediately apparent to anyone not inclined to lump together belief in the supernatural with superstition. Despite this, however, almost all the work of folklorists who deal with maritime beliefs concentrates on "superstitions" and "popular beliefs" and rarely mentions religion as part of that belief system unless they intend to make the point that such beliefs are part of "folk religion."

This paper will look at the manner in which at least one genre of fishermen's folklore—sea disaster ballads—contains religious ideas and information (i.e. matters of religious faith), although such ballads may also contain examples of popular belief. The inspiration for what follows was taken from my observation of the frequency with which sea disaster ballads included references to religious faith and fatalism rather than to popular beliefs considered effective in "calming the fury of the sea which is regarded as being either a divinity in itself or else inhabited by good and evil spirits" (Anson 1932:47). In actual fact, however, we find that belief among fishermen in God, church and "His will" is, at least in reference to sea disaster ballads, even more important than popular beliefs dealing with other supernatural figures, events and practices.

The ballads I refer to here are an important part of the expressive culture of fisherfolk in North America. In G. Malcolm Laws' *American Balladry from British Broadsides* (1957), 9 of 43 (21 percent) of "Ballads of Sailors and the Sea" (K) concern disasters at sea. Again, among "Ballads of Sailors and the Sea" (D and dD) created in the New World, for which see Laws' *Native American Balladry* (1964), 25 out of 52 ballads (49 percent) deal with disasters at sea. To this number many more can be added from the collections of MacEdward Leach (1965) and Kenneth Peacock (1965), published after the revised edition of Laws, *Native American Balladry* in 1964, as well as at least 30 more previously unreported sea disaster ballads (among over 2,700 items) collected by me together with several colleagues in Newfoundland and Labrador since 1977.

Over half of the ballads referred to above contain references either to (A) religion or religious faith, or, even more frequently, to (B) a fatalistic belief in God's way of handling the afterlife of fishermen and sailors who die as a result of sea disasters. I include here, by way of examples, one ballad illustrating the former (A), and one full ballad and pertinent parts of several others illustrating the latter (B).

(A) *Expressions of Religion and Religious Faith*

"The *Rose in June*" is a rarely reported ballad. Perhaps the infrequency with which it has been sung results from the difficulty singers have in making the several changes from a ballad tune to a hymn tune required to sing it. I collected the ballad in August 1982 in Blanc Sablon,

Quebec, just over the border from Labrador, from Bill Dobbin, a 61 year old singer who used to fish for a living but who is now employed, when needed, in a local fish plant. Mr. Dobbin had learned the song many years earlier when working in the lumber woods to which he travelled from his home in Port Saunders in the Great Northern Peninsula of Newfoundland.

Of probable British origin, though unreported in England and Scotland, the ballad is known in vaious parts of Newfoundland and Labrador. Dr. Wilfred Wareham, my fellow field worker from Memorial University in St. John's, recorded a partial version, sung by several members of his family, at a "house time" (party) in Arnold's Cove, Placentia Bay, in February 1975 (Wareham 1982). Wilf and I also recorded a fragmentary text from Jim Keeping of Burnt Islands on the southwest coast of Newfoundland in July 1984. Other singers along the southwest coast, on the Great Northern Peninsula and on the lower Labrador coast knew a few lines or had heard it sung but either couldn't or wouldn't sing it. Bill Dobbin's version is the only complete one, as far as we know, collected to date.

THE *ROSE IN JUNE*

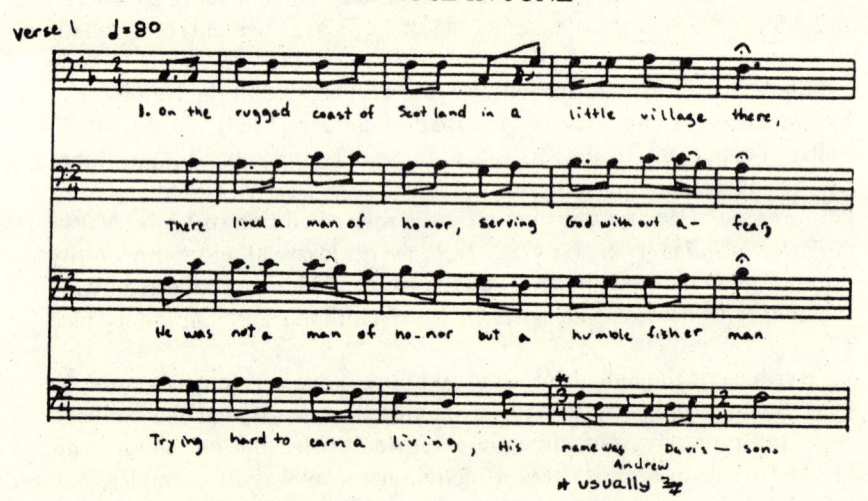

[musical notation: Verse 1, ♩=80]

1. On the rugged coast of Scotland in a little village there,
   There lived a man of honor serving God without a fear;
   He was not a man of honor but a humble fisherman
   Trying hard to earn a living, his name was Andrew Davison.

2. He was master of a vessel and he claimed her as his own,
   She was fitted with all was needed, she was called the
       Rose in June,

And with eager expectation looking forward to the day
When the time would come for fishing and the boats would
    sail away.

3. Andrew had been lately married, just before he left his home
   Andrew and his wife together knelt in prayer before the throne
   Asking God for His protection on his wife while he was gone,
   A-praying nothing would befall her of danger nor of harm.

4. And his wife while kneeling by him listening to his fervent
       prayer
   Asking God for her protection not a word of that for his,
   And her heart did sink within her as she rose from her
       bended knees
   Thinking of those terrible dangers and the perils of the sea.

5. Then the summer winds blew softly, herring fishing season
       came,
   Andrew Davis was preparing, herring fishing was his game.
   Andrew Davis was preparing with his crew to go to sea
   Thinking not 'twould be his last time, friends on earth
       no more to see.

6. Oh, all night long the storm was raging and those angry
       billows roared,
   Many a vessel was tossed and driven out along that rocky
       shore
   While their crews were clinging to them, oh seamen strong
       and brave,
   Praying that the Lord would keep them from a seaman's
       watery grave.

7. All along the coast next morning eager eyes were watch and wait,
   Children of those absent sailors till returning ships were seen.
   One by one those vessels sailed in, oh, from morning until noon
   Till all was in and safely anchored, all but one, the *Rose in June*.

8. Whom the waves turned bottom upwards, dashed against that
       rugged shore
   And the crew were clinging to her thinking the storm would soon
       be o'er.
   Andrew Davis, our captain, in that hour of sudden fear
   Thought on Jesu Christ the Saviour and he bowed his head
       in prayer.

[Musical notation: Verse 9, ♩=80, ♩=96]

9. Saying, "Come and we'll sing God's praises" and at once they all begun:
"I am dying, dear Saviour, what a comfort divine,
What a blessing to know that the Saviour is mine.
Hallelujah, send the Glory, hallelujah, amen,
Hallelujah, send the Glory to revive us again."

10. Those words were scarcely ended when the outwaves struck her side,
Swept our captain from his holdings and he sank beneath the tide,
Gone to join his friends and shipmates on that Heavenly shore
Welcomed by his loving Saviour, singing praise forever more.

11. John Allen was our young mate and he knew he was forgiven,
Said, "Let us keep on with our singing, our captain is in Heaven."
And they sang so loud and shrill till they came to this last verse:
"Slowly onward we'll haste to that Heavenly place,
For this is the Glory and this is the Grace.
Hallelujah, send the Glory, hallelujah, amen,
Hallelujah, send the Glory to revive us again."

12. Those words were scarcely ended when the outwaves burst around,
Swept our young mate from his holdings and his body, too, was drowned.
Gone to join his friends and shipmates on that Heavenly shore,
Welcomed by his loving Saviour, singing praise forever more.

[Musical notation with lyrics:]

11. John Allen was our young mate and he knew he was for-given
Said, "Let us keep on with our singing, our captain is in Heaven."
And they sang so loud and shrill till they came to this last verse:
"Slowly on-ward we'll haste to that Hea-ven-ly place,
For this is the Glo-ry and this is the Grace.
Halle-lu-jah, send the Glory, Halle-lu-jah, a-men,
Halle-lu-jah, send the glory to re-vive us a-gain."

13. And the rest of the crew were rescued but they'll ne'er forget the scene,
In the hour and that moment when the song they tried to sing,
With no sermons ever preached or no experience ever known
In the hour and that moment, the hour of sudden gloom.

14. So sinners give your soul to Jesus, it will never be too soon,
If in Heaven you meet the captain, meet the crew of the *Rose in June.*
So sinners give your soul to Jesus, it will never be too soon
If in Heaven you meet the captain, meet the crew *of the Rose in June.* (spoken)

Religious faith is expressed early and frequently throughout the ballad. In line 2, the captain is introduced as "serving God without a fear." He and his wife pray before a home altar, calling for God's protection (lines 10–15). Once at sea, the sailors pray to the Lord to keep them from a watery grave (line 24). The captain thinks on Jesus and bows his head in prayer (line 32). He then calls for the men to "sing God's praises" (line 33) and the crew joins in a four line rendition of the hymn "Revive Us Again" to its appropriate tune (lines 34-37). Switching back to the ballad tune, the Captain is swept overboard where he joins past friends and shipmates on "that Heavenly shore" welcomed by his Saviour (lines 41-42). The young first mate calls on the crew to continue singing the hymn in honor of the captain's arrival in Heaven (line 42). The men continue to sing, again to the appropriate tune, the final verse of "Revive Us Again" (lines 45-48). Reverting to the ballad tune, the young mate, like his captain before him, is swept overboard and drowned, and joins his Saviour, friends and shipmates on "that Heavenly shore" (lines 51-52). The rest of the crew is rescued without sermons or testimony given at the final hour (line 55). The ballad muse then tells the audience of sinners if they wish to meet the captain and his crew in Heaven, they (the audience) must give their soul to Jesus (lines 57-60).

With 27 of the 60 lined devoted to matters of religious faith or their expression, one might argue that "The *Rose in June*" is a religious ballad rather than a secular narrative song about a sea disaster. Our singer argued otherwise, noting that "religious songs are sung only in church or in praying" and that "The *Rose in June*" is a favorite at non-religious events like house times, concerts, and entertainments. This is confirmed by the ballad having been sung in Arnold's Cove during a house party at which time it was sandwiched between a bawdy song and a satirical ditty (Wareham 1982).

(B) *Expressions of Fatalism*

Newfoundland writers in various fields point frequently to the fact that Newfoundlanders are a fatalistic lot (Gushue 1974: 1; Poole 1982: 5, 92, 95). Those from away translate this to mean that Newfoundlanders passively surrender to the elements, to nature and to other forces beyond their control, and this assumed resignation is then generalized to other behaviours (social and political) as well. Nothing could be further from the truth. The fatalism of Newfoundlanders is based on the idea that it is their lot to live with, fight with and to otherwise deal with the sea and related elements—not to give in to them but to recognize their force and power. As Cyril Poole notes: "Fatalism permits of struggle and battle even though the outcome rests with the Gods" (1982:96).

Closely related is another kind of fatalism, one based in even greater part on faith. This is the fatalism that determines that man's ultimate resting place is with God in Heaven. No matter how bad the weather, how dangerous the sea, how difficult his labor, the fisherman's trials and tribulations will be rewarded by a place on "the Heavenly shore."

In the ballad "The *Rose in June*", this kind of religious fatalism is expressed in lines 40-41, 51-52, and 57-60, and in the two verses of the hymn "Revive Us Again" embedded in the ballad (lines 34-37 and 45-49). Most sea disaster ballads, however, otherwise containing little or no religious elements, will usually have a stanza or stanzas near the conclusion containing a fatalistic request for God's understanding and mercy or a statement of His consignment to Heaven of lost or dead sailors and fishermen.

"The Schooner *Huberry*" is a native Newfoundland ballad whose history we have been unable to trace. Dorman Ralph, a blind singer now in St. John's, was read the ballad from some printed source by his brother, Herbert, in Little Harbour Deep, White Bay, some forty years ago. Dorman later set it to its present tune. I recorded his singing of it in August 1981. The ballad was previously published in the Newfoundland periodical *The Livyere*, Volume 2, No. 1 (August 1982).

THE SCHOONER *HUBERRY*

1. 1. Ye daring sons of Newfoundland, come listen unto me,
   And I'll unfold what's ne'er been told of the dangers of
      the sea,
   Concerning our poor seaman who sail the raging main
   And left behind all dear and kind never to return again.

5. 2. Of a brave and fearless mariner I'm going to relate,
   Of such a hardy seaman and how he met his fate;
   Now let me tell to you quite plain of the mournful tragedy
   That took the toll of five dear souls on the schooner
      Huberry.

  3. She was a ship of sixty ton and trading on our shore,
10   And now that she has vanished and will be seen no more;
   As for Captain Seaward, with me you will agree,
   He was a Newfoundlander but his home was on the sea.

  4. He was a brave and daring man and little did he fear
   Out in his little vessel so late up in the year;
15   And sailing 'round our stormy shore and with the least of
    dread,
   Like all such Newfoundlanders to earn their daily bread.

  5. He left St. John's for Hare Bay in the schooner *Huberry*,
   And little did he ever think it would end in tragedy;
   Off the northeast coast of Newfoundland, beneath the winter
    sky,
20   Captain Seaward and his little crew gave up their lives to die.

  6. Out on the ocean crest, out on the raging foam,
   The sea gulls sing their little songs for those who won't
    come home.
   Now to ye people of New Perlican, to ye I say alone,
   They're anchored on that Heavenly shore where troubles
    there are none.

25 7. It is a sad occurrence but it happens every day,
   The sea takes to the cemetery the live of ones most dear.
   They will be missed throughout our land in summer, spring
    and fall,
   And how they got cast away it's a mystery to us all.
   No more to watch on a stormy deep expecting them to come;
30   They got their call, both one and all, for God has called
    them home.

"The Schooner *Huberry*" is rather typical in its expression of religious fatalism. Line 24 reports the ultimate resting place of the dead sailors is "that Heavenly shore." Though attributing their deaths to the sea (line 26), the ballad muse recognizes that the final decision to "call them home" was God's (line 30).

Other examples of religious fatalism identifying death as God's prerogative include the following:

  17. But God has called him for His own,
    He does things for the best;
    I hope that his immortal soul
    Will find eternal rest.
         ("The *Golden Hind*" in Peacock 1965: 924)

  10. When the Master called our men
    Not one of us can say,
    No doubt we'll know what happened
    To the faithful *Jubal Cain*.
        ("The Loss of the *Jubal Cain*" in Peacock 1965: 953)

Examples of religious fatalism in which a request is made for God's understanding include the following:

> 9. But may the great Almighty God their troubles soon make light
> And ease the broken hearts of those who lost their friends that night.
>
> ("The *Greenland* Disaster" in Peacock 1965: 927)

> 7. Now the *Southern Cross* for twenty days she now is overdue,
> We hope please God she'll soon arrive and all her hearty crew,
> So put your trust in Providence and trust to Him on high,
> To send the *Southern Cross* safe home and fill sad hearts with joy.

> 8. All things do happen for the best, but if they're called away,
> The brave lads on the *Southern Cross* out in the storm that day,
> We trust they reach that heavenly land and rest with Him on high,
> Where cares and sorrows are no more but all is peace and joy.
>
> ("The *Southern Cross*" in Peacock 1965: 974)

I have attempted here to show the value of viewing faith and fate as important *religious* factors in the folklore of fishermen and sailors and to suggest that maritime folklorists give religious beliefs at least equal attention to popular beliefs. Together they form a basis for better understanding the unified belief system of any maritime peoples.

NOTE

[1] I wish to thank the following people for their help and criticism in the preparation of this paper: Dr. David Hufford, Maggie Craig, Diane E. Goldstein, and Dr. Wilfred W. Wareham. I received help with the text transcriptions from Jan Rosenberg, and the musical transcriptions were made by Lucy Long.

REFERENCES

Anson, Peter F.
    1930 *Fishing Boats and Fisher Folk on the East Coast of Scotland*. London & Toronto: J. M. Dent and Sons Ltd.
    1932 *Fishermen and Fishing Ways*. London: George G. Harrap & Co. Ltd.
Gushue, William J.
    1974 "Newfoundland's Unique Culture: The Hunting Tradition." *The Morning Watch*, 1 (March): 1-4.
Laws, Jr., G. Malcolm
    1957 *American Balladry from British Broadsides*. Bibliographical and Special Series, Volume VIII. Philadelphia: The American Folklore Society.
    1964 *Native American Balladry*. Bibliographical and Special Series, Volume I. Revised Edition. Philadelphia: The American Folklore Society.

Leach, MacEdward
  1965 *Folk Ballads and Songs of the Lower Labrador Coast.* National Museum of Canada Bulletin No. 201. Ottawa: Queens Printer.

Peacock, Kenneth
  1965 *Songs of the Newfoundland Outports.* 3 volumes. National Museum of Canada Bulletin No. 197. Ottawa: Queens Printer.

Poole, Cyril F.
  1982 *In Search of the Newfoundland Soul.* St. John's: Harry Cuff Publications Limited.

Wareham, Wilfred W.
  1982 *Towards an Ethnography of "Times": Newfoundland Party Traditions, Past and Present.* Doctoral Dissertation. Philadelphia: University of Pennsylvania.

SINGLEJACK / DOUBLEJACK: CRAFT AND CELEBRATION

Archie Green
San Francisco, California

IN THE AMERICAN WEST, hard-rock miners (gold, silver, lead, copper, and other nonferrous metals) have voiced the linked terms "singlejack"/"doublejack" in daily speech throughout this century. Workers have employed each widely in various forms to name hand tools as well as the acts of hammering and drilling. Beyond technical function, these words have served, also, to denominate a nearly-forgotten ritualized drilling contest. Here, I explore the transitions within occupational speech for these terms as they have encompassed craft and celebration.

Those who have heard the ballad "John Henry" can visualize a hand driller pitted against a mechanical steam drill. Hence, the picture of a muscular hammerman (driller, striker) teamed with a partner (helper, holder, twister, turner, shaker) is not strange to the audience whose members have never seen tunnel men at work. Curiously, neither "singlejack" nor "doublejack" appear in "John Henry's" many texts. While all singers inform us that the driller—properly, a doublejacker—died with his hammer in hand, we are left to guess at his shaker's fate. Among this ballad's ambiguities is the relationship engendered between a driller and his partner, a theme considered within my report.

In 1907, at the very time folklorists began to encounter "John Henry" in the American South, Charles E. Winter, a Wyoming judge and Congressman, published a novel *Grandon of Sierra*. Winter included "The Broken-Hearted Leaser," a poem of his own composition, offered supposedly as a "typical miner's song of sentiment and hope." Indeed, this song has been recovered in oral tradition, altered by miners to whom the composition appealed. The original text opened:

> In a rusty, wornout cabin sat a broken-hearted leaser;
> His singlejack was resting on his knee. . . .
> He lifted his old singlejack, gazed on its battered face,
> And said: "Old boy, I know we're not to blame."[1]

Essentially, this miner who has leased a claim—Happy Joe in the novel—turned an indispensable hammer into a faithful companion, a friendly listener. Solitary workers who have talked to inanimate tools will respond sympathetically to Winter's poem.

In this century's opening decade, Charles E. Wood edited the *Dillon Doublejack* in Carbon County, Wyoming. Only a few issues have survived. One copy, for April 16, 1904, included representative mining news under the headline "A First-Class Reliable Flying Machine Wanted." This offbeat head reported an unseasonal warming of the snowpack, rendering it impossible for outside travellers to reach Dillon.

From my vantage point, the newspaper's unusual masthead retains far more interest than any dated stories or column heads. The *Doublejack*'s printer, or perhaps a local artist, designed an appropriate masthead resonant of ancient heraldry: two crossed long-handled hammers below a long, sharp steel drill. Together, these twined emblems marked both Dillon's actual sweat and sought-after wealth. The mine-town newspaper editor knew clearly which tools were most important to Dillon's fate.

I have called attention to a novel's sentimental poem and a newspaper's graphic art to note long familiarity in the Rocky Mountains with the terms "single jack"/"doublejack." To record meanings conveyed by each, I open with the formal lexical record. The *Oxford English Dictionary* overlooked both words in its original volumes, 1933 supplement, and recent additions. Neither did Rossiter W. Raymond include "singlejack"/"doublejack" in his extensive glossary of 1881. Raymond—an engineer, lawyer, novelist—was intrigued by language. I infer from his glossary that he had not encountered these terms before 1881. His entry for "drill" described the tool then-used by singlejackers and doublejackers; his entry for "rock-drilling" described the machine then replacing hand work:

> Drill—The ordinary miner's drill is a bar of steel, with a chisel-shaped end, and is struck with a hammer.
> Rock-drill—A machine for boring in rock, either by percussion, effected by reciprocating motion, or abrasion, effected by rotary motion. Compressed air is the usual motive power, but steam is also used.[2]

Albert Fay, in his glossary of 1920 for the Bureau of Mines, did report "singlejack" (a light single-hand hammer used in drilling, especially in metal mines) but he neglected "doublejack." During 1926, these two words were first glossed for readers of *American Speech* by Helen Moore, the daughter of a Colorado miner. She noted:

> There are two ways to mine—by hand or by machine. The old hardrock miners (now nearly extinct) were either single jackers or double jackers.

The first held his own steel [drill] in one hand and hammered with the other. In double jacking, one man held the jack [drill] while the other hammered.

A few years later, Levette Davidson elaborated:

> One who wields with both hands a large hammer and strikes the jack or wedge used to separate rocks broken by blasting is called a doublejacker; if he uses a smaller hammer—a single jack—in one hand, he is a single-jacker.[3]

From the earliest discoveries of precious gems, building stone, and metal to the introduction of gunpowder in underground work (about 1620 in Hungary), miners' hand tools changed very slowly in shape and size. Early tools were made of bone, wood, stone, and metal. Archaeologists have found rudimentary implements which anticipated present-day hammer, wedge, gad, drill, chisel, crowbar, pick, shovel, basket, tub, barrow, ladder. Wherever ore cropped at the surface, or was found close to the surface, miners fashioned local words to name their tools.

English-language terms for "hammer" and "drill" have always been discrete. By contrast, "singlejack"/"doublejack" merge to denominate hammering and drilling, tool and technique, person and process. I do not know the time-length for this interchange, nor the exact setting for such proliferation in meaning. However, I feel certain that miners in the West blurred the separate uses of "jack" at the end of the nineteenth century. Perhaps, in writings by miners and mining engineers, we can find their explanation for "jack" as a tag simultaneously applied to implement and action.

To my knowledge, no sleuth has marked the trail of "Jack," the proper name, to "jack," the hard-rock miner's all-purpose friend. We know that English speakers have long used the former to describe a commoner of menial condition and, at times, a knave. Everyday usages rooted in work experience are "jack-of-all-trades," "steeplejack," "jack tar," "lumberjack," "jack-leg preacher," and "disc jockey."

The extension of "Jack" from personal name to mechanical device used by a laborer, or device replacing labor, has taken considerable time. A few examples from the *OED* suffice: Woodcutters propped logs on sawing frames or sawing jacks (1573). Ingeniously, a fire's heat turned a smoke jack or roasting jack (1587). Footboys pulled off their masters' boots by hand until someone invented a boot-jack (1697). Mechanics who lifted heavy equipment perfected screw jacks (1703). In this vein, British coal miners applied "jack" to several devices and structures such as a hand-turned windlass (jack-roll), and an auxilliary small shaft within a mine (jackhead-pit).

With attention to the drilling process, I note that, before 1858, a miner or quarryman in Britain had sounded "jack" to identify a wedge or gad assisting in the cleaving of strata.[4] We learn the age of these "pre-drill" tools from Richard Carew's *Survey of Cornwall* (1602): The Elizabethan tinner's tools include "a pick-axe of yron about sixteene inches long, sharpened at the one end to pecke, and flat-headed at the other to drive certaine little yron wedges." A century later these wedges or gads were described as of "two pounds weight, foursquare and well-steeled at the point, which required sharpening every two or three days."[5]

The noun "jack" naming a wedge/gad stands behind the hard-rock miner's acceptance of the combined terms "singlejack"/"doublejack." Literally, the wedge or gad entered and separated coal and ore formations; one used such helpers to jack apart rocks. The miner's jack, a penetrating servant, took its place in the long line of tools which integrated a personal name with a labor-saving device.

The functional move of "jack" from wedge/gad to steel drill seems obvious; the move from drill to hammer to hammering, less obvious. We search for clues to these linguistic shifts as prospectors seek telltale marks on the land. Where possible we listen to imaginative workers. Acts of pounding, prying, chipping, and drilling have lent themselves well to simile and metaphor. One example makes the point.

In Wales, Cornwall, and the Newcastle district of England, some workers visualized their drilling process as one of jumping and churning. Accordingly, they named an iron drilling bar (that jumped up and down in its bore-hole) a "jumper." Drillers could work this tool with a sledge hammer, or, in soft rock, by hand—raising the bar and letting it fall of its own weight. The bar, five foot or more in length, held a steel cutting edge (chisel). Quarrymen labeled it "churn." A limestone worker at Clydach Vale, Wales, recalled stone boring by hand, a foot each hour: "You kept on turning and turning the bar—dampening down [with water in the hole]. It was like butter making in a churn."[6]

To hear a rockman describe his work by analogy to butter making helps us replay the shift from wedge/gad to jack. To trace this latter naming act, we turn back to the old phrases "single-hand drilling" and "double-hand drilling," literally describing, alternately, how a lone miner gripped his hammer handle, or how a team miner gripped his. In the first instance, the solitary worker held hammer in one hand and drill in the other. By contrast, in the effort of partners, one miner held hammer with both hands while his mate turned a drill with both hands.

Conflict over hand-drilling methods, in 1869, had figured as an issue in the formation of California's first gold miners' union. Soon after Alfred Nobel invented dynamite, Chinese labor crews used the new explosive in the construction of the Central Pacific Railroad. Next, Grass

Valley mining superintendents observing the railroad's progress in the Sierras, also, replaced black gunpowder with giant powder (dynamite). As well, they began to replace Cornish mining teams (doublejackers) with Chinese laborers (singlejackers). This move reduced the work force and lowered pay scales. Such changes were keyed simultaneously to an attack on "highgrading" (miners pilfering ore). Skilled Cornishmen asserted that the issue of single-handed versus double-handed drilling had been settled long ago in Britain. To work alone underground invited danger; to work alone, denied companionship. Accordingly, the experienced Cornishmen banded together into a labor union and called a strike.[7]

We need not be detained, here, by the strike's complex elements: unionism, hand-drilling methods, dynamite, health, wages, highgrading, ethnic rivalry. However, we can use the event to call attention to specific areas of tension as settings in which new words are coined and old words gain fresh meaning. During 1869, Grass Valley journalists described single-handed and double-handed drilling as practices familiar both in the old country and the new.

Storks do not deliver neologisms; words grow in gardens of human need. Wedges and gads, long used in Britain, were called "jacks" by some immigrant coal and metal miners when they followed discoveries from Atlantic to Pacific in the United States. A circumstance, now lost in time and place, impelled a miner to call his drill a "jack." Next, another miner compressed the techniques of single-hand and double-hand drilling into shortland locutions, "singlejacking" and "doublejacking." By back formation, these fresh usages came to identify hammer as well as drill.

This shortening, which I have reconstructed speculatively, could have taken place in daily speech during the Grass Valley strike of 1869, or in a similar dispute, when controversy surrounded drilling methods. Conjecture aside, published accounts from Grass Valley do not record the new words in question. Vernacular usages do not always enter print at their inception. Hence, we shall have to look elsewhere for the baptismal circumstance of the terms "singlejack"/"doublejack."

Whether or not the tag for a Cornish miner, "Cousin Jack," reinforced the novelty of "jack" when extended to bread-and-butter tools, I do not know. Caroline Bancroft has suggested that Cornishmen in America turned the pejorative "Cousin Jack" into an acceptable humorous name during the 1850s. Nearly a century later in Butte, Wayland Hand heard an anecdote that tied tool to ethnic nickname:

> So great was the respect of an old Finn for the prowess of a Cousin Jack with the hammer that he habitually called a single jack a "Cousin

Jack." Once when his hammer fell down the chute, [the Finn] called out: "There's a Cousin Jack in the chute!" Much anxiety and commotion resulted, and subsided only when the hammer was retrieved.[8]

Cornish boys from the Old Country to the New World boasted of the weight and length of their fathers' hammers. A line in a Grass Valley folksong commented: "You ne'er can beat a Cousin Jack for hammering on a drill." This same association aided handily in anecdotes to highlight the customary behavior expected of workers engaged in mutual effort. Solitary work threatened loneliness and danger; shared work required balance and solidarity. A traditional story wryly marks partnership:

> In one hard-rock mine a Cousin Jack was teamed with an American apprentice, who took the easy task of holding and turning the steel while the Cornishman pounded it with the heavy sledge. It was the practice for double-jackers to take turns at the sledge, lest one become worn out, but the American seemed unaware of this. After a half-hour of furious work the exhausted Cousin Jack put down his sledge and remarked, "Thee've good wind for turning, my 'andsome."[9]

Part of the appeal of terminology associated with hand drilling arose out of the introduction of machine drills in the West. New equipment revolutionized practices sanctioned by age, and, in its very newness, gave old words an affective glow. One benchmark in machine drilling dates to 1812, when Richard Trevithick developed a rotary rock-boring steam drill. Four decades later, railroad tunnelers used steam drills in the Alps. Engineers at the Hoosac Tunnel, Massachusetts (1856–1873) converted a steam drill to compressed air. When inventor Charles Burleigh introduced a "perfected" pneumatic drill at Georgetown, Colorado, in 1870, his name became synonymous with modernity in the mines. In time, other machines—Rand, Ingersoll, Leyner—followed.

Technical literature on machine drilling is extensive. Here, I note only that inventors have used steam, compressed air, and electric power to replicate hammering by hand on gad, bar, or steel drill. In some machines, the steel (drill) is tied to a cylinder piston by a rod, and reciprocates back and forth with the piston. More commonly, in others, a free piston strikes (hammers) the steel directly with each forward stroke. Some drills are held in place by a column; others, on legs; still others are reduced in size to become portable.

Machine drills have been classified variously by motive power, operating mode, size, and mounting. Without detailing this full range, I note that manufacturers and miners, together, have applied the word "jack" to different drill parts. Four examples serve from a field of many: In some drills a hand-cranked "jackscrew" advanced the piston/steel mechanism. Drills were mounted on "jackshaft" columns or on tripod "jacklegs." Portable pneumatic drills, at their inception, became "jackhammers." I do not know the exact pattern of interaction for these machine-related terms with those of pre-machine work by singlejacker and doublejacker.

Working stiffs faced with new powerful machines, renamed them "buzzies" after their sound, "wiggletails" after their vibration, and "widow makers" after their unintended effects. Outsiders can understand such argot, but what do they make of "chippy" for a small piston drill? Did a miner, in this naming act, refer to the rock-chipping process or, by analogy, to flashy girls chasing about "on the line"? Despite choice names for power equipment, miners never gave up easily on "jack," a locution which personified their strength and skill.

While "singlejack"/"doublejack" have remained hidden mainly within an occupational community, many Americans, in the 1920s and 1930s, learned the related word "jackhammer" to connect hammering and drilling by a hand-held tool. City dwellers who had never been near a mine could see and hear jackhammers on their streets. The omnipresent jackhammer man, pulverizing rock and carving concrete, came to symbolize both pleasure and pain in technological advance. A jackhammer operator at a New Deal dam project helped bring water and power to "this land." Cheered in topical song and post office mural, he emerged as a 1930s culture hero.[10] Conversely, his fellow worker in city construction, today, reminds us of stress within the urban jungle. One need not wield a pneumatic drill to feel jackhammer blues.

Like other students of language, I have searched for locutions that have illuminated occupational practices and characterized expressive enactments by workers. Hence, I have been especially interested in Western hand-drilling competitions, usually held on the Fourth of July, Labor Day, or a union contract holiday (Miners' Day). Newspapers have reported such events, but no full description is available from a folklorist or ethnographer who has witnessed one.[11]

Virginia City workers established Miners' Union Day in 1874. I believe that drilling contests enlivened this annual celebration on the Comstock Lode, but, presently, I lack details. Victor Noxon, in 1934, recalled Colorado local camp contests at Clear Creek, Gilpin, and Boulder counties during the 1880s. The earliest such event I can date took place at the Boulder Industrial Association Fair in September, 1877, during which the *Sunshine Courier* reported a $60.00 premium to the winning pair of men and $35.00 to the single winner. Local champions, usually "Cousin Jacks," often moved from county events to contests in Rocky Mountain cities.

The State Agricultural Society of California, in 1892, announced a mining exhibition at Sacramento, including, a rock-drilling contest of single-hand and double-hand miners. Exhibit promoters touted this event as California's first drilling contest—winners to challenge Colorado and Montana champions at the 1893 World's Fair (Chicago).

Denver's Carnival of the Mountain and Plain, initiated in 1895, was widely publicized. The *Rocky Mountain News* (October 11-20) offered full reports on two drilling contests: one, outdoors at the Denver Athletic Club Park; one, indoors at the Coliseum. State mining commissioner Harry Lee handled all arrangements, including a tardy contractor late in delivering the Gunnison granite block to a festival site. Miners from the Victor camp arrived in splendid Cowboy Band regalia. One group of miner-musicians carried steel drills, and formed a xylophone-like unit playing these tools. A *News* artist pictured this novelty group in a horse-drawn float. As well, the artist caught a pair of rugged drillers in action on the stone block. Among the many enthusiastic newspaper story heads, my favorite is "Cut Granite Like Ice."

Labor Day announcements for 1900 in *The Miners' Magazine,* the official journal of the Western Federation of Miners, now help readers visualize early drilling contests. The Tuolumne County, California, WFM local planned a brass-band parade, an oration, literary exercises, horse races, foot races, hammer throwing, sack and bicycle races, double-handed and single-handed drilling contests, a supper, and grand ball at the local's union hall in Stent. The Telluride WFM local planned a similar event for the same holiday, extending an invitation to miners and their families throughout Nevada. For its two drilling matches, the arrangements committee stated, "Usual rules and conditions to govern." This terse statement reveals that miners, familiar with contest practices at the turn of the century, needed no reiteration of rules.

It is difficult to step back in time and assert the drilling competition's exact origin. I assume an evolution from informal activity underground to staged matches above ground, and I have treated contests as belonging entirely to the West. However, Angus Murdoch has referred to them at Calumet, Michigan. I do not know whether copper miners carried Michigan practices West, or whether contests reversed American direction by moving from the Rockies to Lake Superior. To my knowledge, no one has explored possible antecedents in Britain for the American matches. For example, a Cornish hand-boring contest during 1888 attracted one thousand spectators. Who can date the earliest such event in Cornwall?

Regardless of origin, the drilling display in the United States can be related to parallel events. I suggest, but cannot document, these connections: hard-rock drilling celebration, cattle rodeo, turkey shoot, anvil throw, county-fair horse pull, plowing contest, lumberjack axe throw, construction riveting display, coal-mine-car loading contest, hard-rock mucking contest. Without venturing into new fields, folklorists still have much to explore in the old province of occupational culture.

Novelist Donald McCaig in *The Butte Polka* (1980) included a drilling contest, set for fictive purposes in the distant past of 1946. His novel concerned the murder of a copper-mine union leader and the crime's unravelling. McCaig's pageant-like contest helped authenticate the victim's class credentials of skills and brawn. We read:

> Even then, they used buzzies to drill the dynamite holes and only the old miners remembered how to use the heavy sledge and rock drill. One man knelt, holding the drill, turning it slightly between the other man's blows so it got a fresh bite on the rock every time.
>
> WPA art: two men, bandy legged, long bodied, shirtless, muscled bulkily across their chests. One's got a hammer coming off his shoulder —the other is concentrating on the drill (eighteen inches of tool steel) and neither attends to nor fears the . . . hammer whistling past his head to strike right above his hands and an inch miscalculation would smash his wristbone to matchsticks, and never a thought now—they've worked together so long—never a thought the driver might miss or be weak or fail in the slightest respect.
>
> When the time's half gone, the timekeeper calls out, and they switch: hammer for rock drill; rock drill for hammer; and damned if they don't pick up a half stroke. Whang, whang, whang, whang, whang, whang, TIME!
>
> And somebody sticks a folding rule in the hole they made, until it bottoms in the tough granite, and announces, "Hardesty and Cole: twenty-eight inches and five eights." And Hardesty is shaking his head ruefully and Cole shrugs, What the hell.[12]

This fictive portrait, with its appropriate analogy to WPA mural art, serves well to introduce a drilling team, a timekeeper, and a judge with his measuring-rod scepter. A Montana State Museum diorama at Helena includes five figures on a model plank-drilling platform (doublejack partners, waterboy, judge, timekeeper). Flanking the glass-encased representation, one sees real hammers and drills, prize makers from the last century. Each tool holds a silver plate memorializing former champions.

Drilling competitions of record from California to Colorado and Texas to Wyoming offered thousands of dollars in prize money to the victors. Contests celebrated, simultaneously, individual work skill and the holiday release from work for the whole community. Generally, the event's planners imported special granite in six-foot blocks from Colorado or, even, distant Vermont. Teamsters hauled some blocks by mule and wagon to remote mountains camps; railroaders moved others. After the El Paso contest (January 16, 1902), the El Paso & Southwestern Railroad carried, free of charge, a seventeen-ton stone to the Bisbee competition (an early example of recycling).

Festive rock needed to be especially hard, uniform, and without visible flaws. Wise drillers sought flaws in granite to gain advantage over opponents. Some contest blocks became cluster points for special attention. The editor of Denver's *Mining Reporter* (October 31, 1901) noted that over $20,000.00 in prizes had been won on the Gunnison granite block used at Leadville. Further, he urged that this "rock should be preserved as a relic and not dumped over the side of a hill." A few blocks, of course, were saved. During 1954, the Almaden Historical Society (Santa Clara County, California) used a drilling rock as a historical marker near the New Almaden Mercury Mining Museum. To this day, visitors at Butte's Mount Moriah Cemetery see one such stone, a tribute to legendary drillers, long gone.

Normally, the phrase "single-hand contest" identified those events in which one miner competed against another's time. Each participant wielded a four-pound hammer and a set of 3/4 inch drill bits for fifteen minutes. The solitary driller held his hammer in one hand and his steel in the other. He finished his work, or "made his time," before rivals began. Similarly, doublejacking pitted competing teams, duo against duo, in sequence. Again, the usual time was fifteen minutes. A winning team might achieve sixty-eight blows or more, per minute, using an eight-pound hammer and a set of 7/8 inch drill bits. These steels were graduated in length by three-inch increments, beginning with a stubby "starter," about a foot long, and ending with a giant five-foot "stick." Winning teams achieved a depth close to four feet.

Contests developed considerable lore. Each participant selected "weapons" (hammers and drills) with great care, and "babied" them constantly. Some camp blacksmiths made a good living by supplying steel forged and tempered to each contestant's personal specifications. During 1892, two Butte "Cousin Jacks," James Davey and Peter Teague, won a $700.00 purse in an out-of-town contest. Arriving home to a tumultuous welcome, they presented $100.00 and a gold chain to their tool sharpener, John Pryor.

Nothing was left to chance. Of the many techniques displayed, one remains especially interesting to folklorists. Singlejackers rotated their steel clockwise. In doublejacking, the kneeling partner also rotated his steel clockwise, holding it in a perfectly vertical position. Holders believed that an angled drill, or a counterclockwise motion, might "fitcher" (bind or jam), thus losing time. The colloquialism "fitchering" described either a hole filled with rock dust, or one, three-cornered rather than circular. Eventually, a fitchered hole fouled the steel; in effect, making it impossible to continue drilling.

The matter of turning steel clockwise made absolute sense to a right-handed singlejacker. In turning with his left hand, he flexed his wrist naturally from left to right. Workers in many crafts—sailors, electricians, riggers—have long coiled line and cable "with the sun." Similarly, fishermen in the Northern Hemisphere have rowed "with the sun." The English word "withershins" asserts that it is unlucky to defy the heavens by working against the clock or sun's direction. Rock drilling contestants, of course, accepted this ancient taboo as they twisted drills in search of glory.[13]

Although these competitions did not attract participants from outside the hard-rock fraternity, some champs virtually gave up work to follow the circuit. A winner's name spread from camp to camp as "ten-day stiffs" (itinerant miners) moved from job to job, turning experience into anecdote. With each contest under way, viewers surrounded the drilling platform, encouraging their favorites with cries and cheers. At times, the phallic association in rock drilling stimulated pungent commentary.

For some in the audience, the event's attraction was the possibility of human error. Marjorie Brown recalled a Tonapah contest where a hammerman struck his partner's hand. "The blood crept down his arm until it looked as though it had been thrust into a pot of red paint.... The platform looked like a slaughtering block." Fortunately, such accidents were infrequent held in check by long experience on the job, and by intense practice by contestants.

The audience usually flocked to the saloon after the drilling event, paying off huge wagers. Needless to say, John Barleycorn was always present at the drilling platform's edge. Although work contests dominated the day, drilling shared position with flamboyant rhetoric on Labor Day and Miners' Union Day. During Independence Day, thought turned to flag and country. Joe Duffy, in Celtic bardic tradition, wrote a poem and a prose sketch to picture one Butte Miners' Union Day (June 13) from town parade to "dhrillin'" contest at the Columbia Gardens' picnic.[14] Such accounts of past holidays are now invaluable in charting the contours of workers' expression.

Drilling celebrations masked ethnic, class, or regional rivalry. While mine operators advanced the prize purse, union men often won contests. It was especially sweet to take the company's money after a set-back on the economic front. Over the years the names of winning drillers reflected shifts in the hard-rock labor force. Drillers carried figurative banners embroidered in Cornwall, Wales, Scotland, Nova Scotia, Ireland, Finland, Sweden, Italy, Bohemia.

The initial competitions of the 1870s essentially rewarded dazzling hand craftsmanship, and long familiarity with demanding work. However, employers and air-drill manufacturers also used contests to extoll their equipment. I cite reports from three continents to glimpse these events: A) Falmouth (September, 1882), a contest staged at the Jubilee

Exhibition of the Royal Cornwall Polytechnic Society called attention to five types of air drills. B) Idaho Springs, Colorado (July 4–6, 1902), promoters announced this event as the first Western air-drill contest. C) Johannesburg (February, 1908), the *South African Miner* noted a contest's value in replacing "Chinamen" and "Kaffir hammer-boys." D) Tonopah, Nevada (July 4–5, 1917), a journalist reported nostalgically that brawn of old days had given way to modern machine drilling.

The post-war decade of Fords, radios, and talking movies weakened many community rituals, including hard-rock drilling. However, a few contests survived after World War Two; these generally dropped machine drilling by returning to hand skills. In recent years, some Chambers-of-Commerce, engineering colleges, and folk festivals have revived hard-rock competitions. Unfortunately, no hand drillers have displayed their craft on the National Mall at the Smithsonian Institution's annual Festival of American Folklife.

Today, we learn about hard-rock drilling from early journalistic accounts and recent histories of the mining West. Such current books hold excellent photographs of drillers in mines and at contests. Fortunately, Louis Simonin's classic of 1867, *La Vie Souterraine* (published in English as *Underground Life*), was embellished with more than one hundred fine wood engravings and maps. Illustrations 111–121 included miners' tools—hammers, drills, gads—and work scenes of drillers, alone and in teams.

To complement these woodcuts and more recent photographs, we need to search out newsreel film footage, either of hand drilling below ground or of holiday contests. Has any present-day film maker considered showing drilling from hand work in the stope to a staged festival? Good ethnography now demands film and monograph as related educational forms.

Here, I return to terminology as a guide to work culture by reiterating that, literally, "singlejack" meant one hand on the hammer handle, while "doublejack" meant two. Colorado miners at Cripple Creek, about 1900, used "oney" and "twoey" to name their different-sized hammers and techniques. Veteran drillers voiced parallel terms such as "single-hand contest," "single-hand purse," "double-hand contest," "double-hand purse." A further refinement in team work projected "straightaway drilling"—one man pounding, one man turning, throughout the contest—and "change drilling"—partners taking short turns at the hammer and the drill. The supreme accolade became "either hand afore" to praise a hammerman who could swing his sledge from right or left shoulder. Lingo varied from camp to camp and decade to decade. That which seemed natural to participants now challenges linguists.

Contemporary perspective in professional sports and commodified leisure often obscures on-the-job ritual that gave, and continues to give, workers some control over their lives. We forget too quickly the long connection of work and play. Not to see a rock-drilling contest on television does not relegate its importance for insiders and outsiders. Where life seemed to offer a worker few alternatives to daily tasks, the celebration of a single task asserted the human condition.

Complex events call for complex analysis. In 1892, the influential *Mining and Scientific Press* denigrated a then-viable tradition:

> The mine owners would be more interested in a competitive trial of rock-drilling machines [than one of hand drillers]. In these days machine labor in rock-drilling has so far displaced hand labor that such personal contests have no longer the value they formerly had. It is only in the smaller mines that this work is done by hand. All mines of any size use the machine drill, of which there are various types. They do the work so much cheaper and quicker than men can do it. . . .[15]

Shades of "John Henry"! Needless to say this utilitarian view has prevailed since the Industrial Revolution. To the extent that cultural documentarians can distance themselves from technology's allure, other perspectives useful to evaluate drilling contests can be found. I see four useful frames to encompass the drilling celebration: building workers' pride and sense of identity; bringing cohesion to frontier communities; sublimating ethnic and regional tension; deflecting revolutionary ardor by circus-like events. Let each reader turn the interpretive glass.

Those who have delved for work tradition (among them—George Korson, Mody Boatright, Ben Botkin, Wayland Hand, Horace Beck) have had to contain outside/inside polarities as they have read meaning into lore gathered and observed. Four of these scholars came to the workplace from the academy; one approached the coal patch from a newspaper desk. No American worker has come from within a mine or mill to the folklorist's calling.

We ask: How do workers and scholars respond to pragmatists who relegate job customs to the antiquary's cabinet? Do we expect workers to generate, maintain, and examine critically their own traditions? Toward what end do folklorists decode occupational culture? Such rhetorical questions pulse when one switches from hammer to pen or, in modern parlance, robot tool to word processor.

This report on a few items in hard-rock vocabulary springs mainly, but not entirely, from academic study. During 1940, I had served in the Civilian Conservation Corps at a road camp in California's Siskiyou Mountains. There, my buddies and I learned to singlejack and doublejack preparatory to handling Hercules powder. Our Forest Service foreman, Lawrence Roberts, a Klamath River "native," taught raw city boys to respect dynamite, work cooperatively, and read nature's books. His standards were exemplary; he was the first of many worker/teachers I have encountered. Roberts helped firm in me a belief in the integrity of skill.

Three decades later, while writing *Only A Miner* (1972), I touched briefly on the CCC experience, but inexplicably, garbled definitions for "singlejack"/"doublejack." I used both terms incorrectly, the former to identify a driller and turner working together, and the latter, two drillers and a turner. Occasionally, drillers did work in trios. Frank Crampton spoke of attempting "two on the hammer and the third turning" in preparation for a Butte contest, 1908. Nevertheless, "singlejack" still connotes a lone driller, and "doublejack," a team.

During 1977, Stan Weir and Robert Miles, in San Pedro, California, formed Singlejack Books to publish workers' writings. After naming the press and circulating initial books, Weir questioned my treatment of rock-drilling nomenclature in *Only a Miner*. Hence, he stimulated the research leading to these findings. Further, he and I seek to gather additional usages, old and new, for "singlejack"/"doublejack." Examples from print and speech are welcome. For the present, I have dated "jack" (wedge) to 1858 and "singlejack"/"doublejack" (hammer) to 1907 and 1904, respectively. Much reading remains in order to reconstruct early transitions from tool to tool.

While continuing to search out vernacular usages for hard-rock hand drills, the drilling process, and drilling contests, I pause to reflect on the role of etymology within occupational folklore. As folklorists study mining practices, Chilean copper is unloaded in Connecticut ports—good news for Chilean miners; bad news for fellow workers in the United States. As I close these remarks, I learn that the giant Bingham Canyon open-pit mine in Utah has closed. Laborlore buffs may know this site and its "copper bosses" by association with Joe Hill—the Wobbly bard with one foot in history and the other in legendry.

Students of tradition can favor the helping nouns, "context" and "setting," by placing cultural enactments within broad experiential frames. Hard-rock miners, too, know the contextual pincer: boom and bust camps, death underground, gallows frame above to lift rock or point to hilltop cemetery. Today's largest context for mine lore is a world market and concomitant science-fiction technology. As we strive to understand new work settings and jobs without "hands," we learn to cross industrial as well as linguistic and territorial boundaries. In our continuous exploration of occupational tradition in global rather than local and national frames, we begin with comparative studies. Two fine openers from Europe are: Gerhard Heilfurth's *Der Bergbau und Seine*

Kultur (Zurich, 1981); Heinrich Winkelmann's *Der Bergbau in der Kunst* (Essen, 1958).

In the past, "ten-day stiffs" carried "bindles" from camp to camp, confident that a fortune lay deep in the next hole. But a little hammering on the drill, but a little churning of the steel, and precious ore was at hand. Singlejackers had as good a chance as any; doublejackers, as well, sought wealth with faithful tools. In the main, folklorists in the United States shared large society's magic optimism with workers. Only a few seekers of traditional lore questioned America's flamboyant promise.

Folklorists probed for song, story, and saying as hard-rockers probed for ore. Miners' creativity became our fortune. Like John Henry and his shaker, folklorist and laborer were bonded partners, not only in the extractive process, but in a joined faith in progress. Metal was abundant; lore was endless. Neither drillers nor ethnographers saw closure in their purpose. As we continue to gather and comment on occupational expression, we do well to contemplate mining emblems in the American West—weathered ghost town and rusting tool—as metaphors for world society. Collector and scribe, singlejacker and doublejacker, now share one future.[16]

NOTES

[1] For Winter's poem, see Richard Lingenfelter, *Songs of the American West* (Berkeley, 1968) 148; Wayland D. Hand, "Songs of the Butte Miners," *Western Folklore,* 9 (1950) 17-18.

[2] R.W. Raymond, *A Glossary of Mining and Metallurgical Terms* (Easton, PA, 1881); also published in *Transactions of the American Institute of Mining Engineers*, Volume 9.

[3] Albert Fay, *A Glossary of the Mining and Mineral Industry* (Washington, 1920). Helen Moore, "The Lingo of the Mining Camp," *American Speech,* 2 (November, 1926) 86-88. Levette J. Davidson, "Mining Expressions Used in Colorado," *AS,* 5 (December, 1929) 145-147.

[4] Peter L. Simmonds, *A Dictionary of Trade Products* (London, 1858).

[5] F. E. Haliday, editor, *Richard Carew of Antony: The Survey of Cornwall* (London, 1953) 92. A. K. Hamilton Jenkin, *The Cornish Miner* (London, 1927) 86. G. Randall Lewis, *The Stannaries* (Cambridge, 1908) 23. See also D. B. Barton, *A History of Tin Mining and Smelting in Cornwall* (Truro, 1967), and *Essays in Cornish Mining History* (Truro, 1968).

[6] Raphael Samuel, *Miners, Quarrymen and Saltworkers* (London, 1977) 40-41.

[7] For strike, see Rodman Paul, *California Gold* (Cambridge, 1947) 326-328; Richard Lingenfelter, *The Hardrock Miners* (Berkeley, 1974) 83-88; John Rowe, *The Hard-Rock Men* (New York, 1974) 119-124. For Cornish practices, see "Single and Double-Handed Drilling," *Mining and Scientific Press,* 18 (June 19, 1869) 392.

[8] Wayland D. Hand, "The Folklore, Customs, and Traditions of the Butte Miners," *California Folklore Quarterly,* 5 (1946) 176. See also Caroline Bancroft, "Folklore of the Central City District, Colorado," *CFQ,* 4 (1945) 315–142.
[9] Anecdote from Robert Wallace, *The Miners* (New York, 1976) 104. Folksong from Duncan Emrich, "Mining Songs," *Southern Folklore Quarterly,* 6 (1942) 103–104.
[10] See, for example, Woody Guthrie's "Jackhammer Blues" in B. A. Botkin, *A Treasury of Western Folklore* (New York, 1951) 770.
[11] In treating drilling contests, I have combined journalistic reports, reminiscences, and recent histories. These sources are arranged sequentially in a checklist appended below.
[12] Donald McCaig, *The Butte Polka* (New York, 1980) 74–75.
[13] The conjunction of work practice and taboo needs elaboration. See Wayland D. Hand, "California Miners' Folklore Below Ground," *CFQ,* 1 (1942) 148, and Archie Green, American Labor Lore: Its Meanings and Uses." *Industrial Relations* (February, 1965) 64.
[14] Joseph H. Duffy, *Butte Was Like That* (Butte, 1941) 249–252; Wayland D. Hand, "The Folklore, Customs, and Traditions of the Butte Miner," *CFQ,* 5 (1946) 164–172.
[15] "A Rock-Drilling Contest," *Mining and Scientific Press,* 65 (August 6, 1892) 90.
[16] Thanks to Peter Tamony, San Francisco; Stan Weir, San Pedro; Richard Lingenfelter, San Diego; each commented on early drafts of this report.

HAND ROCK-DRILLING CONTESTS, A SELECTIVE CHECKLIST

abbreviations: EMJ, Engineering and Mining Journal
MSP, Mining and Scientific Press
MR, Mining Reporter

"Drilling for Prizes in Colorado," (Yuma) *Arizona Sentinel* (January 12, 1878).
"A Rock-Drilling Contest," *MSP,* 63 (December 12, 1891) 378.
"A Rock-Drilling Contest," *MSP,* 65 (August 6, 1892) 90.
"The Miners' Drilling Contest," *MSP,* 68 (May 26, 1894) 321.
[Various Reports], (Denver) *Rocky Mountain News,* (October 11–20, 1895).
"The Day We Celebrate," (Virginia City, Nevada) *Territorial Enterprise* (July 7, 1897).
"The Miners' Drilling Race," (Colorado) *Sunshine Courier* (Oct. 6, 1877).
[Two Labor Day announcements], *Miners' Magazine,* 1 (September, 1900) 41, 44.
Editorial: "No more exhilarating sight . . . ," *MR,* 44 (July 11, 1901) 17.
Editorial: "The greatest drilling contest . . . ," *MR,* 44 (October 31, 1901) 333.
"The Leadville Drilling Contest," *MR,* 44 (October 31, 1901) 340.
"The El Paso Drilling Contest," *MR,* 45 (January 23, 1902) 109.
"Famous Stone Goes to Bisbee," *MR,* 45 (June 12, 1902) 548.
"Rock-Drilling Contests," *MR,* 47 (June 25, 1903) 577.
"Idaho: Shoshone County," *MSP,* 93 (July 14, 1906) 41.
Victor Noxon, "Hard Rock Drilling Contests in Colorado," *Colorado Magazine,* 11 (May, 1934) 81–85.
WPA Writers' Program (William A. Burke, editor). *Copper Camp.* NY: Hastings House, 1943 (221–223).
Angus Murdoch. *Boom Copper.* NY: Macmillan, 1943 (217).

Wayland D. Hand, "The Folklore, Customs, and Traditions of the Butte Miner," *California Folklore Quarterly,* 5 (1946) 169-173.

Joe Chisholm. *Brewery Gulch.* San Antonio: Naylor, 1949 (113-114).

Atha Albert Ritchie, "The Real Facts about Those Famous Old Hand-Drilling Contests," *EMJ,* 152 (November, 1951) 84-95.

Frank A. Crampton. *Deep Enough.* Denver: Sage Books, 1956 (42-48, 56-58, 77-82).

Gosta E. Sandstrom. *Tunnels.* NY: Holt, Rinehart and Winston, 1963 (101).

Arthur Cecil Todd. *The Cornish Miner in America.* Truro: D. B. Barton, 1967 (81).

Mrs. Hugh (Marjorie) Brown. *Lady in Boomtown.* Palo Alto: American West, 1968 (73-75).

Otis E. Young, Jr. *Western Mining.* Norman: University of Oklahoma Press, 1970 (184-186).

Richard Lingenfelter. *The Hardrock Miners.* Berkeley: University of California Press, 1974 (17-18, 54).

John Rowe. *The Hard-Rock Men.* NY: Barnes & Noble, 1974 (274-275).

Otis E. Young, Jr. *Black Powder and Hand Steel.* Norman: University of Oklahoma Press, 1975 (49-56).

Robert Wallace. *The Miners.* NY: Time-Life Books, 1976 (104-108).

Ronald C. Brown. *Hard-Rock Miners.* College Station: Texas A & M University Press, 1979 (54-56).

Mark Wyman. *Hard Rock Epic.* Berkeley: University of California Press, 1979 (87-90).

Patricia Hart and Ivar Nelson. *Mining Town.* Seattle: University of Washington Press, 1984 (26-29).

Note: I list here a few air-drill contests:

"A Rock Drill Contest in Cornwall," *MSP,* 45 (November 4, 1882) 294.

"Rock Drilling Contest at Idaho Springs, Colorado," *MR,* 46 (July 14, 1902) 44.

"Machine Drill Contest at Idaho Springs, Colorado," *EMJ,* 74 (July 26, 1902) 114.

"Recent Rock Drilling Contest," *MSP,* 85 (July 26, 1902) 47.

"Drill Contest on the Rand," *MSP,* 96 (March 14, 1908) 361.

"Drilling Contest at Tonopah," *EMJ,* 104 (August 18, 1917) 315.

TOM PEPPER: THE BIGGEST LIAR ON LAND OR SEA

Herbert Halpert and Violetta M. Halpert
Memorial University of Newfoundland

BOTH AT SEA AND ASHORE the name "Tom Pepper" has been known in the English-language tradition for more than a century and a half as an epithet for a liar. Proverbial sayings, widely distributed, make him a master liar, the "biggest liar" to whom all other liars are compared. This paper brings together the scattered references to Tom Pepper which I have found in a long and sporadic search.

My interest in Tom Pepper the liar began early in my folklore collecting in the Piney country of southern New Jersey. In the summer of 1937 I recorded a song called "Tom Pepper" from an Australian-born ex-seaman, William Tester, aged 76, who lived in Burlington County. He said it was "a very old song. . . . Sailors sung it . . . when I was a kid aboard of a ship . . . a down East American ship, about 1879. . . ."

Tester's song is a tall-tale narrative related by a seaman as his own experience. When a silent stranger appears on deck after a battle at sea, an old tar explains, "From the bow gun of the enemy ship I saw the bugger come flyin'." The sailors christen the speechless stranger "Tom Pepper" in a tub of grog, but his capacity for that beverage is so great that the angered sailors ram him into the ship's bow gun and shoot him away. Several years later, when the narrator is aboard a becalmed vessel, the sailors for amusement haul up a huge shark, which contains in its stomach a two-masted vessel, provisions, and Tom Pepper. This time Tom makes himself unwelcome by his enormous capacity for food, and is flung overboard with a grindstone tied around his neck. In the final episode, the narrator, walking down the Bowery in New York City, is amazed to meet Tom Pepper using the grindstone to sharpen scissors and knives. Asked how he escaped from the "ocean deep",

> "Tom said he didn't care for the billet nor he didn't feel inclined
> to roam,
> So upon the carpenter's grinding stone he took a passage home."

Tester had remarked, before singing this song: "Tom Pepper's supposed to be the biggest liar that ever lived, that's the reason the song was made up about him." This intriguing observation took on new significance when, a few years later, I heard the name Pepper again, from my main informant on Piney lore, Charles Henry Grant, then age 71, who lived on a farm near New Egypt in Ocean County. On January 23, 1940, he started to talk about a notable tall-tale teller he had known.

> Used to be a man around Fork-ed River—Old Joe Britton. They said he could beat Old Jack Pepper in lyin', and Pepper was kicked out of hell three times for lyin'.

When I asked who Jack Pepper was, Grant could only tell me, "They used to say that; that's all I ever heard about Jack Pepper."

Although the first names were different, "Jack Pepper" and "Tom Pepper" seemed to be versions of the same character. I decided to try to trace this big liar to see if he appeared elsewhere in folk tradition.

To my surprise, despite Grant's association of Pepper with a tall-tale narrator, I have never found any tall tales or legends in which Tom or Jack Pepper was the main character or storyteller. Nor, despite my expectations, have I found another published version of the lying-song, or any other song that mentions his name. So far as I can determine, Tom Pepper figures only in folk speech.

I shall present first the evidence for the use of "Tom Pepper" simply as the name for a liar, and continue with examples of "Tom Pepper" or closely related names in proverbial comparisons dealing with liars. In each section most of the items are presented in chronological order by date of publication.

The oldest printed reference located is in a long narrative poem about the British Navy, published by Alfred Burton (1818, 247-48).[2] Captain Teak, an overbearing naval officer, was transferred to a new ship where he met a set of officers who wouldn't "stand his nonsense." He was brought to trial,

> . . . and his deeds in spite
> Of all his cunning brought to light;
> For maugre a Defence which might
> Have made *Tom Pepper* blush outright,
> The charges all were proved, and he
> Was broke at last for Tyranny.

The italics and capitalization are in the original.

The next report, also from the British Navy, this time from below decks, appeared in 1844 in a collection of sea sketches by M. H. Barker (1844, 18-19), in a piece entitled "Dick Fitton, A Reminiscence."[3] While drunk, Dick Fitton, a gunner, captures a French three-master singlehanded. After he has explained his feat to the apparent satisfaction of the Captain, and is beginning to tell his story to his messmates over afternoon grog, the boatswain's mate says, "So d'ye see, Dick, why just overhaul the consarn to us; not as you did to the skipper in Tom Pepper fashion, to make him think you was sober; but let's have the right arnest jometry of the thing. . . ." One concludes from this that in sailor usage an explanation in Tom Pepper fashion was a deceptive rearrangement of the truth.

The third reference found was a straightforward definition given by Russell (1883, 148), in his nautical dictionary: "*Tom Pepper.*—A liar."

Yeoman (1960, 19) reported the use of the term in Shields, Northumberland. After discussing what a "downright liar" might be called, he added: "If a less harsh note of condemnation were adopted he would possibly be called . . . a 'proper Tom Pepper'."

Tom Pepper showed up again in 1966 in Australia, the farthest limit of the English-language tradition, in Bill Wannan's collection of tall tales (Wannan 1966, 79), in which Julian Stewart, referring to Crooked Mick, the hero of a series of tall tales, pointed out that "Mick's name was generally brought to light for the purpose of putting the kibosh on anyone who was emulating Ananias or Munchausen, or Tom Pepper."

Stewart's association of Tom Pepper with Munchausen, the tall-story teller, may help to clarify the next example, from Joseph Farnham's memories of his boyhood days on the island of Nantucket, off the coast of Massachusetts. Farnham (1923, 92) quotes a poem composed in the 1860s by a high school student, containing the names and nicknames of many local characters, including

". . . Peter Raymond, often called Tom Pepper Tell-a-fellow. . . ."

Since Farnham adds nothing more about Peter Raymond, he must have assumed that the nickname was self-explanatory, that everyone would know that Raymond stretched the truth.

A few other texts in which "Tom Pepper" is used as an epithet for a liar include the comment that he was kicked out of hell for lying. These examples have been considered with the proverbial comparisons which follow, most of which contain the same motif.

The two earliest examples in which the "kicked out of hell" motif occurs were published in the 1860s and frequently reprinted in later dictionaries. The following excerpt from Yorkshire appeared in an anonymous 1862 book on Leeds dialect that has been ascribed to C. Clough Robinson (1862, 405):

A noted propagator of untruths is "as big a liar as Tom Pepper," who, as the legend runs, was turned out of his Satanic majesty's dominions for lying.

W. Carew Hazlitt ([1869] 1907, 65) reprinted the simile in an early edition of his proverb dictionary, but replaced Robinson's "legend" with: "The devil is said to have given up Tom in despair."

The second reference was printed in 1867 in Admiral Smyth's dictionary of nautical terms (Smyth 1867, 685):

> *Tom Pepper.* A term for a liar; he having, according to nautical tradition, been kicked out of the nether regions for indulging in falsehood.

R. Pearse Chope (1892, 368) sent an inquiry to *Notes and Queries:*

> I should be glad of any information concerning the persons referred to in the following Devonshire proverbs:-. . . .
> 3. "As big a liar as Tom Payne (or Pepper), and he got kicked out of hell for telling lies."

Apart from the naming of "Tom Payne" as an alternate for "Tom Pepper," this is the first example that includes what happened to Tom as part of the comparison, and discards the Victorian euphemisms for hell used in the two preceding texts.

Andrew Cheviot (1896, 418) published this shorter version of the comparison in his compilation of the proverbial sayings of Scotland: "Ye're as big a liar as Tam Pepper." Cheviot commented: "This saying is common in Berwickshire, and Hazlitt gives it in his collection as of Leeds origin. I have not met with it elsewhere." He then quoted Hazlitt's rephrasing of Robinson's "legend".

The following text appeared in a nautical dictionary compiled by Bowen ([1929], 143): "*Tom Pepper.* A liar, the old tradition being that Tom Pepper was the seaman who was kicked out of Hell for lying."

Haggard (1972, 46) cited the following comparison from Herefordshire: "You're a bigger liar than Tom Pepper, as were turned out of hell for telling lies."

At the end of a group of explanations of various nautical sayings, Margaret Baker (1979, 178) adds: ". . . 'Tom Pepper,' say those who know, was kicked out of Hell, for being a bigger liar than Satan."

In a Sussex version given by Tony Wales (1979, 78), "Someone very dishonest was 'as big a liar as Old Tom Pepper, and *he* was thrown out of Hell for lying.'"

A recent reference in Widdowson (1984, 118) shows that the comparison is still current in the North Country of England. At the end of a list of proverbial comparisons from Lincolnshire is the following item:

> Last, but not least, the elusive Tom Pepper . . . retains his immortality in "He's a bigger liar than Tom Pepper"—a proverbial comparison also still frequently heard in Yorkshire.

The only comparison that closely resembles the New Jersey text cited earlier, in which Pepper is bounced from Hell three times for lying, is another North Country saying published in Pickles (1955, 308): "Tha's as big a liar as Tom Pepper an' he were pawsed aht o' hell three times afore breakfast for lying."

Although a story seems to be implied in many of these statements that Pepper was kicked out of hell for lying, the evidence to date suggests that no such narrative exists, and that the saying circulates in tradition simply as a *dite* (the term proposed by von Sydow 1948, 106–26). Furthermore, I have found only one example in print of the use of the "kicked out of hell for lying" remark in connection with a tall-story teller. It appears as a comment at the end of a group of tall tales told about Daniel Stamps, a well-known storyteller from western Illinois.

> ". . . ol' Dan'l Stamps is gone." Where he is now the river folk don't know, for it is common knowledge that he was kicked out of hell for lying. (Walker et al. 1954, 160)

This is the only reference given in Baughman (1966, 408) for Motif X909.1(e), "Incorrigible liar kicked out of hell."

The versions from Hazlitt and Baker both attempt to explain *why* the Devil kicked Tom Pepper out of hell for lying, but these gratuitous interpretations are unsupported by any other examples presented in this paper. The sayings may well be based on the familiar proverbial tradition about the Devil, reinforced by generations of clergymen, that "The Devil is the father of lies."[4] (See Hazlitt 1907, 415; Stevenson 1961, 564, No. 4; Whiting 1977, 104, D127.) Perhaps Tom Pepper was kicked out of hell simply for having the impudence to lie to the Master-Liar himself.

Four of the five Tom Pepper references published before 1930 have either been reprinted or referred to in compilations of proverbial sayings or in dictionaries: the Robinson text from Leeds in Hazlitt ([1867] 1907, 65), Cheviot (1896, 418), Lean (1902–04, 2:2, 206), and Apperson (1929, 47); the Devonshire one from Chope, only in Lean; the Smyth nautical one in *The Oxford English Dictionary* (1961, 11: 118b) and in Partridge (1967, 895); the Bowen nautical version only in Partridge. The Smyth text is not in the form of a proverbial comparison, so its absence from collections of proverbial sayings is understandable; but it seems curious that both *The Oxford English Dictionary* and Partridge cite only nautical versions.

References to Tom Pepper can still be found occasionally in oral tradition. Although he is specifically named in only a couple of the following proverbial comparisons about liars, the other examples are useful for supplying the contexts in which similar sayings were used. All of these are unpublished texts from two folklore archives.

E. Plummer, of Wickersley, Yorkshire, contributed the following comparison to the Centre for English Cultural Tradition and Language (CECTAL)[5] in Sheffield in April 1976: "He (she) is as big a liar as old Tom Pepper." She recalled hearing it from her mother, Mrs. A. Plummer, born at York, who had learned it when a child and used it frequently since.

Folklore students contributed the next three items to the Memorial University of Newfoundland Folklore and Language Archive (MUNFLA).[6] Louise Mullally, of Northern Bay, Newfoundland, reported the following comparison, which she had heard from her mother, in February 1977: "He tells more lies than Pepper." She said that her mother didn't know where the saying came from nor who Pepper was. (FSC 77-28/6)

Whether the names "Tom Pop" and "Pippy" in the next two examples are echoes of the name "Tom Pepper" (which is likely) is less important than the excellent descriptions of how the sayings were used. Both were contributed in 1970.

Mrs. Terry Gullage, age 23, Corner Brook, wrote the following report:

> My mother [Mrs. Eileen Hiscock, Corner Brook] would often say to someone: "You tell more lies than Tom Pop." It was not used in a serious context, such as when someone told a big lie; it was used more often in a lighter matter, such as little white lies, or when someone exaggerated. It was used when talking to children, or in an adult group when someone said something like, "You're getting younger every day." I often asked who Tom Pop was, but no one seemed to know. (FSC 71-16/62)

Mrs. Florence Barnes learned this one from the old-timers on Change Islands when she was about 15. It was recorded by her daughter, Stephanie Barnes, St. John's.

> "He's a bigger liar than Pippy."

> On Change Islands, if anyone told deliberate lies or exaggerated in any fashion, he was considered "a bigger liar than Pippy." Pippy was presumably a person who lived years ago and always stretched the truth. My mother was not certain of who Pippy was, but says this was the general belief. He lived about two hundred years ago on the Islands. (FSC 71-47/57)

Although, as I mentioned earlier, I was surprised not to find any tall tales told by or about Tom Pepper (or Pop, or Pippy), it is worth emphasizing that the "as big a liar as . . ." comparison is closely related to the whole American tall-tale tradition, in which someone who exaggerated or told tall stories would be called "as big a liar as . . ." or "a bigger liar than . . ." the most noted local storyteller. For example, a famous nineteenth-century tall-story spinner, Abraham "Oregon" Smith, was known in Illinois as "Lying Abe", and people in Indiana would say "You're a bigger liar than Oregon Smith." (Jansen 1948; Jansen 1977, 151-73; Thomas 1977, 25)

A recent contribution to the Newfoundland archive (MUNFLA) presented the same comparison applied to a living storyteller, and makes clear that "lie" equals "tall tale" in narrative tradition. A student, Arch White, wrote in 1970:

> The most common expression that I have heard around home to denote a big liar is: "You're a bigger liar than Clad." Clad is Clarence Thompson of Point Leamington, and his ability to lie is known among almost everyone I know. He became famous for one lie.
> On the road between Point Leamington and Botwood, there is a bump in the road that makes your stomach come up in your mouth if you go over it fast. Well, one day Clad was telling a few stories, and he said that that morning he was going over the bump so fast he stayed in the air fifty-seven seconds. And then he said: "Boy, it's not a word of a lie; ask the wife, she timed me." This was said with an absolutely straight face. . . . From that day forward he became known for telling lies. (FSC 71-35/41)

In summing up the evidence presented in this paper for Tom Pepper in oral tradition, we find that, not counting reprintings, there are sixteen published and four unpublished references specifically using the name Pepper—not a very large number to show for a term that has been circulating for more than a hundred and fifty years. This figure will, I am sure, increase when other folklorists and archives continue the search. Of the twenty examples, there are seven reports specifically from sea-going tradition: one from New England, the others from Great Britain. Among the other reports, there are three from North America, eight from England, and one each from Berwickshire in Scotland, and from Australia. In short, we may reasonably conclude that "Tom Pepper" as an epithet for liar "is widely but thinly distributed" in the English-language tradition, on land and sea.

Notes

[1] Herbert Halpert collected or compiled the examples in this paper; Violetta Halpert edited it.
[2] Mention of this early reference to Tom Pepper was communicated to Partridge (1967, 1425), April 26, 1929, by Colonel Albert F. Moe (retired), U.S. Marines.

[3] Gerald Thomas discovered and gave me this reference.
[4] The saying is probably derived from "The Gospel according to Saint John," 8:44.
[5] J.D.A. Widdowson allowed me to use this reference from CECTAL.
[6] Each MUNFLA reference is followed by its Archive designation.

REFERENCES

Apperson, G.L.
   1929   *English Proverbs and Proverbial Phrases: a Historical Dictionary.* London: J. M. Dent and Sons Ltd.

Baker, Margaret
   1979   *Folklore of the Sea.* Newton Abbot: David & Charles.

Barker, M. H.
   1844   *The Old Sailor's Jolly Boat.* London: W. Strange.

Baughman, Ernest W.
   1966   *Type and Motif-Index of the Folktales of England and North America.* Indiana University Folklore Series, No. 20. The Hague: Mouton & Co.

Bowen, Frank C.
   [1929] *Sea Slang. A Dictionary of the Old-Timers' Expressions and Epithets.* London: Sampson Low, Marston & Co.

Burton, Alfred
   1818   *The Adventures of Johnny Newcome in the Navy; a Poem in Four Cantos.* 2 vols. London: W. Simpkin and R. Marshall.

Cheviot, Andrew
   1896   *Proverbs, Proverbial Expressions, and Popular Rhymes of Scotland.* Paisley and London: Alexander Gardner.

Chope, R. Pearse
   1892   Personal Proverbs. *Notes and Queries* 8th Ser. 2:368.

Farnham, Joseph E. C.
   1923   *Brief Historical Data and Memories of my Boyhood Days in Nantucket.* 2nd ed. Providence, R.I.: Privately printed.

Haggard, Andrew
   1972   *Dialect and Local Usages of Herefordshire.* London: Grower Books.

Hazlitt, W. Carew
   [1869] *English Proverbs and Proverbial Phrases.* Rev. ed. London: Reeves
   1907   and Turner.

Jansen, William Hugh
   1948   Lying Abe: A Tall-Teller and his Reputation. *Hoosier Folklore* 7:107–24.
   1977   *Abraham "Oregon" Smith: Pioneer, Folk Hero and Tale-Teller.* New York: Arno Press.

Lean, Vincent Stuckey
   1902– *Lean's Collectanea.* 4 vols. in 5. Bristol: Privately printed.
   1904
   1961   *The Oxford English Dictionary.* 12 vols. Oxford: Clarendon Press.

Partridge, Eric.
    1967   *A Dictionary of Slang and Unconventional English.* 6th ed. New York: Macmillan and Co.

Pickles, Wilfred.
    1955   *My North Countrie.* London: George Allen & Unwin Ltd.

[Robinson, C. Clough].
    1862   *The Dialect of Leeds and its Neighbourhood.* London: John Russell Smith.

Russell, W. Clark.
    1883   *Sailors' Language.* London: Sampson Low, Marston, Searle, & Rivington.

Smyth, (The late Admiral) W. H.
    1867   *The Sailor's Word-Book: An Alphabetical Digest of Nautical Terms.* Revised by E. Belcher. London: Blackie and Son.

Stevenson, Burton.
    1961   *The Home Book of Proverbs, Maxims, and Familiar Phrases.* New York: The Macmillan Company.

Thomas, Gerald.
    1977   *The Tall Tale and Philippe d'Alcripe. An Analysis of the Tall Tale Genre . . .* Memorial University of Newfoundland Publications, Monograph Series No. 1. St. John's: The Department of Folklore, Memorial University of Newfoundland in association with the American Folklore Society.

Von Sydow, C. W.
    1948   *Selected Papers on Folklore.* Edited by Laurits Bødker. Copenhagen: Rosenkilde and Bagger.

Wales, Tony.
    1979   *A Sussex Garland.* London: Godfrey Cave Associates.

Walker, Warren Stanley et al.
    1954   Dan'l Stamps: Tall Tale Hero of the River Country. *Midwest Folklore* 4:153–60.

Wannan, Bill.
    1966   *Crooked Mick of the Speewah and Other Tall Tales.* Melbourne/London: Lansdowne Press.

Whiting, Bartlett Jere.
    1977   *Early American Proverbs and Proverbial Phrases.* Cambridge, Mass.: The Belknap Press of Harvard University Press.

Widdowson, J. D. A.
    1984   Lincolnshire Traditional Sayings and Proverbial Expressions. In *A Prospect of Lincolnshire,* edited by N. Field and A. White, 114–18. Lincoln: The editors.

Yeoman, James.
    1960   *Shields Sayings.* South Shields: Privately printed.

THE FOLK BELIEFS AND CUSTOMS OF SAN PEDRO'S FISHERMEN

Wayland D. Hand
University of California at Los Angeles

THE TECHNOLOGICAL ADVANCES of American commercial fishing during the past fifty years or more is graphically reflected in the dwindling repertories of folklore found among the country's fishermen. The loss of this colorful lore of the sea, coinciding with the serious decline of the fishing industry itself, is no better seen anywhere in North America than among the decimated fleets plying out of San Pedro and other California fishing ports.

In view of San Pedro's long leadership in the fishing and canning industries, the plight of its fisheries is particularly painful to the proud and self-contained community nestling on the eastern slopes of the Palos Verdes peninsula. San Pedro had not only pioneered the West Coast sardine industry at the turn of the century, and had brought the sea harvest of this elusive species to record tonnage between 1930 and World War II, but had early on likewise begun the pursuit of tuna, with a wide-ranging fleet of up to eighty vessels by 1960. Pole fishing for tuna soon gave way to purse seining, and it remained for Portuguese crews fishing out of Point Loma in San Diego to develop super fishing vessels that ranged far into Mexican and South American waters. They brought in record hauls, and latterly these big ships have begun to venture as far from port as American Samoa and other South Sea Island fishing grounds, with catches approaching one thousand tons per voyage. A few of these canny Portuguese fishermen chose to settle down and remain in San Pedro.

Natural forces and man-made disasters, to be sure, have also figured in the decline of the San Pedro fishing industry that has seen the number of canneries drop from sixteen to twenty in the heyday between 1930 and 1950 to a mere two today. The closing of the Starkist Tuna cannery in October 1984 was the last in a series of vicissitudes to befall San Pedro over the years. To the pollution of coastal waters in the greater Los Angeles area that has been going on for decades must be added the lack of consistent economic policies by the federal government and unworkable regulatory practices imposed by the State of California. Natural factors of weather and climate, principally the appearance of the warm El Niño ocean currents of 1957-1958 and of 1983-1984, also exacted a heavy toll at critical periods in the San Pedro fleet's troubled history.

The plight of the industry, of course, has given many a plucky fisherman ample time to reminisce about the glory days of fishing when San Pedro's sons went down to the sea in ships—the Portuguese, the Yugoslavians, the Italians and Sicilians; also the Japanese before the war, the Mexicans, the Anglos and others who carry on what many San Pedro fishermen claim as the world's second oldest profession. Bumper stickers around town proclaim that even Jesus was a gillnet fisherman.

Because of its ups and downs, but particularly because of the steady advance in its technology, San Pedro's fishing industry makes an excellent case study for the testing of occupational folk beliefs and customs. There is a well-known thesis that folklore develops from man's relationship, not only with fellow humans and his environment, but also with the unseen forces that intervene in his life. With regard to fishing, and the folk beliefs and customs that have grown up with this ancient occupation, the noted British anthropologist, Bronislaw Malinowski, was able to show over sixty years ago that as fishermen by their own technology and practical sense learned to control the physical aspects of their work, they laid increasingly less store by the superstitions and traditional folkways that were calculated to neutralize or control the unseen forces that beset them.[1] On inland waters or in gulfs and estuaries protected from the open sea, therefore, the fisherman relied mainly on his own experience and sagacity to avoid mischance. Exposed to the dangers of unknown and unfriendly waters from land, however, he instinctively reverted to his old ways, propitiating the gods and the forces of nature that were thought to govern wave and weather, and observing myriad ritualistic acts to avoid harm and to secure good fortune.

In a remarkable updating for a modern industrialized country, Patrick B. Mullen was able to show only fifteen years ago that Texas Gulf Coast fishermen tended to be far more wary of the sea, and far more superstitious than otherwise, when they ventured beyond inland coastal waters.[2] Mullen's findings are paralleled for commercial fishing along the California coast except, of course, for shrimping and shellfish operations that are not well developed in Pacific waters. His finding list of the folk beliefs and customs of Texas Gulf Coast fishermen lacks a few of the old traditions, but is still the richest posting of such materials for North America.

Following Mullen's lead I have tried to deal with Malinowski's anxiety-ritual theory, but taking up for particular emphasis the modern high technology as it relates to fishing. (Many of these developments had not found wide applicability in Gulf Coast fishing practice when Mullen began his memorable work.) These innovations deal not only with improvements in the manufacture and outfitting of boats and ships, but with the fishing gear itself, including powerful hoisting apparatus and nylon nets. More important for the fisherman's peace of mind was a whole range of radio and communication devices that were put at the command of even the smallest fishing boats. With continual weather reports and storm warnings, these miracles of modern communication made it easier for the fisherman to deal with wind and weather, and steeled him against the prospect of disaster at sea. Timely help from the Coast Guard and other vessels within range provided assurance and security unknown to earlier generations of fishermen and mariners.

More striking in economic terms than anything that had ever gone before, however, were the new technological means of locating schools of fish. This was done mainly by sonic depthfinders and by aerial spotting. Of these ship-to-ship and ship-to-shore communications and of the short wave hook-ups that kept aerial fish spotters in constant contact with skippers in the fishing fleet, Larry Bozanich, Manager of San Pedro's Fisherman's Co-op and sage observer of the port's fishing life, recently noted that the shortwave radio equipment "boasts more frequencies than the CIA, and boats sprout more antennae than a spy ship." Whereas fishermen had held fast to the time-honored lore of their fathers, blending the skills of fishing folk from Italy, Sicily, Yugoslavia, Portugal, and elsewhere, they were loathe at first to discount these old-country ways, but they did begin gradually to yield to the new technology. There came a day when they were forced to do so just to survive. In practical terms, for example, if one could fish in the light of the moon, as well as in the dark of the moon, as old fishing maxims decree, and as their own experience had confirmed many times over, then why not try the new way, even if such a voyage eliminated the well established fisherman's furlough that began two days before the new moon and lasted until two days after?[3] By the same token, if the fishing had been poor in recent forays, but if now fish were known to be running in certain waters, what was to keep the skipper from summoning his crew for a Friday sailing, or even for an unprecedented departure from the wharves on saints' days and other special days of the sacred calendar? The erosion of the folkways of the sea was gradual, but inexorable, even to a point where religious principles had to be compromised. One veteran San Pedro fisherman faced the dilemma this way: "In the end I would sail, but I'd make sure that my wife went to church."

It was not the new technology per se that wrought the sweeping changes in the craft of the customs of fishermen, but the economic pressure to stay in business. Overcapitalization and exploitation of the sea's bounty to meet the needs of canneries—a demand multiplying almost exponentially—hastened the decline of the fisheries.

Learning of the sweeping technological changes in fishing almost on the first day of my fieldwork in San Pedro, and sensing the concomitant loss of the folklore of the sea, I soon found myself looking not only for heirlooms of the old craft of fishing that had survived, but also making a rough census of the kinds of beliefs and customs that had been known, if not actually practiced, by an earlier generation of workers. That this kind of historical reconstruction was not without merit was confirmed time and again when some informant, after recalling something that he had either seen or heard in his time, would remark, "You ought to have been around asking these questions fifty years ago when all those oldtimers were still here." But for fishing traditions within families, and the closeknit life of the port, much folklore that might not otherwise have survived can still be arduously pieced together.

It is interesting to note that fish spotters, five or six of them flying in close formation, but at different altitudes of up to a thousand feet, like fishermen themselves, try to keep the sun or the moon at their backs. The phosphorescent glow of fish near the surface of the water, of course, could be more readily detected on dull days and moonless nights. Fishermen normally fished on the dark of the moon anyway. Sonic detection, of course, was a separate operation, but the findings of the skipper by interrupted depth soundings could be coordinated with information obtained by aerial surveillance. In the old days it was the spotter in the crow's nest of the boat who would provide as much information as he could to correlate with the observations of the skipper and mates at different stations on the boat.

Rain portended good fishing, whether by day or night; so did cloudy and moist weather. Wind, on the other hand, unless it were soft southeasterly breezes laden with moisture, usually drove fish from the wave-tossed surface of the water to greater depths. Santa Ana winds, hot winds from the desert, were particularly bad, especially since they continued for several days, or even a week on end. The resulting warmer surface temperatures drove fish to deep water. Although almost everyone interviewed knew about good-luck coins secured beneath the mast at the time the keel of the boat was laid, few knew about the coin's "buying" wind whenever needed.[4] This old belief goes back to the days of sail, and although the forebears of the San Pedro fishermen in the old country generally fished by sail, the use of wind-driven fishing boats was all but unknown in San Pedro waters.

Now that we have seen the effect of the high technology that permeates modern fishing, and assessed in a general way why as a consequence the rich folklore of the sea has fallen into desuetude, we can now proceed to a systematic investigation of fishermen's folklore that is still believed and practiced by individual boat owners and common fishermen, or remembered by both active and retired workers. The financing and building of boats are business matters not unlike the construction of buildings, with canneries often holding the mortgages and amortizing them by taking a percentage of every catch. There is little or no folklore in these transactions, to be sure, but there is quite a bit of lore connected with the naming, blessing, launching, and outfitting of ships, particularly with regard to quarters for religious devotions, the mounting of good luck symbols and apotropaic agents, and a provision for minimum conforts for the crew, confined, tense, and ever alert. The communication and security systems so vital to modern fishing have already been treated.

The name of the boat is usually chosen somewhat before completion of the vessel, and is most often painted on the bow before the formal christening and blessing.[5] The owner of the boat, in consultation with family members and friends, usually makes the choice, but the legal owners may have a hand in the naming if the ship is of considerable tonnage. As a matter of courtesy, however, the final choice often rested with the owner's wife. Yugoslavians, Italians, and Portuguese all named their boats after family members, usually women and children, with distinctions of age, such as Frankie Boy I, Frankie Boy II, Angelina, Angelina I, Angelina II, etc. The Yugoslavians were proud to name their boats after their natal villages, and after rivers, islands, and other geographical features of their homeland. For their part Italians frequently chose the names of patron saints, or saints of their native towns. The taboo against renaming a boat seems not to have counted for much in the San Pedro fishing fleet.[6] As a matter of fact, the sale of boats almost always entailed a new name for the vessel and a blessing at the new owner's wish. The new name would be mentioned in the blessing just as it had been when originally launched.

The blessing of a vessel is performed by a priest in clerical vestments, reading from a special office in the *Rituale Romanum*.[7] The ship is then asperged with Holy Water from stem to stern, including not only the deck and wheelhouse, but the galley, sleeping quarters and other areas below deck, including the hatches and engine room. The launching, at high tide when possible,[8] often on Sunday,[9] but usually not on Friday, then followed, with a girl or woman "wetting the ship's nose" with champagne. One Sicilian informant likened a boat's christening to the baptism of a child, with the observation that the boat became "a member of the family." Old and dignified members of the family, male and female, served as sponsors and even as godparents,[10] though untitled. The person actually christening the boat would herself become a godparent by virtue of the ritual act. According to tradition, a charmed life for the vessel was promised when it took three swings to break the champagne bottle properly.[11] In Catholic countries, a boat not blessed by a priest was sure to be unlucky, and it was difficult to muster a crew to man such a vessel.[12] In San Pedro, even non-religious skippers and near atheists are reported not to have risked sailing with an unchristened ship.

The blessing of fishing fleets themselves, as well as individual boats, is encountered in many parts of Europe and elsewhere,[13] and California is no exception.[14] The festive and almost carnival atmosphere of these annual fishermen's festivals is not present, of course, when fishing fleets make ready to sail on long voyages,[15] or when individual fishing vessels request a blessing when embarking.

Since favorable auspices were sought for fishing voyages, old-time fishermen kept an eye out for all kinds of happenings on the day they set out. They were particularly intent on occurrences that did not bode well. There soon developed a whole range of negative signs and portents. Principal among these was the so-called "encounter." Most of these notions about "the encounter" have been little remembered among San Pedro's fishing folk, perhaps for the reason that for as long as people can remember the fisherman did not walk to his boat, but was driven there. At one time this walk to the boat was a solitary trek in which the fisherman didn't want to see anyone. The curious could learn or surmise where he was going, and possibly frustrate his plans or otherwise thwart his purpose by some magical means.[16] The secrecy surrounding whither fishermen are bound still persists, of course. It is a matter of common knowledge that when a cluster of fishermen on the wharf suddenly fall silent at the approach of a rival, or even a stranger, it's a pretty good bet that they are talking about where fish are to be found.

Long since forgotten in San Pedro are ominous encounters with flat-footed or pigeon-toed people,[17] squint-eyed or cross-eyed people, or those who deviate from normal in some way, such as cripples, or even imbeciles.[18] Only Gypsies seem in recent times to have been viewed with suspicion in the port, and sometimes hunchbacks, "but that goes back to before the War," as one Italian fisherman told me. No one seemed to know about the bad luck connected with the commonplace of meeting a woman,[19] much less with meeting a barefoot woman,[20] one wearing a white apron,[21] or a woman carrying an empty water pail. Red-headed women widely feared elsewhere when a chance encounter ensued,[22] seem not to have evoked any such feelings in San Pedro's fishing colony. Even though a few women fish with their husbands and women are welcome aboard ship on festive occasions, there is still a lingering antipathy to having them come aboard a fishing boat.[23] The modern rationale is not that ill-will or magic in anyway attaches to the woman, but rather that men are diverted, and either show off or fail to pay attention to what they are doing.

The widespread dislike of meeting a priest near the boat or his casually coming aboard,[24] is not shared among San Pedro fishermen, although individual skippers are reported to have been discomfited by such a sighting. This antipathy to sailors' meeting or seeing priests and other clergy beyond their appointed rounds has never been satisfactorily explained. The Reverend Arthur Bartlett, Director and Chaplain of San Pedro's Episcopal Seamen's Center, was quick to think of St. Paul's connection with a well-known shipwreck, as reported in Acts of the Apostles, and Beck also gives the apostle to the Gentiles high rank among the jonahs of ships at sea.[25] An even friendlier view of the religious in connection with ships and the sea is reserved for nuns, at least in San Pedro where as youngsters many fishermen were instructed by Sisters of Mercy in the town's parochial schools. No one apparently looked askance at nuns appearing near the boats,[26] and some counted such an appearance actually as a sign of good luck.

Apprehension about unauthorized people near the boats has long since died out, but few fishermen, as I myself have learned, are completely indifferent to having strangers come aboard. On San Pedro's Fishermen's Wharf, even at high tide, the decks are far too low for one to go aboard without help. There still lingers in the port, however, ambivalence about a woman's coming aboard,[27] and likewise a clergyman boarding without invitation.[28]

Fishing boats are more compact than other kinds of craft because of the need to carry bulky nets on deck, and likewise a good-sized skiff to help deploy them. If the fishing had been bad the skipper or mate might urinate on the nets to change the luck, or a Negro prostitute would be paid "to change the luck,"[29] as the saying goes. Another way to turn the wheels of fortune was for someone to pee into the hold. Apotropaic devices of various kinds were employed on ship either to ward off evil, or to turn it back upon ill-wishers. We have already heard of coins being inserted beneath the mast. This was done for good luck as well as for buying wind.[30] Likewise, horseshoes were powerful good luck symbols on boats and were thought to protect the vessel and crew from harm.[31] They were affixed to the mast or the bowstem, nailed to the wheelhouse, or even mounted in the galley. The horns of deer and other animals, with antlers or horns extending forward, making the sign of the "horns," were fastened to the mast at the crow's nest, serving notice to rivals that evil wishes would be returned to the sender. Making the sign of the "horns" as a hand gesture was avoided, of course, since the person to which the horns were pointed was thereby designated as *cornuto*, or cuckolded. Some Sicilian fishermen are reported to have painted the horns on the mast red. In many trips to the wharves I was never able during a three-month period to see a pair of animal horns of any kind on the mast. Fishtails nailed either to the mast or to the bridge, or the skeleton of fish displayed on a wall in the galley, likely served some protective purpose, but my informants could not speculate exactly what. The wings and feet of gulls nailed to the mast, however, were supposed to keep birds from alighting on and befouling the rigging.

Occuli, or eyes,[32] painted on the bow, were supposed to abate the evil eye and other kinds of magic. One skipper had a big black "wicked eye" painted on the stern of his boat because, as he said, "Someone has eyes on us." Nowhere could I find that crosses were ever painted to the bow or stern of a boat in San Pedro, or daubed on with tar as in parts of Europe.[33] Skippers themselves have been known to sprinkle with salt a ship that is beset by bad luck, and Portuguese fishermen would also fumigate the ship with incense wafted from a bucket. These ministrations were performed below deck as well as on deck and in the wheelhouse.

Whistling aboard ship is a taboo known almost everywhere,[34] and this old belief is also widely observed among fishermen in the San Pedro area. The principal reason behind the taboo, perhaps, is that one would whistle up a breeze or a storm, if not the devil himself. In Ireland, for example fishermen were known almost to throw one of their number overboard for whistling, even though they had no objection at all to a mate's singing.[35] Beck reports that whistling could be counted on to bring on enough wind to move a becalmed vessel.[36] Before the days of radio communication there was no objection to whistling on board a ship, of course, when it was necessary to hail other ships in the area.

We have spoken about people who were considered unlucky on the way to fishing boats, on the wharves, or as potential passengers. Now we can speak briefly about actual jonahs aboard vessels, that is, fishermen who for one reason or another were thought to jinx a boat. Beck himself has written the best general treatise on the subject,[37] stressing the circumstance of being different from the rest of the crew as the primary cause of suspicion and ultimate ostracism. In Nova Scotia, for example, such a person might simply be a "bad luck man,"[38] but among San Pedro's Italian fishermen he might be referred to as a *scomunicato*, though not literally being regarded as an excommunicant. Boats likewise might be jinxed,[39] whether from a disaster or series of disasters suffered earlier, or from some impediment attaching to the skipper or the crew. Such a boat was said to be under the blight of *mala fortuna* for which there was little help. According to a crusty old Portuguese fisherman, the only way to deal with such a boat was to raise it up and scrape off all of the paint.

Other beliefs and customs dealing with life on board a fishing vessel including certain beliefs known on land that in course of time became seaborne. Returning for things forgotten, for example, was frowned upon.[40] In the galley it was the custom not to sweep after dark.[41] Reasons were not given, other than the fact that the men were tired and that the work would keep until morning when it could be taken care of with greater dispatch. If the more ominous notions of fire (Puckett, No. 17298) or death (Puckett, Nos. 27550-27553) ever dictated the decision not to sweep until morning, these ideas never came out. Of more consequence than either of the two matters taken up is the taboo against turning bread on its back (round side down, flat side up). The fact that Italian children were taught not to turn a loaf upside down lest they incur the wrath of God,[42] probably accounts for this reverence for bread, God's greatest daily bounty to man. Witches on land, of course, are supposed to be able to capsize a boat at sea simply by turning a loaf of bread upside down, or for that matter, symbolically turning any cup or other hollow vessel bottom up. Close questioning of many informants failed to connect the inadvertent act of turning a loaf of bread on its back with ominal or causal magic involving witchcraft. That no one had ever heard this well-known idea about the ability of a witch on land to work evil at sea shows how rapidly these old notions are passing from view. Two other old taboos, little remembered these days (perhaps because they pertain more to sailors that to fishermen), are the notions that umbrellas and suitcases should not be taken aboard vessels. Umbrellas, I was told, are taboo aboard a vessel because they are useless among men clothed to face the severest kinds of storms at sea.[43] A suitcase, a bane on merchant ships, likewise has no place on board fishing vessels,[44] where a fisherman's garb is easier to manipulate from a bag of some sort than from a case designed for much lighter and less sturdy clothing and footgear.

Fishermen's clothing is usually weather worn and battered; so a greenhorn would guard against going aboard a boat with an entirely new outfit. Experienced hands would say: "Where in hell did that guy come from?" Greenhorns who preferred to bed down by at least taking their boots off, very soon learned that it proved easier in the end to sleep in one's boots, what with the need for quick action when the boat came upon a school of fish, or when disaster threatened. Although pranking was generally frowned upon, a brand new hat, for example, might end up in the sea "by accident" before the day was done. If there are traditional fool's errands on which rookie fishermen were sent, apart from hunting the golden spike in the keel, I could not learn what they are. This tightened discipline aboard ship, even in leisure hours, likely reflects the tense economic situation prevailing in the industry.

Inauspicious times for fishing boats to set out was mentioned at the beginning of this article in connection with the economic squeeze and the new technology of "fishing around the clock." Let us now look more closely at the decline of some of the most inveterate beliefs and customs of fishermen and sailors who put out to sea.[45] From early times sailors have been reluctant to sail on Friday and this fear of the day has likewise extended to fishermen. Friday was an ominous day even in pre-Christian times, but the crucifixion of Jesus on this day, and the institution of Good Friday, a corruption perhaps of God's Friday, have conspired to mark Friday as a day of ill-omen. Sanctions against starting many other kinds of things on this day extend, to be sure, to many kinds of activities besides setting out on a voyage.[46] Good Friday, likewise, is a day when many things should be avoided. Planting and other acts of husbandry, by way of contrast, are prescribed for this day, perhaps from the fact that the continuing cycle of life, beginning with death and extending to the resurrection and newness of life, begins on this darkest day of the Christian year. Local fishing in San Pedro and Catalina waters nowadays may begin on Friday, but fishing voyages to Mexico do not leave port until after midnight on Friday. Men would be told to report by ten o'clock, but the sailing would invariably be delayed for one reason or another. One experienced Sicilian fisherman tells of a case of a pilot's being eager to jump the gun a little. The engine is reported to have conked out. A second try took them as far as the breakwater, but they were stalled again, and the boat didn't actually leave until after midnight. Friday sailings were discouraged for other more compelling reasons, namely, a wage scale of time-and-a-half on Saturday and double-time on Sunday. At one time the aversion to transacting business on Friday was so strong that many a fisherman would not accept a check on Friday. Friday the thirteenth as a bad luck day had its own special groups of adherents.

An even stronger aversion to leaving port for the fishing banks, of course, attached to Good Friday and certain of the saints days. If a fishing boat were already at sea on Good Friday, for example, the crew would spend a quiet day unless the fish were running. This went for all of the special feast days at sea. The Sicilians will ordinarily not put to sea on St. Joseph's Day (March 19), and the Dalmatians and other Yugoslavian fishermen like to be at home on the day of their patron saint, St.

Nicholas (December 6). "If they go out on the Assumption of the Blessed Virgin (August 15)," one Sicilian fisherman told me, "they're in for trouble." He likely spoke for all of the fishermen who worship at Mary Star of the Sea church. The Virgin Mary, along with St. John Joseph of the Light, is a patron of the San Pedro fishermen. Easter, All Saints, and All Souls are quiet days among the town's fishermen.[47] Saint Lucy's Day (December 13) at one time was a day when all boats were to stay in port, but this feast is little observed these days by working fishermen. If boats were named for saints, it was customary for the boats and their crews to remain idle on the saint's natal day, as for example, the San Antonio III, named in honor of St. Anthony of Padua (June 13). Finally, in most Christian countries Sunday itself is an inauspicious day for fishing.[48] Even so, with expenses so high and rewards so low, many fishermen will not only fish on Sundays, but will venture out on the saints days as well. There were not enough Spanish, Mexican, and Greek fishermen in San Pedro's fishing crews for the taboo against setting out or fishing on Tuesday to gain ground.[49]

In the recent past considerable store was laid by the first fish caught, for it portended the course and magnitude of the haul. The practice of tossing the first fish back in gratitude for the sea's bounty, however, was little observed.[50] More likely, the fish was examined, broken open to inspect the roe, and then tossed into the hatch. Kissing the first fish full on the mouth, was a salute observed by many fishermen in days past, and when as especially heavy catch was being brailed aboard, many an exuberant fisherman has been known to jump right into the flopping mass to grab a fish and kiss it.

When men were fishing on shares—the usual way in many parts of the world—the division was made by weight registered at the cannery, with the processor automatically taking a substantial percentage of the haul, depending on the money still owing on the boat. Schedules were then worked out for the skipper himself, expenses for the boat, and also for the gear. It there were an engineer aboard he would get a special partial share, likewise the spotter in the crow's nest who was aloft all night, often in wind and storm, when the crew was in the galley or cosily billeted in the sleeping quarters. Remembered in part, but barely, is a way of dividing fish before fish were sold to canneries and weighing scales came into general use. For local market catches only one person remembers hearing about blind men being pressed aboard to pull fish from barrels or gurneys one by one, and pass them around, without fear or favor, to the assembled crew. On some of the small Yugoslavian boats a similar arrangement was made whereby the fish were counted and placed in piles aggregating the number of participants in the catch. Since weights varied somewhat, names were arbitrarily assigned to each pile and a sort of lottery was conducted by the skipper. The piles were usually laid out in the galley, and the skipper, going on deck and forward on the vessel, and, looking straight ahead, pulled his coat up over his head as a blind. He would then call out, "Pile No. 1 goes to so-and-so, Pile No. 2 to so and so," etc., etc. With smaller catches the skipper could pick out several of the largest fish for himself and then the crew chose them one at a time in 1-2-3-4-5 order, or whatever. The order was then reversed: 5-4-3-2-1 so that things got pretty well evened out after a few helpings.

Catches seem never to have been tithed in San Pedro, but the church frequently got percentages of the catch, and claimed special gifts when churches were built or other charitable ventures pursued. The poor were welcome to obtain fish whenever they came to the wharves, but there were never provisions for pregnant women and others especially in need. Fishing boats also contributed to civic undertakings such as the building of the San Pedro Library and the YMCA.

Apart from the evil eye and the jinxing of boats not much magic seems to have found its way into the folklore of San Pedro fishermen, and even less into the witchcraft that once might have been far more considerable. One story, almost unparalleled, is made a part of this present record to show the rich kind of material that might have been lost before it occurred to anyone to preserve it for posterity. It comes from a retired Portuguese fisherman still living in San Pedro, and was current some thirty-five to fifty years ago.

> One time I had a *feiticeira*. I was on the ship, and we were out to sea, and we had the worst luck you ever did see. We weren't catching any fish whatsoever, and as we were fishing there were three fish following us. They were yellowtail. These three fish were following us, and every day we'd stop, and they'd be there. We'd go, and then we'd stop, and the three fish would be there. This one older man said, "You know what these fish are?" and I said, "No, I didn't know who they are," and he said "they're this here woman. The other two are her sons. She's mad and she's throwing a jinx on us because the skipper didn't hire them to go fishing with us. And they're watching us to make sure we don't catch any fish." This happened every day for about a week, and those fish did not leave us. One day this guy made a harpoon and said, "I'm going to catch them!" He harpooned one of them and hurt it badly. He hit the other one, but we didn't see it any more. He said, "George, you mark my word, and you'll find out what I tell you." Just for the hell of it, I memorized what day it was, and the time. I remembered it, and we finished the trip, and we came home. Then I didn't think anything more about it, but my sister said, "Did you hear that so-and-so had an automobile accident? She was hurt bad, and the other son was hurt bad, and other son took off, in fact he . . . " "When did that happen?" Then it came to mind who it was. And this is the truth. She told me the date, and that's who it was."[51]

Fish as familiar spirits of witches is a phenomenon of utmost rarity in the literature, but in this story the essential relationship of the familiar spirit to the witch comes out when the witch herself is seen to suffer the harm visited upon the creature whose shape she had temporarily assumed. Moreover, the motivation for the witch's *maleficium*, her bedeviling of the boat to get even, is established by the fact that the skipper had refused to take her two sons along on the fishing voyage.

The fabric of religious belief that underlies many of the folk beliefs and customs encountered among San Pedro fishermen, and their awareness of the numinous forces at work in their lives, can, unfortunately, only be touched upon here. Despite the many scientific aids that have been put at the fisherman's command, as discussed earlier, the hazards of ocean fishing are always present. A woman deck hand, fishing with her husband only two years ago, spoke of the constant anxiety at sea, particularly during storms. "I've said a lot of prayers," she said once in an interview, "you're really close to God, when you're out there in bad weather." In face of the uncertainty and danger of their work and the prodigious forces of nature set loose in storms and tempests at sea, sailors and fishermen alike have always depended upon God and sought the solace of the church. In their daily and weekly devotions at San Pedro's Mary Star of the Sea Church, with its motto *Maria Stella Maris —Ora pro nobis*, their eyes fall easily on an imposing statue of the Holy Mother under a baldachin behind the High Altar cradling a small fishing boat in her arm. As their eyes look upward and around they can see beautiful stained glass windows depicting the feeding of the multitudes with the loaves and the fishes, and the Master calming the waves. Among the many saints adorning stained glass windows in the church walls just below the vault of the roof are Saint Andrew, who dropped his nets to become a fisher of men, and St. Nicholas, patron saint of Greek and Slavic fishermen.

Now putting out to sea, and far from the church, as fishermen look back at San Pedro from the Angels Gate breakwater, they can get one last glimpse of Mary Star atop the church steeple looking solicitously out to the open sea. This same stately figure, crowned with a nimbus containing nine stars, and beckoning from a hill, is the first thing that catches their eye from beyond the harbor as the sons of the sea return. Private devotions take place in the home before embarking, of course, and most of the larger ships provide small but well-furnished little chapels for men at sea, with bibles, prayer books, and other religious utensils at the disposal of suppliants. Divine providences at sea, miraculous deliverances, and personal revelations of God's bounty, are not easily talked about; neither are one's promptings and hunches. To assemble these myriad stories and accounts and fit them properly into the fabric of folk belief and custom that I have sketched in these pages, but all too briefly, must alas, fall to abler and more patient hands. Meanwhile, I hope to take Horace Beck to San Pedro one day to see the sights that mean so much to him.*

NOTES

[1] This essay on "Magic, Science, and Religion" was written in 1925 and later selected as the title article for a series of essays, entitled *Magic, Science, and Religion and Other Essays*, ed. Robert Redfield (New York: Doubleday, 1948), pp. 30-31: "An interesting and crucial test is provided by fishing in the Trobriand Islands and its magic. While in the villages on the inner lagoon fishing is done in an easy and absolutely reliable manner by the method of poisoning, yielding abundant results without danger and uncertainty, there are on the shores of the open sea dangerous modes of fishing and also certain types in which the yield greatly varies according to whether shoals of fish appear beforehand or not. It is most significant that in the lagoon fishing, where man can rely completely upon his knowledge and skill, magic does not exist, while in the open sea fishing, full of danger and uncertainty, there is extensive magical ritual to secure safety and good results."

[2] These theories were adumbrated in a fine article, "The Function of Magic Folk Belief Among Texas Coastal Fishermen," *Journal of American Folklore*, 82 (1969), 214-225, and followed up with a more detailed statement in his book, *I Heard the Fishermen Say: Folklore of the Texas Gulf Coast* (Austin and London: University of Texas Press, 1978), pp. 3-22, esp. pp. 6-11, *passim*.

[3] Even modern timekeeping and payroll accounts are reckoned by the lunar month.

[4] Horace Beck, *Folklore and the Sea* (Mystic Seaport, Conn.: The Marine Historical Association, Inc., 1973), pp. 12, 78, 101; Mullen, pp. 18, 35, 66, 69, 71, 90, 160, No. 107.

[5] See Beck, pp. 18-23, for a discussion of the naming of vessels; Mullen, pp. 20-21, 160, No. 104.

[6] Beck, pp. 20-21; Peter F. Anson, *Fisher Folk-Lore* (London: The Faith Press, 1965), p. 97; Mullen, p. 156, No. 31.

[7] The blessing is entitled *Benedictio solemnis navis piscatoris*. See Anson, pp. 96-97, No. 15.

[8] Anson, p. 94.

[9] Paul Sébillot, *Le Folk-lore des Pecheurs* (Les Litteratures Populaires des Toutes les Nations, tome 43, Paris: J. Maisonneuve, 1901), p. 142.

[10] Anson, p. 94 (France).

[11] *Los Angeles Times*, January 21, 1964. Cf. Mullen, pp. 20, 79, 160, No. 102.

[12] Sébillot, p. 141; Anson, pp. 92-93. Cf. Mullen, pp. 20-21, 160, Nos. 103-104; Beck, p. 305.

[13] *Journal of American Folklore*, 14 (1901), 209; Charles Speroni, "California Fishermen's Festivals," *Western Folklore*, 14 (1955), 78-79 (Sicily and California ports); *Journal of the Folklore Institute*, 7 (1970), 132 (British Isles); *National Geographic*, 104 (July 1953), 75-84 (Gloucester, Mass., Illustrated); *Southern Folklore Quarterly*, 29 (1969), 134 (Greek sponge fishing fleet at Tarpon Springs

Florida at Epiphany); Elizabeth Brandon, *Les Moeurs de la Paroisse de Vermillon en Louisiane* (diss., Université Laval, Quebec, 1955), p. 254; Mullen, pp. 21, 65, 160, No. 105.

[14] See Speroni, pp. 77-91. Treatment of the San Pedro Fisherman's festival is to be found on pp. 83-89, with an excellent photograph facing p. 88. Cardinals McIntyre and Manning have officiated at the blessing of the fishing fleet over the years, as well as other high church dignitaries.

[15] *National Geographic*, 101 (May 1952), 565 (blessing of Portuguese cod fishing fleet before it sets out from Lisbon for the Grand Banks off Newfoundland); *Southern Folklore Quarterly*, 29 (1965), 135 (blessing of Greek sponge fishermen before each trip).

[16] *Folk-Lore*, 20 (1909), 322-323.

[17] Sébillot, p. 180; Anson, pp. 79, 101; Beck, p. 303.

[18] E. Radford and M. A. Radford, *Encyclopedia of Superstitions* (London, n.d. = 1947), p. 153; cf. Beck, p. 303.

[19] Helen Creighton, *Bluenose Magic, Popular Beliefs and Superstitions in Nova Scotia* (Toronto: Ryerson Press, 1968), p. 124, No. 53.

[20] Robert Morel and Suzanne Walter, *Dictionnaire des Superstitions* (Paris: Bibliotheque Marabout, n.d.), p. 109, s.v., *femme*.

[21] Radford and Radford, pp. 122, 213; Beck, p. 310.

[22] Sébillot, p. 180; Anson, p. 101.

[23] Creighton, p. 124, No. 54.

[24] Morel and Walter, pp. 185, 199; Sébillot, p. 179; Anson, p. 104; Beck, p. 310; Radford and Radford, pp. 186-187. Robert Georges reports that if Greek sponge fishermen in Florida sighted a priest suddenly appearing on the docks on the morning of a planned departure, they would postpone their trip to another day (*SFQ*, 29 [1965], 136).

[25] Acts 27:10-44; Beck, p. 303.

[26] Anson, p. 104.

[27] Beck, p. 310; Creighton, pp. 123-124. Cf. Mullen, pp. 5-6, 157, No. 37.

[28] Morel and Walter, pp. 185-199.

[29] With its earlier allusions in folklore, as set down in Stith Thompson's *Motif-Index of Folk-Literature*, etc. 6 vols. (Copenhagen: Rosenkilde and Bagger, 1955-1958): N131.1. "Luck changing after cohabitation," this notion found its way into cards and gambling, whence it was no doubt taken up into the lore of fishermen. As the best kept secret in town, several fishermen knew of the saying, but I could find only one or two fellows who were willing to vouch for the practice. One of these had at one time fished out of New Bedford.

[30] Beck, pp. 12-27; Mullen, pp. 7, 20, 79, 160, No. 97: *ibid.*, pp. 18, 35, 66, 69, 71, 90, 160, No. 107.

[31] Anson, p. 95; Mullen, pp. 7, 18, 79, 89, 159, No. 81.

[32] Beck, p. 15.

[33] Anson, p. 75.

[34] *JAF*, 10 (1897), 214 (Newfoundland); Mullen, pp. 3, 18, 66, 68, 70-71, 89, 155, No. 2, 160, No. 106. Cf. Beck, p. 101.

[35] *Folk-lore*, 8 (1897), 14.

[36] Beck, p. 101.

[37] Beck, pp. 303-304; Mullen, pp. 23, 157, No. 42.

[38] Creighton, pp. 125-126.

[39] *Ibid.*; Mullen, pp. 23, 157, No. 42.

[40] *Popular Beliefs and Superstitions: A Compendium of American Folklore from the Ohio Collection of Newbell Niles Puckett.* Ed. Wayland D. Hand, Anna Casetta, Sondra B. Thiederman. 3 vols. (Boston: G. K. Hall and Company, 1981), Nos. 7570-7573; 20894-20911, *passim*; Mullen, pp. 15, 156, Nos. 12-13.
[41] *Ibid.*, Nos. 20010-20014.
[42] *Ibid.*, No. 3150; Mullen, pp. 16, 156, No. 29.
[43] Beck, p. 312.
[44] Creighton, p. 121; *National Geographic*, 91 (1947), 127; George Carey, *A Faraway Time and Place: Lore of the Eastern Shore* (Washington and New York: Robert B. Luce, Inc., 1971), p. 183 (black satchel); Mullen, pp. 5, 15, 66, 88, 157, No. 35.
[45] *Folk-Lore*, 35 (1924), 347; Sébillot, p. 164; Beck, pp. 20, 313; Creighton, p. 128, No. 105; *ibid.*, No. 110; *SFQ*, 33 (1969), 84; Mullen, pp. 6, 14, 27, 66, 71, 88, 155, No. 3.
[46] Puckett, (Index), III, 1694, s.v. "Friday(s), beginning on; beginning a job on; beginning a trip on," etc., etc., with many other activities not recommended to be undertaken on Friday, such as being born on Friday, a woman coming downstairs for the first time after bearing a child, hanging curtains, sweeping, whistling, etc., etc. Included is: launching a ship on Friday: Nos. 19097-19101.
[47] Sébillot, p. 166; Anson, p. 113.
[48] Sébillot, p. 162; Mullen, pp. 8, No. 157, No. 32; 9, 156, No. 11.
[49] *JAF*, 52 (1939), 123; *SFQ*, 29 (1965), 135; Mullen, p. 155, No. 4.
[50] Mullen, 9, 157, No. 33.
[51] A *feiticeira* is a worker of evil, a witch.

*I am indebted to many active San Pedro fishermen, and to even more retired men who plied the boats, shot the nets, and gathered in the catch for more years then they can remember. For giving me much practical advice and protecting me from the errors that are the lot of the landlubber, I gratefully acknowledge the help of John Davies of the San Pedro News Pilot, Bill Oleson of the Los Angeles Marine Museum (in San Pedro), and Lawrence Bozanich of the Fishermen's Co-op. Frank Iacona, one of San Pedro's most respected skippers and a ship's engineer, patiently explained many of the technical aspects of commercial fishing to me.

"THE MAN WHO PLUCKED THE GORBEY": A MAINE WOODS LEGEND DEBATED IN SLOW MOTION

Edward D. Ives
University of Maine, Orono

AT THE 1958 ANNUAL MEETING of the American Folklore Society in New York two things happened, neither of them very significant either singly or in their concurrence—not, at least, until this very moment. First, I read a paper entitled "The Man Who Plucked the Gorbey"; second, I met a man named Horace Beck. The paper went on to be published in the *Journal of American Folklore* in 1961[1], and over the years Horace and I became fast friends; I never told anyone he was a poacher, and he never let on I occasionally fished with worms, which is a kind of mutuality one does not often find here along the edges of the great boreal forest. The gorbey article sat in quiet obscurity for thirteen years until in 1974 Bacil Kirtley published a note suggesting an alternative to my conclusion that the story was of British provenience.[2] More about that in a moment.

Then I was asked to contribute something to Horace Beck's *festschrift*. I said I had nothing suitable either at the ready or in the works, but the editors would not be dissuaded. Then I bethought me of the gorbey article and Kirtley's response. Would a brief rejoinder be suitable? There was a certain rough justice, I added, in presenting it to Horace now, since he had happened *not* to be present when I read the paper, even though he had been at the 1958 meeting. The editors agreed.

My original article concerned itself with the story of a Maine or New Brunswick woodsman who caught a gorbey (Canada Jay), stripped it of its feathers, and let it go into the winter cold, saying (in many of the tellings) something like "Now go to hell and get a new suit!" The next morning when he lifted his head, all his hair had fallen out and lay on his pillow. I gathered over one-hundred versions of the story, mostly by mail, almost all of which located it in a Maine or New Brunswick lumbercamp and most of which claimed (in one form or another) that the story was "true." I concluded that it was of rather recent (post-1900) origin and came to New Brunswick along with settlers from Ireland, Scotland, and North-Country England. From thence it came to Maine in the late nineteenth century as many of those settlers and their sons crossed the line to work in the lumberwoods, and with the story came the bird's new nickname of "gorbey," for which cognate dialect terms could be found in the old country: "gorb" for "glutton" and "gorbling" for "an unfledged bird." The story then attached itself to several utterly bald woodsmen—particularly a well-known character along the Penobscot by the name of Archie Stackhouse—as accounting for their glabrous plight.

A quarter century has now passed since I first put it all together, during which time I have had ample leisure to reconsider what I called my "house of cards," and I find it has held up extremely well. However, there are a couple of points that were not made as clear as they should have been in the article, the first of them being the highly cautionary quality of the story. Canada Jays are utterly intrepid little birds, as anyone who has been where they are can testify. They used to become so thick around lumbercamps as to become a tarnation nuisance, and they were easily caught and victimized. Usually, though, the worst that happened was some kind of joke. Someone would trick one into picking up an overheated biscuit, burning the bird's beak and causing it to fly off into a nearby tree, where it would scold the perpetrator amusingly; or someone would catch one and make it a collar out of baloney rind or something similar which would stay there all winter. Angus Enman, one of the first people ever to tell me the story, said it was told to him by an "old fellow" at a lunch ground in the woods after he himself "pretty near caught one."[3] The thrust of the story, and it is the thrust of a good deal of legendry, is not to entertain or even to maintain belief but to *convince* someone to leave this bird alone.[4] If ever a bird needed the protection of a cautionary tale, it is this amiable little gray burglar, and the tale it received has served it well for most of a century.

Second, why is this story not found throughout the Canada Jay's entire coast-to-coast range? Since it is so clearly a lumbercamp story, why did it not follow the westward migration of the logging industry? Both questions have the same answer, and it is the same explanation I gave for Joe Scott's ballads remaining localized to Maine and the Maritime Provinces. The story is a fairly recent one that entered into oral tradition long after that westward migration had stopped but during a time when there was still a great deal of back-and-forth between Maine and the Maritimes.[5] No question about it, the story is solidly localized. The event it celebrates is always located in a limited area of Maine and New

Brunswick, and the story has hardly ever been found outside Maine and the Maritimes, a range, by the way, that is just about identical with that of the bird's nickname of "gorbey," which, as I pointed out in the original article, is also a recent arrival.[6]

Finally, we come to Bacil Kirtley's suggestion that the story "is an account of an Indian practice exposited in the formulae of European narrative tradition." His evidence is a passage from John W. Cooper's "Field Notes on Northern Algonkian Magic"[7] describing a Northern Algonkian ritual for bringing on cold weather in which "a Whiskey Jack, or Canada Jay, is caught, some of the feathers plucked from the bird and it is set free again."[8] To this he adds the belief found both among the Northern Algonkian and the Indians of Labrador that it is bad luck to find the Canada Jay's eggs, a belief that Fannie Hardy Eckstorm suspicioned *might* exist among the Indians of Maine, since she could find no one willing to bring her these eggs, even when she offered two dollars apiece for them.[9] "That the gorbey was employed for a magical rite of weather control in the Maine-Maritimes area is eminently likely," says Kirtley; "that a rumor of the rite would be known in this region, even if the rite itself were not actually enacted, is a near certainty." Unfortunately—for Kirtley was one of my first mentors in folklore—I can accept neither the eminence of the likelihood nor the nearness of the certainty.

There is no need here for any extended discussion of the myth/ritual theory, but if we simply assume for argument's sake that a narrative *can* have its origins in a ritual, then the connections between the two in any specific instance should be *prima facie* evident, clearly demonstrable, or—best of all—both. In the present example the connections are neither evident nor demonstrated. A ritual to call up cold weather by pulling "some" feathers from a bird who is then set free (hardly what Kirtley calls "the grisly practice of mutilating the bird") and a widespread reluctance to collect that bird's eggs are adumbrated as somehow related to a story of a man who plucked a bird clean and is supernaturally punished for that deed by losing his own hair. This adumbration is put forward even though neither the ritual nor a specific belief that finding the eggs brings bad luck can be shown to have existed in the same area where the story is found. If my theory of British origin is a house of cards, Kirtley's is far too tenuous even to be called that. Beyond a pinch of feathers from the same bird, I see no connection between rite and story at all.

Furthermore, there is nothing in the belief system of the Penobscot or any other Wabanaki group to indicate that the Canada Jay was treated with any special respect. Song birds in general were not appreciated at all. One singing near a camp was an omen of sickness, Speck reports, but if the bird could be killed, its beak torn off, and its throat cut open and spat into, the curse was annulled. Children were praised for killing song birds too.[10] But the crucial passage in Speck's study is the following:

> It is unfortunate, however, from the point of view of the ornithologist that the whiskey-jack's fondness for the society of man is requited with cruelty. The Indian boys persecute the bold bird with their bows and arrows. It seems a natural archery target for the young hunters. But the white woodsman has refined the practice of cruelty to its extreme. It is no uncommon thing for the men of the lumbercamps to bait a pole with a piece of meat and balance it over a log. When the whiskey-jack alights on the meat to tear a piece off, the tormentor strikes the other end of the pole a blow with a club, driving the bird stunned and wounded into the air. The helpless victim is then picked up, plucked bare of feathers and turned loose to enjoy the cold of an arctic winter shorn of his warm plumage.[11]

It is, of course, possible that *some* rumor of the rite Kirtley alludes to just *might* have been abroad in the story area, but its connection with that story is somewhere between dubious and nonexistent. There is no need for such a connection anyway. It is a white man's story that sprang up to counter white man's cruelty in an area and industry whose folklore shows strong homogeneity. Maine frequently shows stronger ties with the Maritimes than it does with the rest of the United States. And the first person I know to have pointed that out was Horace Beck.[12]

NOTES

[1] "The Man Who Plucked the Gorbey: A Maine Woods Legend," *Journal of American Folklore* 74 (1961), 1–8.
[2] "On the Origin of the Maine-Maritimes Legend of the Plucked Gorbey," *Journal of American Folklore* 87 (1974), 364–365.
[3] Ives, "Gorbey," 2.
[4] The point about legend serving to convince was made by Dan Ben-Amos in a paper entitled "Legend: A Descriptive Definition" read at the 1983 Annual Meeting of the American Folklore Society, Nashville, Tennessee.
[5] Edward D. Ives, *Joe Scott: The Woodsman Songmaker* (Champaign: University of Illinois Press, 1978), pp. 415–416.
[6] Ives, "Gorbey," 7.
[7] *Proceedings of the International Conference of Americanists* XXIII (1928), 513–518.
[8] Cooper, p. 516.
[9] "Concerning the Bad Repute of Whiskey John," *Bird-Lore* IV (July–August, 1902), 113
[10] Frank J. Speck, "Bird-Lore of the Northern Indians," *University Lectures, University of Pennsylvania* VII (1920), 370.
[11] Speck, 365–366.
[12] Horace P. Beck, "Folksong Affiliations of Maine," *Midwest Folklore* VI (Fall, 1956), 159–166. For a more elaborate working out of this same point see Ives, *Joe Scott*, pp. 414–419.

CRAFTING THE MODEL: MAINE LOBSTERBOAT BUILDING AS A DESIGN TRADITION

Richard Lunt
State University College at Potsdam, NY

DURING ONE OF OUR MORNING CONVERSATIONS in 1969, Howard Chapelle, the eminent small craft historian and Curator Emeritus at the Smithsonian, leaned back in his office chair and tossed in my direction his vigorous and firmly held assertion that in his experience he had found that generally forty to fifty years pass before an American traditional boat type develops into its mature form. When I asked why, he said something about its usually taking about two generations of builders to perfect the "model." And he left the topic right there, returning to the line drawings he was preparing for *The American Fishing Schooners* (which came out in 1973).

In the next several months of fieldwork and library study on the boatbuilding tradition of the Maine Lobsterboat I came to understand what he was talking about. Subsequently, my research on other boat types and in greater depth on the lobsterboat has confirmed that there was a great deal in that simple assertion of his to interest the folklorist. In fact, as is often the case in the work and thinking of pioneers, Chapelle had pointed the way toward understanding the role of the boatbuilder/craftsman (in contemporary folkloristic terms) as an "internalizer of context" who formulates traditional design solutions to problems posed by the social and physical context with which he has to deal. In the case of the lobsterboat builder the extended context has been the lobster fishery of the coast of Maine.

The task I would like to undertake in this paper is to show how the Maine lobsterboat's developmental history supports Mr. Chapelle's rule of thumb. I hope also to examine how the folk boatbuilder and his traditional methods of design are responsible for the historical record of this boat type. For I believe that in understanding the role of the traditional designer/builder(s) in the development of a boat type we can gain considerable insight into the role of all craftsmen as solvers of the problems presented by context. In addition I think that what the lobsterboat has undergone is typical of the experience of other boat types, not only in North America, but throughout most of the world as well. Although, of course, it remains to be demonstrated, the cross-cultural applicability of what we can draw from the case of the Maine lobsterboat seems a possibility.

The reader will note that both the production of the individual boat *and* the development of the boat type are the results of a traditional design process. The fact is that this process expresses itself in a similar fashion at these two levels, though in the one case we are examining one builder producing one boat, and in the other, one or several builders producing a succession of boats over time. In either case the result is a design formulation specifically calculated to produce suitable boats. The process of traditional boat design appears to be a case of the internalization of context in that the traditional builder, when faced with building a new boat, draws upon his past experience with his boat type, sizes up the requests of the fisherman he is negotiating with, and assesses the current views of his community on proper boat form and performance, and then balances all these factors *in his mind*. He then carves a model, expands its measurements to full size, and finally sets up his boat. This process is a complex one whose essential manipulations occur within the mind of the builder. The boat produced is only the final manifestation of the process. As such its success as an artifact depends upon the astuteness of the builder's thinking. The history of boats built in a given type is thus the record of builders' thought. Since the author has dealt at length elsewhere with the elements involved in the design process (Lunt, 1976 Ch II, and 1971), the present paper utilizes the historical record to analyze the matter of the role of traditional builders in the development of type.[1]

The early thoughts of Henry Glassie on matters of type definition (Glassie 1968:8–17) suggest that the subject of the lobsterboat can be dealt with in terms of matters pertaining to its *form*, its *construction* and its *use*. It is not really possible to separate these matters in a balanced understanding of what the Maine lobsterboat is and has come to represent, but the intertwinings are sufficiently complex to make it advisable to cut them apart for the purpose of analysis. It's also advisable because any of these three can absorb us at length. Because of that I have limited this paper to matters pertaining to boat *form* (with the understanding that construction and use are lurking back there contributing silently to the general mix).

Now let us examine what *in boats* we mean by form. Basically it has to do not only with the shape of boat hulls, but also with their suitability to the job they are designed for, their *model*, if you will. Boat form is concretely seen in the shape of any given hull. It is abstractly seen in the mental formula which gives rise to that shape. That mental formula is what is generally called the boat's model, and it involves a balanced phrasing of all the elements in the builder/designer's mind which he takes into account in his given solution to the problems at hand. It is boat form in both these senses which is our subject. We shall be concerned with what the forms are today in all their variety, what they have been in the past, and how and why the past forms evolved into the present ones.

Boat scholars like Chapelle and John Gardner[2] tell us that by the end of the nineteenth century traditional boats in North America had developed into regional, specifically developed types highly suited to their respective environments. Such was the case with the boats of the coast of Maine. Lobster fishing had been practiced in a systematic way since the mid-1850's and boats had been developed which suited that fishery. Other fisheries had been practiced longer, some from colonial times, such as those for herring, swordfish, cod and other groundfish, menhaden and mackerel, etc., and there was a lot of overlap in the fisheries being pursued by any given fisherman, especially in Casco Bay within reach of the Portland market. Accordingly there were many boat types being used. Each region, indeed every community had its variations on skiffs, peapods, wherries, sloops, dories and such, and they were all driven by oar and sail. The total list of recognized types was long, though adequate descriptions of many are lost to us today. They themselves descended from a smaller group of boat ancestors present at the end of the eighteenth century, and thus back to the shallops, pinnaces, yawl boats, wherries, batteaux and canoes of colonial times. The late nineteenth century boats represented a full, mature stage of the flowering of traditional craftsmanship. Most boats were suited to their work, thanks to the evolution of their models by their builders over lifetimes of careful innovation and preservation of what worked.

My research has led me to conclude that there came to be four principal lobster fishing types (with some minor variations) which were dominant by 1890: The Reach boat, the Friendship sloop, the Hampton boat, and the peapod. The first three of these were found in relatively confined sections of the coast, and the peapod, being a very old type, was ubiquitous and had a number of sub-types.

The Reachboat, rediscovered only recently by the author,[3] was found on the easternmost section of the Maine coastline in the waters surrounding Moosabec Reach (a thoroughfare oriented southwest to northeast between Beals Island and Jonesport which gives the boat type its name). These were round-bottomed, square-sterned, lapstrake-planked skiffs fitted for sail with the customary spritsails of late nineteenth century

Maine coastal craft. Three varieties existed, a ten- to eleven-foot size which was only rowed, a fourteen- to sixteen-foot size with two rowing stations and a spritsail, and an eighteen- to twenty-foot size with three rowing stations and spritsail. The most popular variety for lobstering was the mid-size boat (see figures #1 and 2). These were powerful sailing craft, with full mid-sections, strongly built on sawn frames. They were capable of speed under sail and could withstand remarkably severe weather for so small a boat.

The mid-section of the coast from Schoodic Point westward to the western reaches of Muscongus Bay near Boothbay was the range of a larger sailing craft called the Friendship Sloop. Evolved from an earlier predecessor called the Muscongus Bay Sloop, the Friendship was a powerful, deep-hulled, gaff-rigged sloop of some twenty-four to thirty feet in length which was more of a sea boat than the Reachboat, and very popular along the midcoast (see figure #3 for lines plan). Most were built in Friendship and Bremen, both on Muscongus Bay, at the western extremity of its range, so we may note that these craft had spread eastward in use due to their popularity among the fishermen.

The western section of the coast from Boothbay to Kittery, including the waters of Casco Bay around Portland, was dominated by a third type which derived its name from the Hampton Beach area of the New Hampshire coast (see figure #4 for lines). These boats had evolved early in the century through a complex series of events involving the Newfoundland fisheries and the east coast of Nova Scotia, finally becoming popular in western Maine adjacent to the New Hampshire fisheries. Usually cat-ketch rigged, these craft were relatively shallow, fast, and square-sterned. They ran around twenty to twenty-four feet in length, and were used in other fisheries as well as in lobstering (for instance the daily fishing for the Portland fresh-fish market).

The peapod, named for its double-ended, canoe-like form, was found everywhere on the Maine coast (see figure #5). The most popular size was around sixteen feet in length. Some were fitted with spritsails as well as oars. The numbers of regional sub-types of this boat were numerous, and they varied from very heavily built, wide, rather hard-bilged working boats, to narrow, slack-bilged, lightly-built, fast-sailing craft. Picked up by yachtsmen early as suitable for tenders, they were subject to a good deal of architectural experimentation, and by the 1890's could be found in both working and yacht versions.

By contrast, today in the 1980's all along the coast of Maine, a modern, relatively unified form of the lobsterboat is found, the workhorse of our fisheries (see figure #6). These boats vary in length from

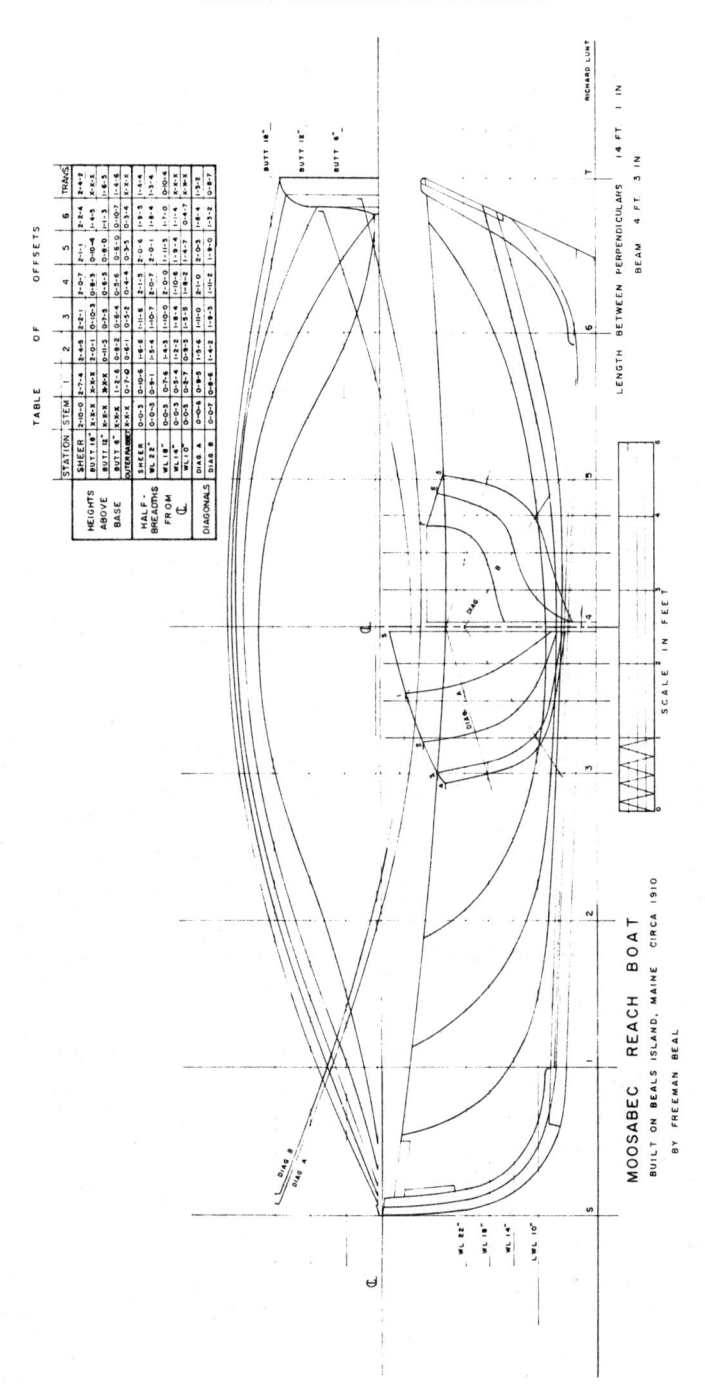

Fig. 1. Reachboat Lines

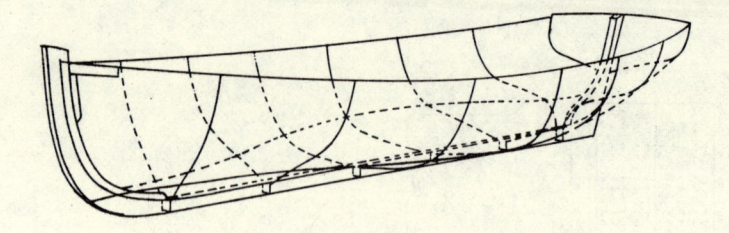

MOOSABEC REACH BOAT
14'- 0 x 4'- 3"
built by Freeman Beal
Beal's Island, 1910

measured perspective by S. F. Manning
from lines by R. Lunt

Fig. 2. Reachboat Perspective

twenty-odd feet to forty-six or forty-eight feet. Many are wood; many are fiberglass. Most are the distinctive Maine round-bottomed hull, but there are some "V" bottomed ones. Some are skeg built, others planked down.[4] In Casco Bay there are strip-built as well as planked craft, while Down East in Jonesport/Beals we typically find boats heavily powered with Oldsmobile, Lincoln and Cadillac engines. There is a great deal of this kind of variety, and yet we all agree that there *is* a Maine Lobsterboat, easily distinguished from the Massachusetts-built or Nova Scotian-built craft. Thus we have a concept of type, based mostly on hull form, which allows us at least to agree on what we are talking about.

I should point out that the variety we see in the modern boats is of several kinds. First we can observe that there are still regional sub-types of the modern lobsterboat, principally the Jonesport/Beals Island-built boats (near the Canadian border), the Penobscot Bay-built boats (including everything from Mt. Desert, Stonington, and the Fox Islands), the mid-coast region boats from Camden to roughly Damariscove Island, and the boats of Casco Bay to Kittery (at the New Hampshire border). The subtypes merge into each other sometimes, but they are distinguishable enough to the builders and fishermen, and even to some

Fig. 3. Friendship Sloop

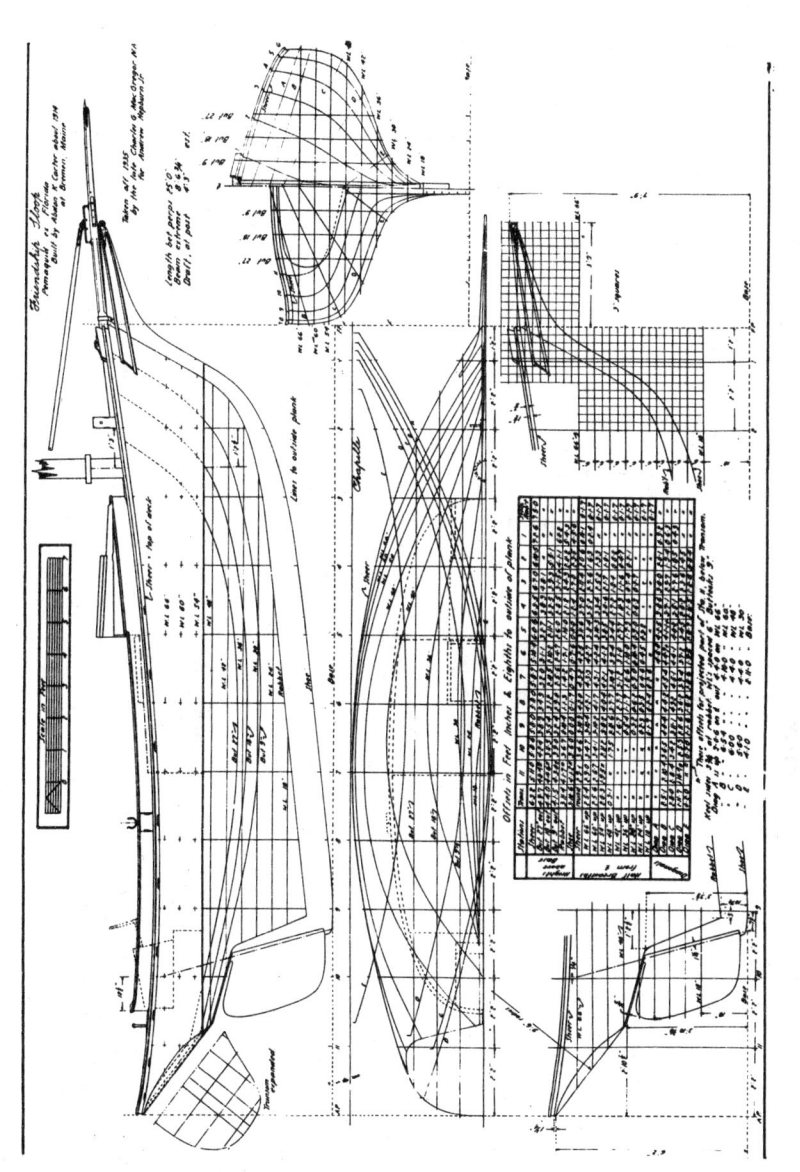

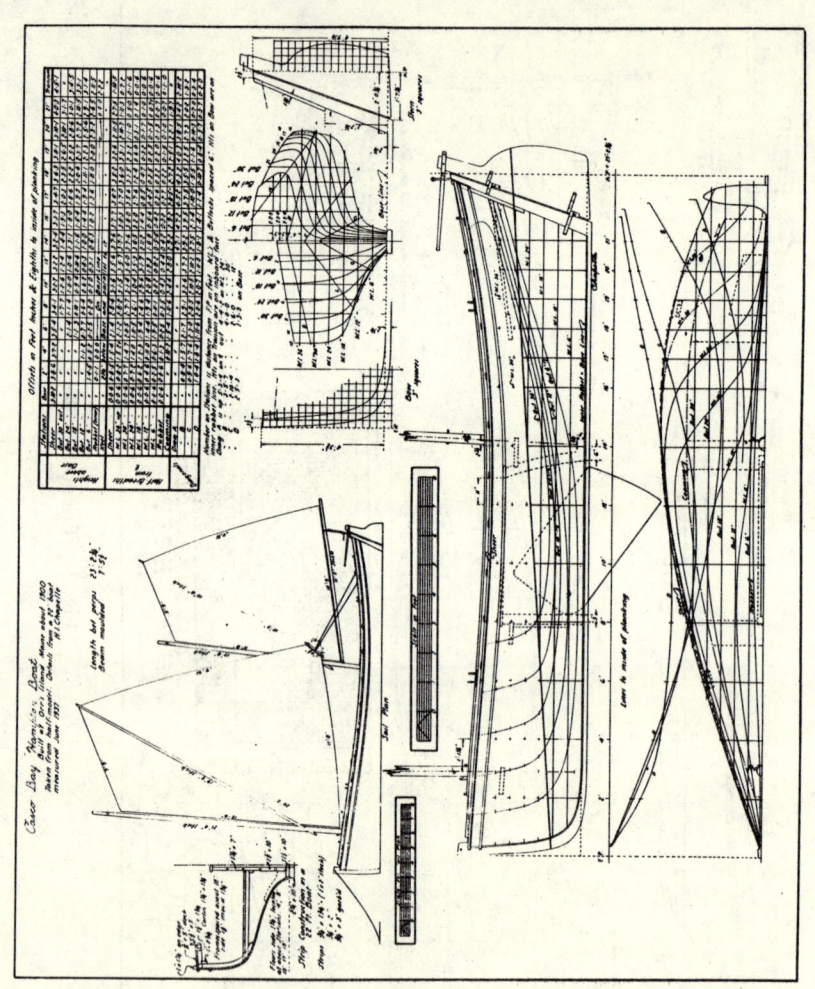

Fig. 4. Hampton Boat

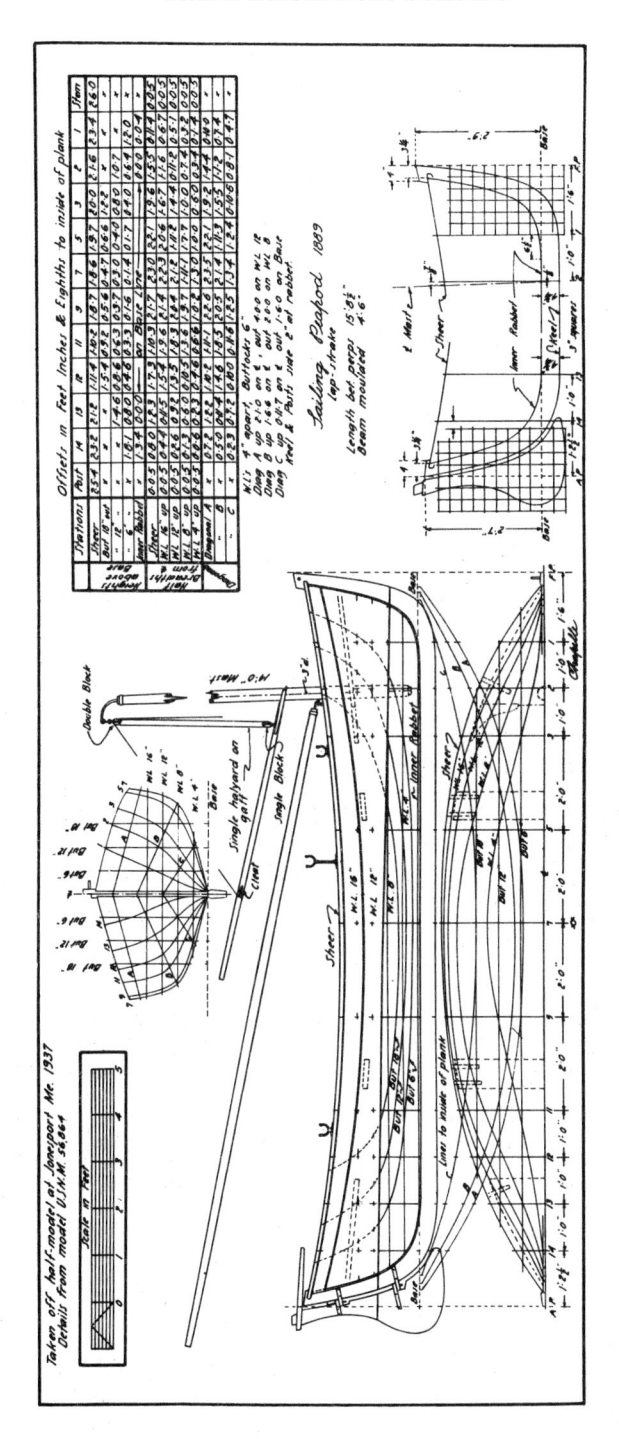

Fig. 5. Peapod Lines

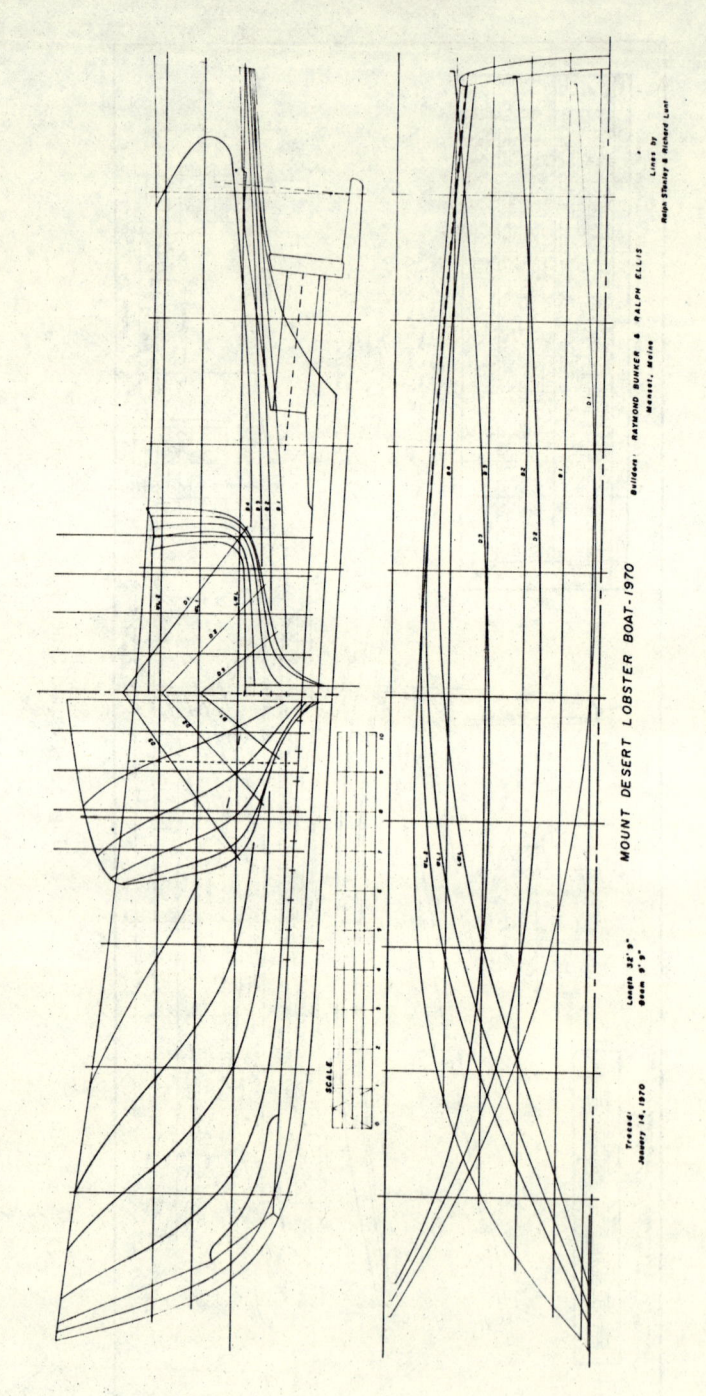

Fig. 6. Modern Maine Lobsterboat

of the rest of us. The next interesting observation is that boats built in these regions don't necessarily stay where they are built, but are found scattered about the coast of Maine and the Maritimes, sharing their domain with no small number of Novi (Nova Scotia built) boats and occasional mongrels of one sort or another of unknown origin.

A further apparent difficulty with the study of these boats is the fact that we often see side by side in a given modern harbor lobsterboats of widely divergent characteristics. It is superficially difficult to see any rhyme or reason to this diversity. As a way of coping with this problem, let us recall a concept used by engineers called "state-of-the-art" which refers to ideas, techniques and ways of doing things from relatively primitive to more advanced stages of development. I am not referring here to boat building skill, but again to concepts of hull form and model. If we think in terms of state-of-the-art when looking at a harbor full of boats, we will be able to see boats representing different states coexisting side by side, some states as far back as thirty to forty years ago. Sometimes we will see quite recent boats built or set up according to states which precede them by decades (as in open-hulled smaller boats often used by part-time fishermen and youngsters).

Now the question we are confronted with is how the Maine lobsterboat got to its present form after having established previous high development in its antecedent types of the 1890's. What brought about this further development? What factors were involved? I believe we can look to the process of traditional design utilized by the lobsterboat builders for our explanation. There were important changes in the context which forced builders to adapt, using their design process as a means of coping or responding to new challenges in the fisheries. The most important challenge was the introduction of the internal combustion engine for boat use. Its effect was revolutionary and caused major reformulations in boat model. It is this revolution on which we must focus to understand the development of the modern lobsterboat and the craftsman's role in this process.

It is my contention that the development of the modern lobsterboat is best understood in terms of an evolution of boat form. In fact, we can follow such an evolution back as far as we can find any data to work with. Beyond the oldest boats which survive we can find there are sometimes half-models, or there are the memories of elder builders and fishermen, or there are photographs. These kinds of data and the methods used to interpret them can get us back well before the turn of the century in some instances (builders can talk intelligently about their grandfather's boats, photographs survive, half models do remain). Much is lost, but enough remains to give us something to go on. Now, let us return to the challenge presented by the internal combustion engine.

The advent of the twentieth century brought with it a new form of power in the gas engine. It was first utilized in stationary form as a donkey engine, but by 1895–1900 mechanics began applying it to the driving of all sorts of vehicles; automobiles, bicycles, trucks, boats, and ultimately even to aircraft. Thus the powered lobsterboat is a fairly recent phenomenon; only eighty-five to ninety years have elapsed since the earliest experiments. Our discussion will focus on the direct results of this innovation, the whole giving rise to the modern lobsterboat of today.

This new motor, an industrial innovation, was both cheaper and less complicated than the steam and naphtha engines which preceded it. In its early form as a two-cycle, single-cylinder "make-and-break" engine the gasoline, internal combustion engine turned out to be aptly suited for use in fishing boats. They were compact, and though heavy, could if placed correctly, function as helpful ballast.

Accordingly, in the first decade of the century "make-and-breaks" were tried in everything. Differing brands of motor like the Myannis, Lathrop, Hartford and Acadia were dropped into peapods, Reach boats, Friendship sloops, dories, Hampton boats, yawl boats, scows, seine boats, life boats, whitehalls and various of their sub-types until practically every nook and cranny of the coast had seen these experiments. Some were successful from the outset, as with the Hampton boat with its square stern (see below); other types took some modification to complete the wedding of hull and engine, and still others just never came out right and were abandoned as unsuitable for power (as in the Friendship sloop —see below). These experiments were not easy because of several factors. The engines were heavy, on the average of 100 lbs/horsepower. Even though they ran at low rpms they presented the problem of vibration which sail and oars did not, and they required rudders behind the propellor for steering. The engines got in the way if placed in the middle of the boat, but fortunately as two-cycle engines have no crankcase they could be installed at a fairly steep angle, so stern mounting was possible. Propellor shafts had to pass out through the hull without leaking, so shaft logs and stuffing boxes were devised with all the appurtenant problems of leaks. And finally, there was electrolysis. These were all new problems to the Maine lobster fishermen and the men who built the boats.

These people were seldom at a loss, however, and innovations in hull design and construction as well as deck arrangement were rapid between 1900 and 1920. Chapelle reports that most of the Hampton boats in Casco Bay were converted to power in the ten to fifteen years after 1900.

(Chapelle, the Hampden [sic] Boats. *Yachting*. July 1938:40 ff. [in the Thirties a debate raged over the correct spelling of the type's name]). This shows that the fishermen were choosing in large numbers to convert to power, a factor that the builders could not ignore.

Thus, the basic problems consisted of strengthening hulls against vibration, dealing with engine weight, getting the engine out of the way, and installing proper propellor shafts and steering gear. These the builders dealt with in two ways, by adapting existing boats to the engines, and by building new boats more suitable for engine use.

Vibration problems were handled basically by building the boat heavier. Pre-existing boats were often strengthened by sister framing and double fastening. New ones were built heavier because light weight was no longer the premium it used to be when a man's back or a light air was the only propulsion. Also, boats could be built larger now that old make-and-break was doing the rowing. So sixteen-foot rowing pods became eighteen- and twenty-foot powered peapods. Eighteen-foot Hampton boats gave way to twenty-one and twenty-four foot models. The old balance between easy driveability of a hull and carrying capacity was altered, now that a man's muscle was no longer a limiting factor. Many types came to be decked for the first time, and some were fitted with spray hoods now that speed to windward was possible.

Engine weight presented another problem. The first boats receiving engines had difficulty holding up that weight. Even a two horsepower motor weighed two hundred pounds. In a peapod or a skiff anything that big could only conveniently go right in the middle of the boat, and that cluttered up valuable space in a fishing boat. The smaller engines could be shoved back in the stern of such boats, but it became clear that increased weight-bearing capacity aft would be necessary if any of the double-ended types were to be successful. The Hampton boats had already evolved square sterns by 1900, so they were easily adapted to power. Whitehall boats were successfully adapted, and so were dories.

The peapod was the most widespread of the types being adapted and can thus serve as a good example of how a motor's weight could be accommodated. In the illustrated eighteen-foot peapod (built in Milbridge in 1907 and now in the collection of the Penobscot Marine Museums in Searsport), (see figures #7 and #8), we can see the placement of the engine well aft, the outboard rudder, the shaft log, and the general trim down by the stern occasioned by the motor's weight. In the lines we can see something very interesting and typical of what builders did. Comparing cross sections in fig. 8, we note how the sternward sections (nos. 6 and 7) bulge out at the waterline to increase bearing width aft. That's

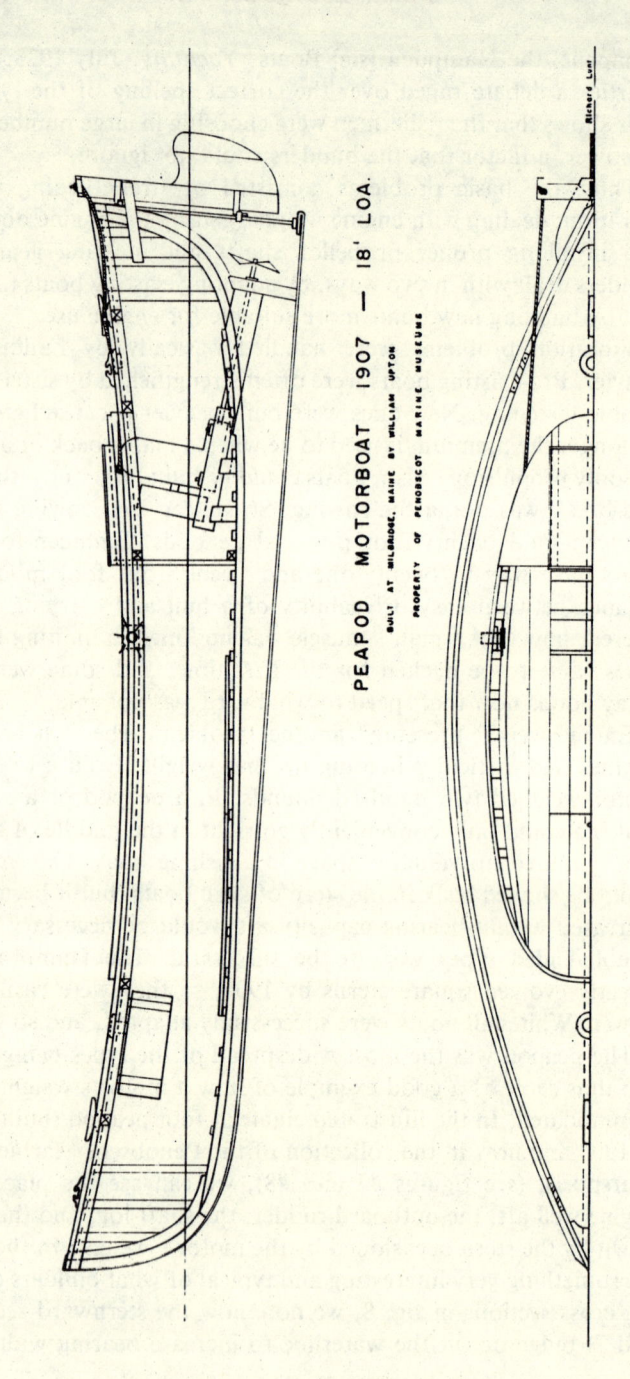

PEAPOD MOTORBOAT 1907 — 18' LOA.
BUILT AT MILBRIDGE, MAINE BY WILLIAM UPTON
PROPERTY OF PENOBSCOT MARINE MUSEUMS

Fig. 7. Power Peapod (Construction Plan)

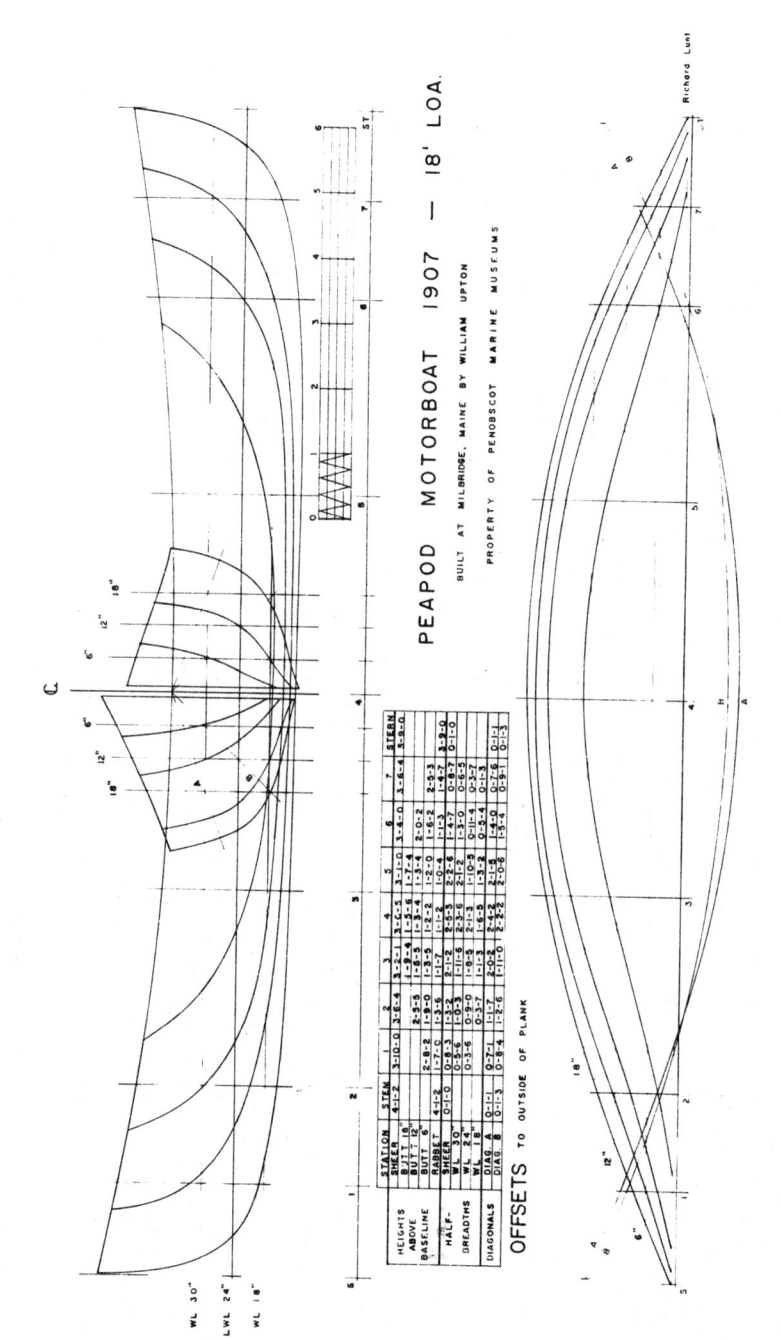

Fig. 8. Power Peapod (Lines)

how they did it. This particular hull is a classic example of the peapod hull form in the early stages of being modified for power. The next illustration (figure #9) shows a Mt. Desert hull from 1915, just eight years later, showing how much further along the modifications had progressed. We notice here now the whole hull has been widened aft to markedly increase the bearing. These boats came to be called melon-seed or pumpkin-seed hulls, and though they were still double-ended, they were hardly symmetrical.

As any builder will testify, however, as long as a boat is double-ended one is still not getting full use of the stern area or getting full bearing, so in some regions, particularly in Jonesport/Beals, a fully round stern was adopted. This could accommodate the weight of even larger engines and allowed the fisherman to pile far more traps on the stern.

However, even though widespread along the coast, the peapod was not the only boat successfully adapted. The Casco Bay Hampton boat with its square stern (see figure #4) underwent the simple changes of the deepening of the transom and the consequent flattening of the stern quarters to give all the bearing necessary. The outboard rudder of the early boats was simply tipped more vertically outward from the sloping transom and held by a triangular piece of deadwood called the jib piece, thus leaving space for a propeller on a shaft that simply pierced the stern post. Later Hampton builders straightened the transom, creating an overhang aft of the stern post, and went to a built-on rudder. Proper shaft logs came in due course.

By contrast the Friendship sloop presented considerably greater difficulties with its substantial deadwood and deep keel. The problem of boring through three to four feet of oak to run a propeller shaft through was so great as to prompt many fishermen and builders to run the shaft out by the deadwood on one side or the other and mount the engine off center. Predictably, that didn't please many fishermen, because it affected handling and caused a list. The additional problem of drag because of the deep keel also tended to limit the Friendships as only auxiliary conversions. Other local sloops with shoaler keels and less deadwood made much easier conversions, I would expect, though I don't happen to have seen any evidence of it.

The Reach boat (from Eastern Maine) as a type is now known to have had a form quite suitable for power in its largest eighteen- to twenty-foot size. These bigger craft seemed adequately built to take an engine. Indeed, the hull form as indicated by surviving photographs is not too far off the ideal hull form to support the early engines (see figure #1 Reach boat lines). The only problem is that there is no clear evidence to show that they were in fact successfully converted. Power lobsterboats were

Maine Lobsterboat Building 157

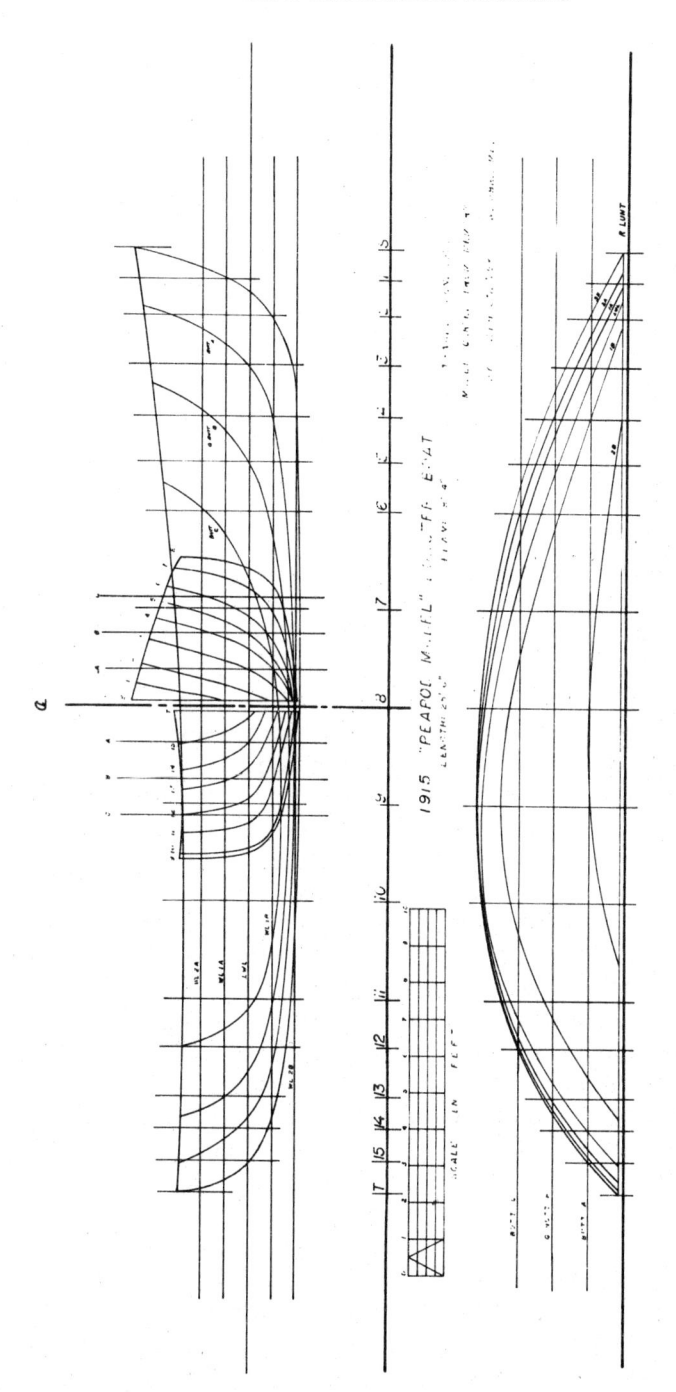

Fig. 9. Power Peapod (1915) Lines

actively built in Jonesport/Beals until 1914 or so when Will Frost moved there from Digby Neck, Nova Scotia and began to change things. These rather tubby early craft were likely the descendants of the Reach boats of ten and twenty years before, but I am not certain about it, and surviving photographs show that some of the grace of the earlier craft was clearly lost in the process.

We have now reached a point where we can assess the true regional ancestry of the modern lobsterboat. I have stressed the peapod, the Hampton boat and the Reachboat, and I have given reasons why not to consider other types. Because of their unsuitability to power conversion or matters of aesthetics or lack of familiarity, other types like the Friendship sloop, the dory, the whitehall, the wherry, the Quoddy boat, the yawl boat, and other miscellaneous sloops turn out to be not so much ancestors but simply *antecedents* like the Dutch uncles of our own childhood days, friends of the family, perhaps even contributors to the general well-being, but not the clear progenitors. I believe this situation obtained until World War I, when new factors entered in to change the picture greatly.

With the coming of the War and the passing of the builders' early attempts to adapt these existing ancestral boat types to the two-cycle engine before 1920, two factors affected lobsterboat development substantially during the 1920s and 1930s. These were the further development during World War I of the new, lighter and more powerful four-cycle engine (with the clamoring desire of the fishermen to have those engines) and the immigration into eastern Maine of a builder named William Frost (mentioned briefly above), who was from an adjacent area of Canada. Frost's arrival represents an infusion of new, regionally somewhat foreign, and yet ultimately successful ideas into the lobsterboat building tradition of eastern Maine and thus deserves special comment.

According to family reports Frost first moved to Beals Island (near Jonesport) in 1914, in order to find a better market for his boats. He was already a capable builder in Whales Cove, Digby Neck, on the southwest coast of Nova Scotia, but one who was short of work in the prevailing Canadian economy. His cousin, George Addison, who lived on Beals Island in Maine, pursuaded him to cross the Bay of Fundy, since in Addison's view there was a market for good boats on Moosabec Reach. We wonder now at his prescience. Will came over and began building a boat in a herring smokehouse on Beals. He had learned his craft in another tradition than that on Beals, and being a Canadian in pre-World War I coastal Maine he was pretty much left to himself. No record remains of the boat he built save the story that he hand sawed every plank in her and built on speculation in hopes he could interest a buyer. One old captain (reputedly Capt. Charles Henry Beal) did visit the shop and liked what he saw enough to offer Frost an engine and a shaft to put in her, with a promise to buy her if he liked the result. The author has seen a photograph of a boat built in 1918 at Tiverton, N.S. (from the Barnes collection at the Mariner's Museum, Newport News, Va.) showing a boat forty-six feet long and nine feet wide(!), powered by a ten horse Hartford. This may be a comparable boat since it comes from Frost's home area. Certainly it gives us some idea of the boatbuilding climate from which he came. Frost's boat was doubtless narrow also, but not as long. The story goes that when he launched her, people up and down Moosabec Reach slipped their moorings to go out and see if they could outrun her on her trial run. Another Beals Island builder, Harold Gower, himself of Nova Scotian origin, said she about doubled the speed of any other craft on the Reach.[5] Those who know Jonesport/Beals fishermen know that from then on Frost had his market. Unfortunately, soon after his triumph, Canada entered the Great War and he was drafted back to Nova Scotia to build wooden military craft for the duration.

When the war ended in 1918 he moved back to Beals, this time with his family, and set to building in earnest. We now know he introduced a new breed of power boats in eastern Maine which became a force to be reckoned with. The only surviving data from this early period is fortunately the most important. The lines of the "Redwing," built in 1924 (see figure #10), document the boats he began to build at this time.[6] She was apparently part of a sales campaign he and George Addison developed for their new franchise for the "Redwing Thoroughbred" engine. Addison built a similar craft, called the "Thoroughbred," which some fishermen preferred, though she wasn't as fast as the Redwing. I am told that nearly one hundred craft were built to the lines of the Redwing.[7] The point is, Will Frost took Jonesport by storm. I think he really eclipsed the development of the Reachboat-derived power boats and supplanted it with his own, just at the critical moment.[8]

That indeed critical moment was the changeover from two-cycle make-and-break engines to the new four-cycle engines developed during the War. The new engines were both lighter and more powerful by a factor of ten! That is, a fifty horsepower engine weighed the same as, or even less than the old two cycles of five horsepower. Further, they could be throttled and fitted with a reverse gear, all technological spin offs from the burgeoning automobile industry that received such a shot in the arm in the War.

Frost and the other builders found themselves in the middle of a technological acceleration unlike anything dreamed of before the War. In that heady decade of the 20s all along the coast the new engines

Fig. 10. The "Redwing" Lines

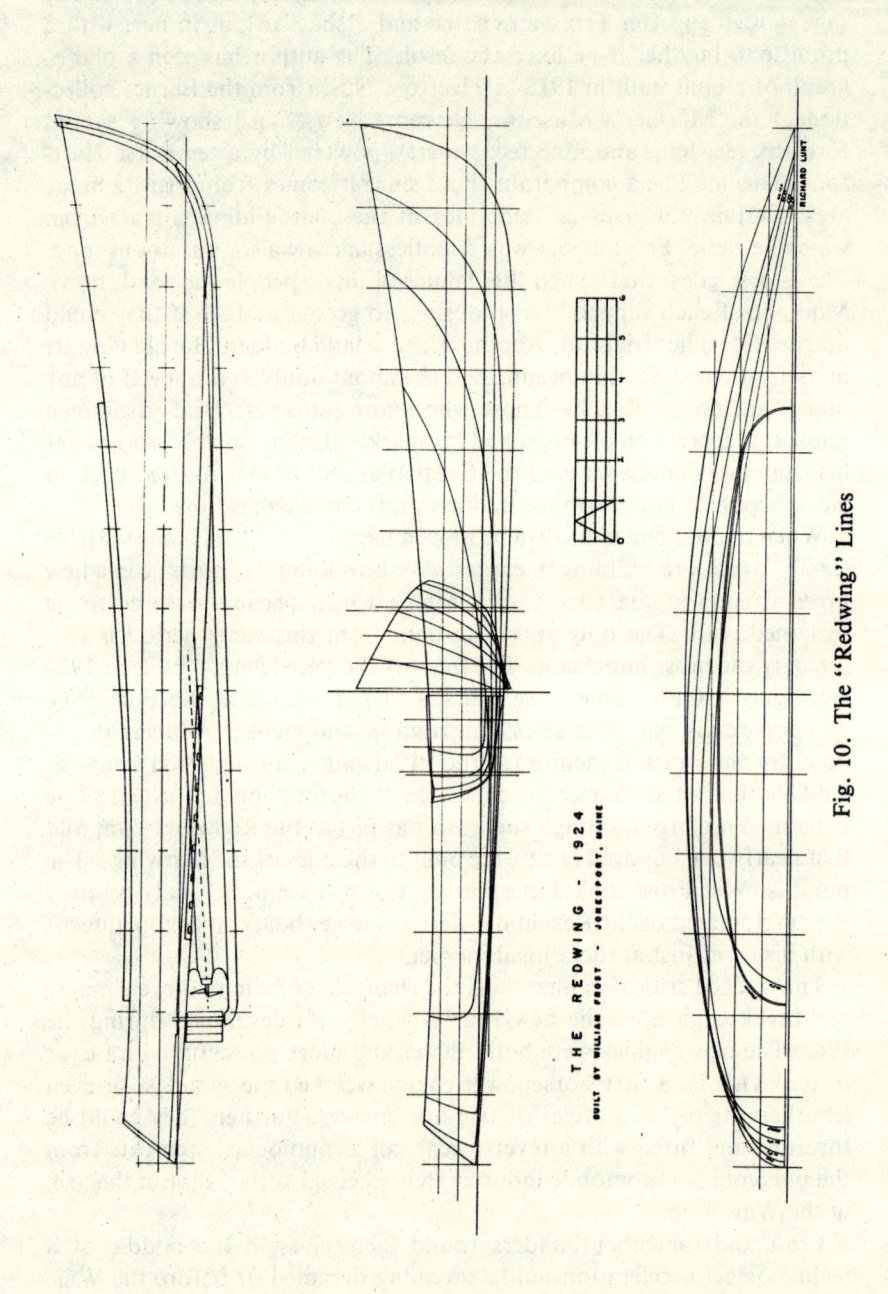

wrought major changes in the lobsterboat hulls. Outside Washington County few builders built such narrow hulls as Frost, though they did confront the same new problems he did, the problems of increased horsepower and the crankcase engine. This new engine couldn't be tilted sharply enough to be installed in the stern anymore. In fact the limit of tilt of 15 degrees required that the engines go well into the middle of the boat. The smaller size of the engine helped out, and the new idea of installing power winches on the motor to haul traps with was made easier by the new engine position, so it was easily accepted.

One would think that the builders could go back to a double-ended hull, now that the engine was out of the stern. But that was not to be, because increased horsepower can drive a boat up to hull speed. Any increases of power beyond that and the stern hauls down and the boat mushes along, getting no additional speed, unless the builder keeps that bearing aft and makes sure the rear part of the hull (the "run" to purists) is as straight as possible, allowing the hull to plane. Thus, the trend toward the wider stern simply continued, though now the cause was different; weight was simply replaced by horsepower.

The round sterns that Frost and others built eventually gave way to the square stern by the mid thirties, because the round sterns were hard to build and proved not durable. Furthermore, square sterns gave even greater bearing. Many fishermen eventually cut off their leaky round sterns themselves, replacing them with homebuilt, squared sterns, probably giving rise to the modern term "cut off" stern.[9]

Frost continued to build in Jonesport until 1933 when his business failed. He went to Rhode Island and Massachusetts, building draggers, returning in 1945 when he set up shop in Portland and built lobsterboats again, seeding that area of the western coast of Maine with his ideas and innovations until his death in 1965. He brought up a whole new crew of builders, the Lowells, whose influence is strong today. Frost was, to my mind, the fifth major influence on the modern lobsterboat, after the Hampton boat, the peapod, the Reachboat and the four-cycle engine.

A final factor to consider is the influence of architect-designed craft conceived by men like Herreschoff. His launches, those of his competitors, and military craft introduced ideas into Maine which were often translated into hull form by conservative but enterprising Maine builders. And we should not forget the rum runners. The only other surviving model of a Frost boat is probably of a rum runner. This last group of influences from outside the tradition is hard to calculate or measure, but it's nevertheless still there.

The history of the Maine lobsterboat continues with many interesting eddies and asides to this day, carried along by the minds of the builders and fishermen. Hull forms stabilizied in the late fifties, but the innovations in construction and use are very significant of late. Fiberglass hulls, extensive use of the boats in shrimp and scallop dragging, diesel power; all these are having their influence on the shapes of the boats, and the craft of building them. As a way of visualizing the past ninety-five years of lobsterboat history I have prepared a chart that outlines the basic lineage which I have presented, showing the ancestral and more important antecedent types arranged regionally and chronologically from 1890 to 1970 (see figure #11). Clear transmissions are shown in solid lines, antecedents are shown by dotted ones. Ones that died out are shown, and merging strains are shown as double lines. This chart essentially makes clear that out of several nineteenth century antecedent types only a few are really ancestral, having survived the selective influence of the internal combustion engine. These three or four regional types have since merged into what we collectively call the modern powered lobsterboat. Even today, however, subtle regional sub-types survive in the modern boats. We see the skeg-built, strip and carvel planked Casco bay boats of the Western coast, the planked down craft of the Penobscot bay area, and the skeg built, "V" mid-sectioned craft from Down East in Jonesport and Beals Island. Within these basic form sub-types there are many smaller variations of form in such things as a builder's distinctive sheer line or stem and stern profiles. Differences in structure and significant construction detail vary from builder to builder. The variety in boat use is even more complex and worthy of its own treatment, but that we'll have to leave to another day.

We return now to Howard Chapelle's rule of thumb about the maturation of a boat type over time. I believe that in the Maine lobsterboat we have a very interesting case that shows how the development of type occurs. Furthermore, it appears to have occurred twice in succession, in a kind of first and second phase development. Several lobsterboat types evolved by the 1890s into a regional maturity suitable to the needs of the fishery at that time. This forty year development (from the earliest beginnings of lobster fishing) corresponds to Chapelle's rule. Then the introduction of the internal combustion engine in 1900 spurred another phase of type development characterized by an abandonment of some of the considerations so important in the earlier types (ease of rowing and sailing, small size), in favor of new possibilities placed within reach by the power and economy of the new mechanical powerplants (increased size, speed, boat weight, payload etc.). This resulted in the development of a new type of lobsterboat, plying the waters of a much larger region than its ancestral types, indebted to all of them for its form, and yet transcending them in order to exploit mechanical power. Thus, with the introduction of an industrial powerplant, and vigorous ideas on how to

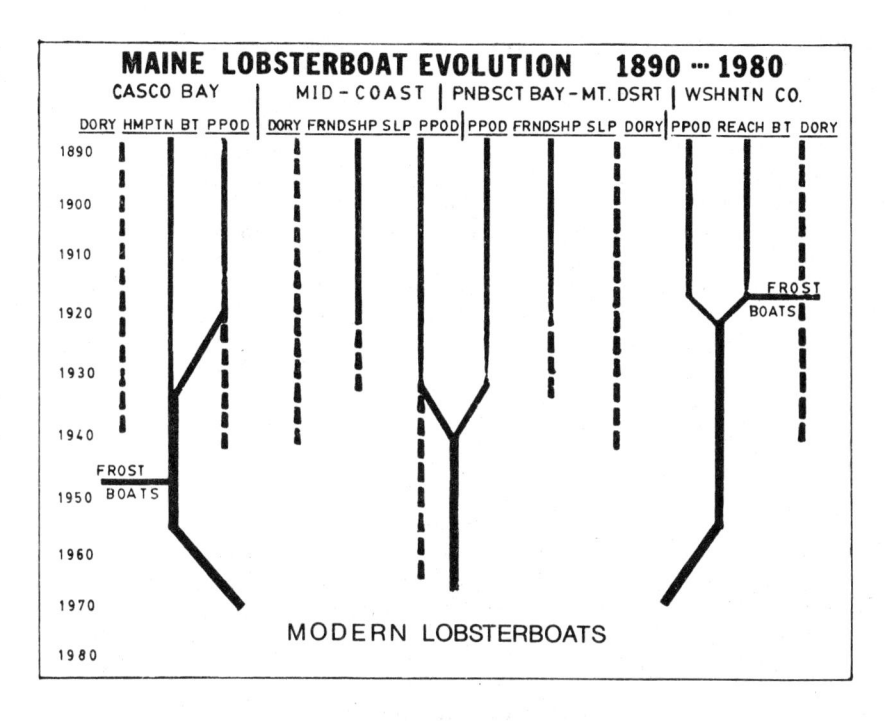

Fig. 11. Historical Chart

best exploit that power, the builders again took about fifty years to produce a mature, unified result. It is a testament to the creativity and coping ability of the traditional boatbuilders who made it possible. Most interesting for folklorists (perhaps used to the notion of traditional craftsmanship simply surviving in an economic backwater?) is the clear evidence in the case of the lobsterboat that traditional craftsmen/boatbuilders have simply exploited the advantages offered by industrial innovations and continue to re-formulate their model to suit the new realities. Thus they have survived to provide several more generations of fishermen with the boats they need to continue fishing. And incidentally, the boatbuilders themselves have stayed alive to meet the challenges of another day. Canny, these Yankees.

NOTES

[1] When I first began studies of the Maine lobsterboat in 1969, I was interested in lobsterboat building as a living laboratory of the more general topic of craftsmanship in wood. I picked lobsterboat building because it had all the earmarks of

traditional craftsmanship and was very much a living practice to be observed, and since I had grown up around boat shops and boat yards it seemed both a logical and convenient thing to study. It was both these, and much more. I have learned about craftsmanship from some fine boatbuilders, many now gone, many others now retired or driven out of business by economic forces beyond their control. I also learned to love what they built, or rather what they and their mentors before them collectively created, the Maine lobsterboat itself. What began as the study of a process has come now to include the study of a class of objects as well. Over the years my research has depended on tape-recorded interviews, extensive photography of the building process (principally in eastern Maine), the taking of lines from half models and boats and the drafting of these, study of the collections of several museums, and endless conversations. I've been helped in particular by the Maine Maritime Museum's ApprenticeShop (sic) which supported field research around Casco Bay on the Hampton boats and who made it possible to gather the information on the Reach boat. Lines from one of the boats in the Penobscot Museum's collection have been crucial to my argument as have been lines taken from one of the models from Old Mystic Seaport's collections. A great many people have contributed to this story.

[2]Howard Chapelle, a naval architect turned historian, who was Curator of Small Craft at the Smithsonian Institution from c.1950 to 1965 and thereafter for some years as Curator Emeritus, should be credited with most of the best work in this century ferreting out evidence of nineteenth century boat types. His work most relevant to this paper is *American Small Sailing Craft, Their Design, Development and Construction*, W. W. Norton, 1951. It presents information on some ninety boat types from the last century which would have been lost without his research. His drawings present a definitive standard.

John Gardner, Curator of Small Craft at Old Mystic Seaport Museum and Technical Editor of the *National Fisherman*, a trade journal for professional fishermen (which contains valuable articles on traditional boatbuilding and other technological concerns) is a boatbuilder turned scholar. His work appears mostly in articles in the *National Fisherman*, dating from the early 1950s until the present day. He has also done monographs on specific boat types (as in *The Dory Book*, International Marine Press, 1978, illustrated by Samuel F. Manning).

[3]Chapelle included the Reach boat among the lost nineteenth century types. Through good fortune, good timing, and the support of the Maine Maritime Museum, in April of 1979 I was able to do the necessary fieldwork in Jonesport/Beals Island to recover enough information to accurately define the type. One fifteen foot boat was recovered and now resides in the collections of the Maine Maritime Museum, where they also have a scale model of the type now recognized to have been built by the same builder who built the recovered boat, Freeman Beal. The drawing presented in figure 1 is of this craft and was drawn by the author. In the collections of the Old Mystic Seaport Museum in Mystic, Connecticut there is another variant example of the type, now acknowledged to be a Reach boat as well.

[4]"Skeg-built" and "planked-down" are terms that refer to variant methods of keel construction. The skeg is the sternward end of the keel of a lobsterboat. In skeg-built construction the skeg is entirely solid wood, or "deadwood," whereas in the planked-down hull the skeg is hollow and somewhat wider than a deadwood skeg, thus displacing more water, creating more drag, and producing a slower, more buoyant boat. The author apologizes for the use of such technical terms when they seem to be unavoidable for technical accuracy. With a topic

such as this and a readership not versed in boat terminology there is an audience problem. The author is sensitive to it and is doing his best to strike a middle course between strictly accurate usages and the non-specialist reader's needs.

[5] Extreme narrowness in fast boats was a trait devised early in powered yachts and military craft of this period (thus the result of naval architecture). Perhaps Frost had an eye for such innovations and borrowed the idea, or perhaps he came to it on his own. We can't know which, but we do know that among the fishermen it was a popular innovation.

[6] Only two of Frost's models survive. This one is in the collection at Old Mystic Seaport Museum and was graciously lent for these lines to be taken. The other, of a forty foot "rum runner" is privately owned by Frost's granddaughter, and has been documented by the author as well.

[7] I believe I know where one is on Great Cranberry Island today, though somewhat structurally changed when replanked some years ago. Frost boats of any description are becoming increasingly rare, and one to the Redwing's lines is particularly valuable to those interested in the Maine lobsterboat's history.

[8] However, in 1970 one elderly builder, Oscar Smith of West Jonesport, was still building boats which bore visible form traits traceable to pre-Frost boats of the second decade of the century. Oscar had worked on his own boats all his life, first with his father and then alone after his father's death. They appear to have been holdouts who resisted the local boatbuilding revolution (and provided an alternative to it, though it passed them by). All of the other local builders appear to have joined the Frost bandwagon, many of them working in his shop at one time or another.

[9] It should be stated that another paper could (and probably shouldn't) be written on the topic of the varieties and complexities of lobsterboat sterns. This paragraph greatly over simplifies a matter that involves several stages of development, varying in the different regions of the coast, and involving significant factors of aesthetics and craft technique.

REFERENCES

Chapelle, Howard I.
    1938   The Hampden Boats. *Yachting*. July 1938:40-44.
    1951   *American Small Sailing Craft*. New York: W. W. Norton.
    1973   *The American Fishing Schooner: 1825-1935*. New York: W. W. Norton.

Glassie, Henry.
    1968   *Pattern in the Material Folk Culture of the Eastern U.S.* Philadelphia: University of Pennsylvania Press.

Lunt, C. Richard K.
    1971   Lobsterboat Building in Maine: Design Aspects. A paper presented at AFS meeting in Washington, D.C. Nov. 14, 1971.
    1976   *Lobsterboat Building on the Eastern Coast of Maine: A Comparative Study*. Bloomington, Ind.: Indiana Univ. doctoral dissertation.
    1981   "The Origins and Evolution of the Maine Lobsterboat," Paper presented May 3, 1981 at the 9th Annual Symposium on Maritime History, Maine Maritime Museum, Bath, Maine. This paper was the germ plasm from which the present study grows.

ILLUSTRATIONS

Fig. 1. Reachboat in the collections of the Maine Maritime Museum. Bath, Me. Lines by author.

Fig. 2. Reachboat perspective of author's lines by Samuel F. Manning.

Fig. 3. Friendship Sloop. Construction plan of "Pemaquid" by Howard I. Chapelle. By permission of the Smithsonian Institution.

Fig. 4. Hampton Boat. Lines by Howard I. Chapelle. By permission of the Smithsonian Institution.

Fig. 5. Jonesport Peapod. Lines by Howard I. Chapelle. By permission of the Smithsonian Institution.

Fig. 6. Modern Maine Lobsterboat. Mount Desert Island, 1970. Lines drawn by author after plans by Raymond Bunker.

Fig. 7. Power Peapod. Milbridge 1907. From collection of the Penobscot Marine Museums. Construction plan by author.

Fig. 8. Power Peapod. Milbridge 1907. From collection of the Penobscot Marine Museums. Lines by author.

Fig. 9. Power Peapod. Mt. Desert 1915. From carved model by Ralph Stanley, builder. Lines by author.

Fig. 10. The "Redwing." From model in the collections of Old Mystic Seaport Museum. Lines by author.

Fig. 11. History of the Maine Lobsterboat. Chart by author.

METHODS OF CATCHING MARINE EELS IN THE GILBERT ISLANDS (KIRIBATI)

Katharine Luomala
University of Hawaii at Manoa

Introduction. BECAUSE THEY VALUE EELS AS FOOD, the people of the Gilbert Islands (now Republic of Kiribati), Micronesia, have various methods of catching them which will be discussed here. Of the four eel families present, the Muraenidae with six genera are well represented with the morays (*Gymnothorax*) especially plentiful. Although many reef eels are small, the smallest the length of a man's forefinger, others are as much as thirty inches long. Eels from deeper waters may be well over three feet long, and, as Sabatier (1939:104) puts it, "... *plus grosses que les bras d'un lutteur*," larger than a wrestler's arm. All are marine eels, for the Gilberts have no fresh-water specimens.

That islanders have over sixty names for eels, a few relating to developmental stages, indicates the importance of this food. Probably more names can be collected. Fishermen do not agree on all names, and differences occur even on the same island. An unfamiliar specimen is simply called *te rabono*, "an eel." Specialists in noosing and trapping them recognize their characteristics and compare their tastiness. In 1948, Naiti, an eel expert on Tabiteuea Island, recited to me eighteen names, four of them for large ocean eels, briefly described them, and compared the tastiness of the four. The tastiest, he said, are the all-black and the "mixed color" eels—black and white, red and white, and other color combinations. These he considered superior in flavor to the all-red; "the all-white are all right but the two-color are best of all" (Luomala 1985:Ms.).

In 1953, Takaria (1953-1954), an eel fisherman from Nonouti Island, asked rhetorically, "Who has not yet eaten eel? The eel is first in fattiness and is sought for because it is life-giving." Grimble (1933:25-26), an administrator from 1913 to the 1930s in this former Gilbert and Ellice Islands Crown Colony, wrote: "Of all qualities most prized in food, fattiness (*nenea*) comes easily first. Nevertheless, this is not listed as a gastronomical preference, inasmuch as the native, though admittedly fond of the taste of fat, sets an even greater value upon its food-properties, and, despite its scarcity in the atolls which he inhabits, regards it not as a luxury but as a necessity. . . . The deep-sea conger (*rabono-ni-man*) is esteemed for its fat to a degree hardly less than the porpoise, and is eaten either fresh-cooked or dry-salted. Though highly prized, this creature is the object of no socio-religious reservations comparable with those connected with the porpoise."

Grimble does not mean that there are no socio-religious observances relating to eels. An eel god is a primal figure in creation mythology. There are still members of clans having Eel as an ancestor, god, or totem who do not catch or eat eels. Men of other clans who are specialists observe many rituals and taboos in making and using their equipment (Luomala 1981).

Little has been reported on preparing an eel for a meal. The "fresh-cooking" mentioned by Grimble perhaps resembles that described by Hambruch (1915:109) for Nauru Island. First the eel's head and fins are cut off, the viscera removed, and the eel tied in a circle. After the coral stones piled on a coconut-wood fire in a funnel-shaped earth oven are hot all except those along the walls are taken out and set near the oven. When the eel has been deposited in the middle of the oven, these glowing stones are used to cover it. Finally a layer of leaves and a mat is placed over the top. The eel, Hambruch states, is ready to eat in a short time. Sun-drying any fish that cannot be eaten in one meal is common, and any excess is sold on the island or elsewhere. On Nonouti, large eels are cut up and sundried, and the "rather smelly, very greasy pieces of fish are sold for a remarkably high price to the Chinese on Nauru" (Cooper 1964:427).

Gilbertese and other Pacific islanders for whom eel is a favorite food have learned that eating large specimens may lead to death or acute and sometimes lengthy illnesses from ichthyotoxism that primarily affects the gastro-intestinal and nervous systems. Since World War II, scientists have intensified research on ciguatera, poisoning from toxic fish, and for the Gilberts, Cooper's report (1964) is comprehensive. Eel poisoning may be true ciguatera or "caused by a different, although perhaps allied, toxin" (Cooper, p. 414). Neither heat nor gastric juices will destroy any toxin in the flesh. Although some Gilbertese know that the viscera is particularly likely to be toxic, they do not always bother to remove it. Cleaning and gutting may, however, be insufficient if the toxin is also in the flesh.

Morays, Cooper found, were clearly implicated among the various fish, large and small, reported to have caused poisoning in ten of the sixteen islands of the Gilberts. Cooper (p. 439) suggests that during an eight-year cycle of toxicity, a few species first become toxic, then almost all, and finally "only large eels, certain snappers, and groupers." According to islanders, morays become toxic because as they grow large their voracious appetites lead them to eat so many smaller toxic fish that they become deadly from the stored toxin (Cooper, p. 414).

Toxic fish are limited to the western lee sides, and "usually confined to open sea reefs and anchorages in this area, seldom penetrating into lagoons" (Cooper, p. 439). Certain reefs, according to tradition, have always been toxic; others have become toxic in this century. The most recent scientific explanation is that the toxicity is caused by dynoflagellates, small organisms, that attach themselves to algae that reef-dwelling fish eat. The poison-causing alga, it is thought, is the first to grow on wrecked ships or dumped war materiel of World War II. Areas that became toxic years before may have been sites of wrecked ships from earlier times.

Cooper (pp. 414–415) cites two examples of eel poisoning. In 1961, at Betio, Tarawa, two men ate part of a large cooked moray they had found in a home from which the family was temporarily absent and had not tasted the eel. It had been neither cleaned nor gutted and had come from a toxic reef. The older man died within a few hours, the younger lingered for two weeks before dying. Gilbertese and others temporarily located in the Phoenix Islands have also had eel poisoning. In 1949, a Caucasian administrator, a newcomer at Canton Island, became ill for three weeks or more after eating with five other men "a big, black moray" caught in the lagoon. The others, Cooper conjectures, had given the newcomer what they considered choicest, the fatty part of the belly. The five who had no ill effects advanced their belief, which is scientifically invalid, that they had developed a partial immunity to ichthyotoxism during their months at Canton Island. A large black eel also made ten members of two families at Sydney Island ill for a day in late 1949 or early 1950 (Groves 1951:19).

Many cases of ichthyotoxism escape the attention of medical officers who are not consulted until the patient is at death's door. People first try out herbal remedies, some of whose value is emetic (Cooper, p. 415; Lobel 1979). Islanders have tests to determine if a suspected fish is toxic. They first try it out on a domestic animal, and then on an elderly person. Children are not permitted to eat strange or suspected foods. Among several other tests, these of no scientific validity, one is to bake a grated coconut with the suspected fish, and if the coconut turns green it is assumed that the fish is toxic.

Because fish, including eels, are a major part of their food supply, the islanders continue to fish, with ichthyotoxism only one of the hazards that come from the reef and the ocean. Following are the major methods by which they catch eels.

Te kaukamea, a method and a device for catching small eels on reef flats, is one of several different methods and devices that men, women, and children use in daytime fossicking, or gleaning, to add both variety and quantity to their food supply. As they walk and wade at ebbtide on either the eastern, or ocean, side of the island or the lagoon side to grope for small edible marine creatures, they frequently bend over to scrutinize the tidal pools, lift away any loose rocks, and probe in, under, and around coral boulders exposed by the reflux of the tide.

At Aiwa village, central Tabiteuea, Koch (1965:28) observed the gleaners looking for small eels on the eastern reef and using a *kaukamea*, a foot-long piece of hard *ngea* wood (*Pemphis acidula*), to probe, draw out, and kill small eels that hide near rocks. In northern Tabiteuea, I found that a *kaukamea* (its literal meaning was not learned) refers both to the method and a hooked device for pulling a small eel or an octopus from its hole. For unidentified islands, Sabatier's dictionary (1954:71) calls the method *te au-rabono*, "the extracting of eels," and a hooked iron instrument, *te kai-n-au-rabono*, "the thing for extracting eels."

The device may be a wooden stick with a curved piece of metal at one end, but, according to my Tabiteuean informant, it is more likely these days to be either an umbrella rib with one end curved into a barbless hook or a pencil-thick wire, two to three feet long, with a half-inch curve at one end. No bait is used. Generalizing about several islands, Catala (1957:123) also reports the use of "an umbrella rib or some other metallic spike curved at the end" to prod out a small moray and then whip it until it can be safely handled. To kill it, a fisherman bites it behind the head or strikes it against a rock and then puts it in an open-topped basket tied around his waist or across his chest.

Fishermen (and women) often have two devices, one to probe and one to hook an eel. Some people, a Tabiteuean said, can determine by means of a wooden probing stick the size and kind of fish the stick touches. It is dangerous to put one's hand into a hole or crevice for it may harbor a biting or stinging creature. On Onotoa Island, a fisherman uses "two metal rods" (vernacular names not given), each about two feet long; one rod has a sharpened point, the other a hooked end (Banner and Randall 1952:54). Knowing that a certain species of moray is common well up on the outer reef flat on the ocean side, the fisherman turns over coral boulders and with his sharpened stick checks every crevice for an eel before inserting his hooked rod to pull it out. These eels, identified as *Gymnothorax picta*, are "white, densely speckled with black except ventrally" (Randall 1955:11). The vernacular name is not stated but eel names vary. At Hull and Sydney Islands, Gilbertese call *G. picta te wiura*; those at Fanning call it *te rabono-mai* (*mai*, "whitish"), and an Arorae islander calls it *te mauti* (Luomala 1985:Ms.).

Although Koch does not mention seeing a hooked device in the Tabiteuean villages he visited, he saw a Nonouti woman, Kirara, lay aside her wooden probing stick to catch a small eel *mit einem eisernen Haken*, "with a metal hook," called *te kai ni kareke* (Koch 1969:24). It is "the thing for catching" which Sabatier (1954:334) defines as an iron rod or wire for catching fish in holes. Kirara's device was surely similar to the "metal hook" employed by Tamoaieta, a Nonouti man, for catching an octopus. Koch (1969:18-20:19,Abb.13,14) first photographed him stooped over to insert his hook into a hole and then showed him erect with an octopus, *te kīka* (*Polypus marmoratus*), on the hooked end of a thick wire which looks to me like an umbrella rib. On Onotoa, men, women, and children catch many octopuses with undescribed "short, hooked spears" (Banner and Randall 1952:41). The "spears" are probably umbrella ribs. Another widespread way to catch an octopus is to let it wind itself around the probing stick.

Octopus and Eel are linked in mythology. When the eel god Rīki was too hungry to continue raising the sky, so one version goes, he got renewed energy from eating two of Na Kīka's ten tentacles. Since then Sir Octopus has had only eight. Sometimes the two tentacles are bait for a noose to drag out Rīki and get him to start lifting the sky.

Not only by day but at night Gilbertese employ the *kaukamea* method and device to catch small morays and octopuses (Luomala 1980:534). This is part of *te kibe*, nocturnal fossicking at ebbtide with light from coconut-leaf torches, or, occasionally, from Coleman lanterns. A small party, usually family members, wade in the shallow and sometimes very deep water on the flats to catch whatever they can. The woman often carries the extra torches of dried and bound coconut leaves, each of which burns only a few minutes. Her husband holds a blazing torch in one hand and, generally on Tabiteuea, a long-handled dipnet to scoop up the light-blinded fish, among them small morays, whch he kills by striking their backs with his metal-pointed spear. In this way, according to Koch (1965:30), a Tabiteuean may catch a dozen different kinds of fish, including morays called *rabono-mai*. On Onotoa, torch fishermen go out preferably to the back ridge trough on the ocean side to catch morays and other fish by scooping them up with a short-handled dipnet or by striking them rapidly with a long knife (Banner and Randall 1952:50). Presumably *kaukamea* is also used but it is not specifically mentioned. As in other islands the catch is ordinarily eaten that night after roasting it on a bed of hot coals.

Te matamea or *kai-ni-matamea* is the daytime noosing of an eel by first using a baited stick to lure it from its hiding place in or near coral boulders, and then as it appears a second stick with a running noose to tighten over it so that it cannot escape. Of the three forms of the method the more common is for the fisherman to walk on the reef at low tide in shallow water to snare an eel, usually a small one. Another way is for him to wade into deep water to look for large eels. In the least common way he dives into very deep water in the lagoon or outside the reef to noose a very large eel hidden in piles of coral boulders.

Few men, however, noose eels either on or outside the reef. One deterrent is that, at least in earlier times and sometimes even now, a man will not catch or eat an eel if Eel or the eel god Rīki is his clan or personal totem or an ancestor and a god (Luomala 1981:227–228). Further, a man who wishes to noose eels must be trained, generally by a kinsman who is an expert and will also share with him the secret knowledge regarded as essential to success. Noosing is often hazardous even for a well-trained, skillful, and experienced man. Small eels can inflict wounds and large ones can kill. Also if a man is noosing at ebbtide far out on the ocean side of the reef he may be swept away by large waves breaking on the rocks. Or if he dives frequently to noose eels he may eventually lose his hearing. That women ever noose eels has not been reported.

In 1948, Naiti of Taku village, Tabiteuea, described to me the method and equipment for noosing. He is not only an eel expert but holds the respected title of Unim'ane, "Old Man," as one of the clan elders officiating in the traditional village *maneaba*, or assembly house.

Naiti calls the noosing method *kai-ni-matamea*, a term referring to the two sticks (*kai*) used. To Naiti, *matamea*, besides meaning "to noose eels," is also the name of a black eel, one of the fourteen kinds that he named which he either nooses or catches in a small eel trap on the reef (Luomala 1985:Ms.). He calls his noosing stick *te kai-ni-kabaebae* (or *kabae*), "the stick for snaring or binding"; in earlier times it was the name for a warrior's lassoo. Naiti's bait stick is *te kai-ni-kabobo*, with *kabobo* referring to its movement up and down to attract the eel to the bait tied on the stick. He also calls it *te kai-n-oro*, "the stick for hitting," because he has a rock tied on the top with which to tap to call the eel and when it shows its head to hit it hard as it enters the noose to get the bait.

Naiti's two rods are of *ngea* (*Pemphis*) with the bark removed, but the set he made for me is of *uri* (*Guettarda speciosa*) and still has the bark on it. *Uri* is not as strong as *ngea* but good enough, Naiti explained, to snare a small reef eel. He made my set as he would one of *ngea* for himself. It is now in Bishop Museum (D 934, 2 pieces).

Naiti demonstrated the correct way to measure the two sticks to get a good catch. It has ritual value for he follows a similar pattern in measuring *Pemphis* sticks for large and small eel traps (Luomala 1983:233-234). To measure the rods he said:

"Measure by placing the first, middle and ring fingers of the left hand across the rod. With the right hand make a notch with a knife on the stick (the noosing stick) where the forefinger is. Then do two finger spans with thumb and forefinger from the notch. Whenever the first span is measured with thumb and forefinger, always take a half span first easy, then stretch the full span. The half span doesn't count in getting the right length (but brings luck). If the stick isn't measured (right), the eel will just bite the stick and run away. The best and proper wood to use for the noose stick is *ngea*. Measure off a second stick for the bait stick in the same way as the first, but don't spread the fingers as much as for the first. The second stick is supposed to be shorter than the first."

The sturdy, well-made Museum set illustrates the construction of the two *kai-ni-matamea*. All cordage on both sticks, according to Naiti, is of tightly twisted two-ply sennit (*kora*) that is thicker than that for lashing a house. The Museum noose stick is 16.50 inches long. On what I shall call its front side, a vertical groove, wider and deeper at the top, is roughly dubbed out for some four inches down the stick starting from the top. Next, work begins on the other side. Naiti, it seems, starts on this side with two sennit cords, a long one to be the noosing line and a shorter, the lashing cord, to intertwine with the other to form two connected casings. These will hold the beginning of the noosing cord rigidly fixed so that it cannot pull out when an eel is noosed. First, a length of the beginning of the noosing line is placed about four inches from the top of the stick and held down by five or six tight turns of the lashing cord around the stick to create the casing over it. My term "casing" for this kind of lashing comes from Finsch's expression *eine Schnurhülse*, "a cord casing," that he uses to describe a Tarawa noose stick (1893:324). The noosing cord, which has somehow been worked into this first casing, is knotted with the second cord, and the two cords continue tautly side by side toward the top of the stick for about a half inch before starting a second casing. This upper casing ends about an inch from the top, and consists of seven parallel turns of sennit around the stick. Then only the noosing cord emerges from it and is passed over the top of the stick to the front to form a loop, the noose itself, which is adjustable to whatever size is needed for each eel. The noose is held open because the cord from which it was shaped slips easily down under the upper casing along the groove cut previously. Then the cord hangs free of the stick and is finished with a wrist or hand loop, over six inches long, made by doubling back the end of the cord and knotting it.

When an eel passes into the open noosing loop the fisherman jerks his hand loop to tighten the noose over the eel. Most eel-catchers agree with Naiti that the noosing cord should be longer than the stick, or handle, to which it is attached. Naiti calls the noose *te b'au*, which can also mean, for example, "the wreath." He has no name for the hand loop. The noosing line is *te ao-ni-kabaebae*," the fishline for noosing."

Naiti's bait stick, 15.50 inches long, differs from any other examples I know of. Most are made by simply looping and tying a sennit cord around the stick about an inch from the top, and letting the short end of the cord, sometimes ravelled, hang free. Bait is tied to this free end, and the baited stick is always put on the far side of the noose away from the eel's hole. Were this baiting end long it might swing through the noose, let the eel grab the bait, and escape. Bait consists of a bit of an octopus tentacle or fish.

Naiti calls his bait stick *kai-ni-kabobo* because it holds the bobbing bait and *kai-n-oro* because its top holds a rock that is tapped to attract the eel's attention and then to hit it on the head. The smooth, light-colored coral rock, just over two inches long, resembles a crude, rather flat, narrow-waisted figure 8 laid on its side. The flat part of the waist is laid directly on the top of the rod, and each end of the rock, thicker and rounder than the waist, is about an inch wide and extends beyond the top of the stick. The rock is held securely by a long two-ply sennit cord, the end of which is laid along one side of the stick, just as for a noose stick, and is held in place by a three-turn knotted casing. The cord then passes up the stick, over the rock, down a short vertical groove cut in the front and under a six-turn casing, and is lashed at the bottom of the stick. The rock cannot slip out because the sennit cord is always kept taut right down to the end of the stick where a casing holds it down. No baiting string is evident on the Museum example but perhaps a short separate cord was threaded through a casing as needed.

To Naiti the bait stick should always be shorter than the noose stick, but a Nonouti man has his bait stick two inches longer than his noose stick, and a Beru man has both sticks the same 18-inch length. Probably each has found what brings him luck and has adapted his motor habits.

Naiti nooses reef eels at ebbtide as he walks either on the windward or the leeward side of the island. He can also catch large eels with his noose by wading in waist-deep water to look for eel holes in any big rock. For such eels he uses thicker sennit. He did not happen to mention if he ever dived into deeper water to snare.

Of how he actually snares an eel after locating it he said:

> "Tap the top of the eel's hole to call it; use the bait stick for this. Then arrange the noose around the hole, with the hand loop of the noose stick across the palm of the left hand and controlled by the left thumb and forefinger. And with the noose stick held in the right hand and with the bait stick in the left hand, you are ready. Tap the top of the eel's hole again with the bait stick, then put it just in front of the hole and the noose. When the eel hears the tapping and sees the bait, he comes out of his hole, passes through the noose. Pull it tight with the left hand while at the same time thrusting the noose stick closer to the hole to help speed up tightening the noose.—Another step after having tapped the top of the eel's hole a second time and the eel is coming out is to strike it on the head with the bait stick, and then pull the noose."

For Naiti and other Gilbertese this is a one-man operation. Anell (1955:56) apparently did not understand this. In his history of South Seas fishing he comments, after much generalizing, that the Samoan equipment for noosing and baiting is like the Micronesian, and that "the bait is fastened to a stick which is evidently manipulated by an assistant to the snarer." He overlooked Buck's explanation (1930:422) that a Samoan holds the bait stick and the free end of the noose line in his right hand and the noose stick itself in his left. The Samoan and Naiti differ only on which hand does what. So far as I can learn, two men work together only in the Marquesas where one man holds the bait stick, the other, the noose stick (Handy 1923:177).

Noose sticks from Tarawa and Maiana are constructed in much the same way as Naiti's. The Tarawa eel-noose, which was collected, briefly described, and poorly sketched by Finsch (1893:324, Fig. 5), is now in Vienna Museum für Völkerkunde (No. 28372, Finsch No. 172). The wooden handle, approximately 28 inches long, has three unconnected casings of sennit cord that is thicker than that of the noosing line. The start of the noosing line is visible below the first casing that begins about halfway up the stick and consists of three turns of sennit around the stick. The second casing has two turns, and the third near the top has four. No knots or other closings appear in the sketch to show why the casings could not slide down. The noosing cord emerges from the top of the third casing, passes over the top of the handle and is shaped into a loop that can be kept open by adjusting the cord that slides down under the upper casing, presumably along a groove as in Naiti's example. The freely hanging line ends with a long hand loop held open by several lashings at the top of the loop.

The sturdy-looking Maiana example, collected and photographed by Krämer (1906:352, Bild 57:355), is now in Linden Museum, Stuttgart (No. L 1502; 60 Krämer). The approximately 23-inch long *Pemphis* handle has the start of the noosing line tightly held by two casings in which some foreign string was used. As in the other two examples, the noosing line goes over the top of the stick, is made into a loop, while the rest of the line slides down under the upper casing, and ends in a long hand loop. A unique feature is that another hand hold has been made by slightly flattening one side of the lower part of the stick.

Neither Finsch nor Krämer collected a bait stick. This is surprising on Finsch's part since he apparently saw reef eels noosed at Tarawa. He called the noose stick *te kainekabobo*, Krämer's orthography is *te kainikabó*.

Another type of attachment of noosing line to handle requires only one casing. Two separate cords are needed. A groove is cut around the stick about an inch from its top. The end of the first cord, the lashing cord, is doubled over, laid in the groove, and knotted twice at what will be the back of the handle. The knotting is done to leave a very small closed loop. For the moment the remaining short and long ends of the lashing cord hang freely. Then one end of the noosing cord is threaded through the small loop at the back and tied tightly. As in the first type, the rest of the noosing cord then passes over the top of the stick to the front to form the noosing loop. This is held open by several parallel rows of the lashing cord that form a casing below it. To hold the casing in place the rest of the lashing cord is tied to the short end at the back and the remainder cut off. The casing has now covered the little loop through which the noosing cord was tied and further strengthens it. As in the first type, the noosing cord in front slides down easily until its long end is free. It is then doubled over and knotted for a hand loop.

Variations occur in details. On Nonouti, Koch filmed the making and use of *Pemphis* sticks and described the process followed by Tamoaieta (Koch 1969:31,Abb.20; 41–43,Abb.26–28; 1965:28,Abb.10) The set is now in Berlin Museum für Völkerkunde (No. VI 47 094–095). The bait stick, the *kai-ni-kabobo*, is about 15 inches long, and the noose stick, which Tamoaieta called the *kai-ni-b'au*, is about two inches shorter. Tamoaieta now buys cord and rope from the store unlike Naiti who prefers the traditional sennit. Formerly, according to Koch (1969:42), the noosing line was made of *taboa*, tough, slippery strips from the epidermis of a coconut-leaf midrib, and, I assume, were braided to make the line.

This second type of attachment is also represented in museums in Stockholm and London. The Ethnographical Museum of Sweden has a set (neither stick named) from Abemama (No. 1924.6.503–504), collected in 1917-1918 by Sixten Bock. He also obtained a bait stick, *te kainekapopo*, from Marakei Island (No. 1924.6.393). The Grimble collection in British Museum, from an unidentified island, has two nooses called *te matamea* (No. 2.21.1921,Gr.Nos.72,73). No. 73 has human hair braid as lashing for the sennit noosing cord. Hair is valued for its strength and magic. I have no data on a set, a *kai-ni-matamea* for noosing and a *kai-ni-kabobo* for baiting, from Tabiteuea in the H. E. Maude collection in Auckland Museum (No. 22905). Maude's attached note states that fishermen attracted an eel's attention by striking the sea with the bait stick. This would simulate the movement of many fish agitating the water.

Tione Baraka of Beru Island (1947:8), who briefly described two *kai-ni-matamea* in a very general way, also made a very crude sketch. He did not name the sticks but the noosing loop is *te b'au* and the action of baiting is *kabobo*. Each *Pemphis* stick is 18 inches long, and the noosing line is of thick, firm sennit cord. The construction resembles that of other sets already described, but whether more than one casing was used cannot be judged from the sketch. The noosing cord lacks a hand loop and is, atypically, much shorter than the stick. One wonders if the fisherman could get a good grip on the line without getting dangerously near the eel's teeth. The bait stick tapers toward the top where four turns of sennit around the stick hold a short, ravelled end for bait.

I have found only two references to Gilbertese diving into deep water to noose eels. Banner and Randall (1952:54) state that Onotoa fishermen dived to noose eels in deep lagoon water. Nearly fifty years earlier Krämer (1906:355-356) wrote, without naming the island, that the Gilbertese like the Nauruans dived to noose congers and morays in deep water on the lee side of reefs. After placing bait in front of an eel's hole and arranging a noose around it, a fisherman snared the eel as its head appeared and then swam to the surface with his prey. Krämer did not state whether the bait was on a stick or consisted of chum scattered on the water.

Perhaps the Gilbertese method and equipment was once like that described for Nauru by Kayser (1936:168-171; 169,Abb.15). The diver, who goes out alone, has a short, thin stick on which to tie bait and a two-foot long noose stick, *ima*. Because his life depends on his noose he carefully checks it after each use, never uses it on the reef, never lends it, and never lets women and children touch it. As each eel has a definite place in a coral jungle from which it emerges only a short distance for food, a diver learns of these places and keeps them secret.

On the surface of the water above an eel's cave, he places a float-pole of *Hibiscus tiliaceus* wood and attaches a fish basket and a sennit rope to it. The length of the rope, whether ten or fifteen spans, is determined by how long he can usually hold his breath under water. After tying his loincloth to the rope, he dives down to the eel's cave, ties the end of the rope to a nearby rocky outcrop, and returns to the surface for air. Then with his baited stick he dives again, guided by the rope, and watches for what he considers the eel's spy, a little fish that when disturbed swims into the cave and is thought to warn the eel of danger. It is one proof of the eel's presence. Another is to put an ear to a small hole to listen for the long, drawn-out sounds made by eels. The diver moves the bait stick up and down to lure the eel to investigate. When its head emerges for a moment, the man has now enough information to go to the surface to get air and his noose stick.

After looping his two sticks over his arm he uses both hands to work his way down on the rope still tied to the rocky outcrop. At the entry to the eel's cave he braces himself against the current, spreads the noose over the cave, and waves the bait stick. When the eel's head appears and gets caught in the noose, the man pulls the noose as tightly as he can and keeps it that way. Were the noose line to slacken the eel, now struggling furiously, would turn on him and kill him. To help him hold the line he twists it around one hand, forces the handle into his palm, and with the other hand catches the rope to pull himself and his catch to the surface. There he repeatedly hits it with the float-pole. Should he be unable to pull out the noosed eel, he must, to save his life, tie the noosing line securely to a boulder, and go up for air and wait for the eel to exhaust itself in the noose. Then he dives to haul it up.

Of the ten kinds of eels noosed by divers that Kayser names and describes most are between three to five feet long and extremely vicious. Some of the names are clearly of Gilbertese origin, not surprising since many Gilbertese have long been settled on Nauru.

Kayser does not describe the noose stick but Hambruch (1915:135, Abb.225) has a little about it. The attachment of the noose line is essentially like that of Gilbertese Type 2 in that there is only one casing and that near the top of the stick. The tapered top has two shallow notches, one vertical, the other horizontal. In the latter the end of a cord of *Hibiscus* fiber is firmly twisted around the stick, while the free end follows the vertical notch and forms the noose in front. To keep the noose from slipping the notches are wrapped with strong braid and netting. Braid encircles the pointed bottom of the two-foot handle, perhaps to make it easier to hold. Octopus is used for bait, and the baited stick is slapped on the water to attract an eel.

The Gilbertese eel-noosing has impressed visitors. Finsch (1893:324) thought the eel noose a singular device he had seen nowhere but in the Gilberts. Krämer (1906:355) also thought it unusual and worthy of special mention. Koch (1969:30) considers the method as undoubtedly old and typical of the Gilberts. Anell (1955:55-56), in tracing the worldwide distribution of pole nooses and hand snares, regards the Polynesian and Micronesian contrivances as very ancient but now fallen in disuse and replaced by more modern equipment. That the eel noose has by no means fallen into disuse is evident from what I have written here.

Whatever the history of Gilbertese eel-noosing and baiting, the people themselves attribute its invention to Na Areau, who as world transformer wanted Rīki, the giant eel, to raise the sky. After the eel had twice bitten messengers, Na Areau invented the bait stick and the noose stick, and with two of Sir Octopus's tentacles as bait and a magical chant, he lured Rīki away from the side of his wife Short-tailed Eel and got him to push up the sky with his snout. When it could reach no higher, one of the primal beings below kicked Rīki in the tail. He leaped up so hard he broke some of the sky-rock which fell into the ocean as islands. Much offended, Rīki remained in the sky as the Milky Way, but parts of his tail became the small eels of today.

Rīki reappears, however, in the migratory period as one of the ancestors leaving Samoa to find a new home to the north. When the headman of a canoe which had Eel as a passenger rejected Na Areau's advice not to take such a dangerous being with them, the world-transformer gave the leader a noose, *te b-au*, and a beating stick, *te kai-n-orea*, to control him if necessary.

Although nothing is said of trouble on the voyage, Rīki caused disaster after the party settled on Nikunau Island. His daughter Nei Baikarawa, offended by her parents, went to live in the bush where she had many lovers. Thereupon, Rīki entered her vagina and bit to death most of the men of two villages. Island elders then sent three experts to kill Rīki. They were Kaenaena, "Mocker or Teaser," with his *kai-ni-kaenaena*, bait stick; Kabobo with his *kai-ni-kabobo*; and Kabaebae (also called Matamea) with his *ao-ni-kabaebae*, noosing line, which perhaps was attached to the *kabobo* stick. The three noosed Rīki, but his violent threshing about formed four ponds on Nikunau and two on Beru before he landed at Kauake, a place either on Aranuka or Abemama. (Luomala 1981:230-231.)

Islanders, it is evident, differ in naming the sticks. Both Finsch and Krämer called the noose stick the *kai-ni-kabobo*, as does Sabatier (1954:333), who adds that it is a synonym for *kai-ni-matamea*, and that the bait stick is *kai-ni-kaenaena*. For Naiti, Tamoaieta, and Maude's informant, the bait stick is *kai-ni-kabobo*, but they differ in naming the noose stick—*kai-ni-matamea*, *kai-ni-b'au*, or *kai-ni-kabaebae*. Some of the same names as used in eel-noosing are applied to the pole nooses and hand nooses, baiting sticks, and other equipment the people use to catch certain large ocean fish (Luomala 1980:552–553; 1983:1207 ff.).

Eel nooses are not limited to the Gilberts and Nauru, but the several from Polynesia in Bishop Museum and described in its monographs are very different from the Gilbertese. The same is true of noosing devices in the former Trust Territory of Micronesia.

Ū is the term for capturing eels in a trap called *te ū* or *to ū*. The baited and weighted trap if large is lowered on a sennit rope from a canoe into deep water, with floats on the surface end of the rope to mark the site. Less often, perhaps, a diver places a trap far out on the reef in deep water where he weights it with rocks to hide it and to keep the current from carrying it away. Trapping large eels in a large trap in the ocean requires specialized equipment and knowledge and at least two men to work together from a canoe, particularly when the loaded trap is raised and emptied of its ferocious captives. Small *ū* needing only one man to handle them are set in shallow water on the reef, and, except for the entrance, are covered with sand and rocks. The first published reference to a Gilbertese *ū* was in a word list by Horatio Hale (1846:467), philologist of the U.S. Exploring Expedition, 1838–42.

Traps vary in shape. Most, it seems, resemble a rectangular, gabled house, longer than wide and higher in front than in back. The roof may be a steep saddle, or flat, or slightly rounded, or a combination of shallow saddle with a slightly rounded front. Certain traps, especially for deep water, are Quonset-shaped, also longer than wide and higher in front than in back. Koch (1969:48,Abb.33–34) has photographs of two traps from Onotoa and two from Tabiteuea of different shapes, sizes, and roof forms (Berlin Museum für Völkerkunde VI 47 117–118, 120–121). He also made a film and described how Timeon, a Nonouti master builder, made and used a medium-sized trap (1965:36–40,Abb. 19–21; 1969:51–53,Abb.29–37).

The size of traps is as variable as the shape. The largest are over three feet long, two feet wide, 18 inches high, and half as high in the back. Small traps may be less than 15 inches long. Baraka of Beru (1947:7–8) states that *ū* vary in length from a cubit (about 18 inches but some are smaller) to an *angauoua*, which is over three feet measured from the fingertips across the chest to the opposite shoulder, while the width is about a third or a half of the length. Some but not all museum examples which have been measured conform roughly to the proportions but more study is needed. Baraka adds, without stating the size or shape he has in mind, that the height in front should be no more than 18 inches and in back eight or nine inches.

The largest traps in museums are between 100 cm to 60 cm long. A Quonset-shaped trap from Tabiteuea is 100 cm long, 65 cm wide, 53.5 cm high (Berlin VI 47 117; Koch 1969:48,Abb.34). A Butaritari trap is 91.5 cm long and 37 cm wide (U.S. National Museum 206239.0.64, Moore coll.). A rounded-roofed, rectangular trap, island unidentified, is 80 cm long, 55 cm wide, 15 cm high on the sides and 20 cm in the middle; the height, middle front, is 30 cm and at each side 23 cm (Schmeltz and Krause 1881:270-271). It was formerly in Museum Godeffroy, Hamburg (No. 709) but since the dispersal of the Godeffroy brothers' collection, its whereabouts is unknown. An old, much used, saddle-roofed, rectangular trap from Tarawa (Bishop Museum C 6388, Wm. G. Anderson coll.) has a 74 cm long ridgepole with each slope 29 cm. The height to the gable peak in front is 32.5 cm and the width across the center of the gable is 44 cm. At the back the height to the ridgepole is 24 cm; the width 34 cm; each sidewall toward the back is 9 cm high and toward the center 14 cm. A rectangular, saddle-roofed example from Onotoa is 64 cm long, 50.5 cm wide, 38.5 cm high (Berlin VI 47 120; Koch 1969:48,Abb.33b). A Butaritari trap with a slightly rounded roof is about 60 cm long, 42 cm wide across the front, 35 cm across the back (U.S.N.M. 206240.0.365, Moore coll.).

Most other traps in museums are between 50 to 55 cm long. They are: Berlin VI 47 118, Tabiteuea, and No. 120, Onotoa, Koch coll.; Ethnographical Museum of Sweden, Stockholm, No. 1885.5.22, unidentified island, from Mus. Godeffroy, and in the Bock coll. No. 1924.6.326, Nukunau, and No. 1924.6.587, Araroa, Aranuka; Linden Museum, Stuttgart, No. Krämer 1295, perhaps Abaiang. I have no island origin or measurements for No. 3329 in Rautenstrauch-Joest Museum, Cologne.

The smallest in museums includes one from Tarawa, rectangular with slightly sloping roof, that is only 37 cm long, 27 cm wide, 14 cm high (Vienna Mus. f. Völkerkunde No. 28371, Finsch No. 171); a 39.5 cm long lagoon trap from Beru (British Museum No. Oct.24,1910,No.306, Christy coll.), and a flat-roofed, rectangular trap from Tabiteuea made for me by Naiti that is 46 cm long, 26 cm wide, 14 cm high in front, 11 cm high in back (Bishop Museum D 933).

"Every trap has its own name," Naiti said, but whether he meant an individual or type name is unclear. The small trap he made for me is *te bukinnongona*, "just a name," but, at a guess, "the tail stopper." His large trap Na Nimatoi, Sir Caterpillar, is "named for an insect like the caterpillar that humps along" and for the way he measures the first large *Pemphis* stick to be one of the *wana*, sleepers of the trap floor. Because curious men, eager to learn his secrets were present, he omitted calling my attention to his "humping," the half-measurement he makes before the first full span as on the noose stick. He said:

> "Measure off the end of one of the three large, longitudinal sticks by placing the three fingers of the left hand across the stick. This is for luck. Then with the right hand mark the point where the forefinger ends, and then put the thumb of the right hand on that point and measure off a finger span with the thumb and middle fingers (he omitted saying to take a half span "easy" before stretching out for the full span). Then measure off a second finger span."

For my small trap he measured off two spans; for his large traps he would measure off enough to get the size he wanted. He had other types of measurement that also had both practical and ritual value (Luomala 1981:233). To ensure luck, Timeon's ritual before beginning his trap was to fill his mouth with grated coconut and put the ends of two of these bottom sticks between his teeth.

The floor, four walls, and roof of a trap are fashioned from tough, wiry branches and shoots of *Pemphis* bushes. Although Finsch (1893: 324) describes one trap as made of pandanus sticks and coconut-leaf pinnules, it was surely of *Pemphis* sticks and twigs. Pandanus wood like *inoto* (*Clerodendrom inerme*) are all right, Naiti says, for traps to catch other fish but not for eel traps because the eels would bite through the soft wood and escape. Timeon used *Pemphis* for all of his new trap except the ridgepole and the platform under the trap. The ridgepole, *taubuki*, was made of a *mao* branch (*Scaevola sericea*), slit lengthwise and the pith removed. The platform of thick shoots of *uri* (*Guettarda speciosa*) was lashed on after the rest of the trap was finished to protect the trap floor from coral cuts. Such a trap has what Naiti calls "its raised floor," *baona*.

The *Pemphis* sticks, which have a diameter of probably less than a fourth of a millimeter, are always doubled to form a pair, *kakauāi*, and treated as a unit. In the frequent counting of sticks during construction and later for baiting, each pair counts as one. A small trap like mine may have an occasional single stick; Naiti pointed out three toward the rear of the trap. Each vertical pair is tautly lashed with each horizontal pair by a special kind of double lashing, *te taeuoua*, "the two knots," done by experts with two-ply sennit cord. After Timeon had made the floor and one side wall, a male relative skilled in *taeuoua* made the second wall but would not know the ritual or procedures for making a trap by himself. Women make the great amount of sennit cord needed, Naiti said, but Timeon's father Rangateaba, as part of his help in much of the work, made the sennit cord that then, with a mesh measure, he made into a piece of netting required inside the trap.

Whatever the shape or size of a trap, an eel enters at the front through a reinforced round hole, *te wi*, "the mouth," or as Takaria of Nonouti calls it, *te mata*, "the eye." The eel passes into a fixed cylinder, *te bua*, "the throat," attached inside with cord and made by lashing together circular and horizontal elasticized *Pemphis* twigs. For a large trap the funnel is approximately eight inches long, for a small trap, five inches. At the end of "the throat" the eel encounters an inner trap, *te kuan*, which is a triangular net, coarsely made, with the wide part fastened above and around the funnel. The netting, Naiti says, is of thicker two-ply sennit cord and made in the same way as for a fishnet. The netting narrows to two flaps, each held by a cord to a side wall. When the eel pushes its way through the flaps to reach the bait hanging inside from the roof, the flaps close behind it and it cannot return. Naiti's large trap has a *bun* shell (*Asaphia deflorata*) lashed to the top of the *kuan* to hold the top down after the eel has passed through. Large, white *bun* shells are sometimes tied on the outside of a trap to make it more visible in the water; whether these shells have ritual value also I do not know.

An *ū* always has square trap doors with specialized functions—baiting, mending the netting, or removing the eels. The squares are cut out of the roof and rear wall and refitted as doors, or flaps, which are secured with three thin but strong *Pemphis* sticks, *kai-n-ti*, thrust horizontally through them. While bait and repair flaps may also be hinged at the top with cord, that for the exit in the center rear wall is sometimes completely removable as in Naiti's trap. Naiti's large trap has three doors on the roof, one on each side toward the front for bait; and a third for mending the *kuan* is just over it, in the middle toward the rear. The rear wall has the door for removing eels. My small trap has two doors, each about two and a half inches wide, on each side of the roof toward the front. The Bishop Museum Tarawa trap has a door about four inches wide on each slope of the saddle roof. Of course, each trap has an exit at the back about the same size as the other openings. Baraka, however, states that the exit should be narrower than the four-inch wide entry. Naiti calls the exit *te buki*, "the tail"; Timeon (Koch 1969:49) calls its flap *ti-ni-bukina*, meaning, I guess, "gushing from its tail." Naiti calls the bait openings *matati*, "small openings," or *mataroa-ne-ni-kanana*, "door places for its food." Timeon calls the flaps for the bait openings *taninga*, "ears."

Lashed on the outside of each long wall of an ocean trap but not of a small reef trap, is either a wooden lattice, or two stout sticks, or, according to Koch (1969:50), a square frame of four sticks with overlapping ends, called *korona*, "crown," Before the trap is lowered from a canoe a stone sinker, *te ati-n-taninga*, "the rock with ears," is securely lashed in each *korona* to anchor the trap among coral boulders or on the ocean floor. Timeon's sister braided a four-stranded rope of much pounded and softened *taboa* strips for a carrying rope, *tiena*, "its swing." After smoothing it and making a large, knotted loop in the middle, Timeon fastened it to each end of the long side of the roof. The Bishop Museum Tarawa trap has a similar attachment and fixed loop but the rope is of hemp or other non-Gilbertese material. My trap has a double sennit rope across the middle and fastened at each short side. Before the trap is lowered a long sennit tow rope, *ro*, is tied through the loop of the carrying rope. Naiti's floats, tied to the free end of the rope, were unhusked coconuts; Timeon had empty, stoppered coconut bottles, *binobino*, and a breadfruit-wood float board, *bukiro*.

When Naiti goes out at sunrise to check the trap he has left overnight, he and his companion haul it into their canoe. He removes the exit flap and uses the sticks to fasten one end of a yard-long, rectangular, closely netted, sennit carrying bag, *kāo* or *kannana*, to the exit. A wide rectangular flap on the other side of the bag is across Naiti's body to protect him from any eel that does not slide immediately into the bag. His companion tips the trap to hurry out the eels and occasionally prods them through the roof. The eels emerge one by one as they are crowded into the lower part of the trap at the back. If the bag is full, and the drawstring below the opening drawn, any eels left in the trap are released. They are too dangerous to carry home on the floor of the canoe. Naiti often gets two or three "big-sea eels," but if he finds a good fishing place he may get more.

Then the trap is baited again, a complex, ritual process, for the *taboa* strings of bait must now be tied in one of two different ways in certain places of the roof which change with each baiting. It is ritually dangerous ever to tie a bait string from the ridgepole. The baiting is extremeley secret and complicated and has been described elsewhere (Luomala 1981). Day baiting, *taeua*, differs from night baiting, *kamatu*. Bait consists of three pieces on a *taboa* strip with octopus providing the bottom piece and fresh fish the two upper pieces. With the trap in his canoe, Naiti has the mouth face land with himself in front. He always starts by tying the bait through the right-hand door before the left-hand.

Naiti checks his trap frequently during the day because large eels eat the small ones. If he finds a stonefish stuck in the entry he uses it as part of his bait. While he waits he fishes for whatever he can catch. With a large metal hook he can hook an eel which he could not do in former times when he had only large *Pemphis* hooks which had been shaped on a growing plant. These wooden hooks were too large for eels to bite and get caught.

He noted that in making a *kāo* for transporting eels, he works from the top to the rectangular bottom. For a large bag he measures from his fingertip to his shoulder, a measurement called *te ang*; a smaller bag is measured from his fingertip to his chest, a measurement called *te bwenawa*, meaning "half-man." For eels from the deep sea he prefers to make the netting with much smaller holes than in a fishnet to protect himself from eels biting from inside the *kāo*. Timeon also has a three-sided shield, *tuka*, made of pandanus roots bound with sennit as protection in removing eels. Examples in the Koch collection, Berlin, are illustrated and described by Koch (1965:39,Abb.21; 1969:52,Abb.36, *kāo*, and 1965:38,Abb.20; 1969:50,Abb.35, *tukan te rabono*). Contrary to Schmeltz and Krause (1881:270-271) eels are not removed from the roof openings as well as from the back; it would be difficult and dangerous. Although small eels can also bite, they are simply emptied out on the sand from a small trap, and gathered up from there.

On finishing his trap Timeon's ritual at dusk was to offer a *babai* corm (*Cyrtosperma chamissonis*), a prized food, to the trap while he faced the trap mouth and ate grated coconut and fish. A coconut torch burned beside him, perhaps to keep off mischievous spirits who might bring bad luck to the new trap.

Naiti, after using a new trap for the first time, does not eat eel for three days. He and his son-in-law also have a renewal, purifying, and perfuming ritual for a trap after it has been repaired. The night before taking it out the fisherman sets the trap mouth facing landward, east for a lagoon trip, west for an ocean trip, and makes a fire in front of the mouth with "dry stuff"—Tebina prefers coconut husk, coconut "cloth" from the base of a leaf, or twigs; Naiti swears by dry *Scaevola* leaves. Then the fisherman, holding his breath, dips a fresh *Scaevola* branch into the fire and slaps it three times on and above the trap mouth to make the eels go inside the next day. He eats a little bit of any kind of food before he goes to sleep. At sunrise he holds his breath as he puts three handfuls of the ashes and the branch into the trap mouth. On his way to his canoe he stops three times, each time to hold his breath and throw three handfuls of sand into the trap mouth over the ashes and the branch. On the third stop the back part of the trap must touch the water. (This is probably another way of saying the mouth faces landward toward which the captured eels will be brought.) In the canoe the trap can face any direction until time to bait it when it must face land. Before dropping the baited and weighted trap the fisherman takes out the things in the mouth and drops them in the water. There is no taboo in eel fishing about what one may eat while fishing and waiting for the trap to fill.

Naiti had no special instructions about where to find eels although they are usually in and around coral boulders. Takaria of Nonouti, however, explained exactly where in the midst of a very smelly kind of coral, *enga*, to deposit a trap and the direction, depending on certain conditions, the trap mouth should face. He is probably of Teuabu village (formerly called Tekaman) for he says it and the Tewaeraba people are the most successful in trapping eels and their success results from their knowledge having come down from their ancestors. Eels can be caught day or night in good weather throughout the year. Family claims to certain fishing areas receive less consideration since modern times although village and island administrators may put certain channels or reefs out of bounds for fishermen.

In many villages today, according to Koch (1965:36), only one man may know how to build an eel trap or how to bait it. The master builder's helpers would feel unable, Koch adds, to make a trap by themselves, largely because one must know the secret rituals, formulas, and taboos connected with making and using it. Success is believed to depend on this knowledge.

Both Naiti and his son-in-law, companion, and student Tebina of Taungaeaka village are two of an undetermined number of eel experts on Tabiteuea. Naiti's father Obaia had trained him in the methods, equipment, and rituals, and Obaia had been taught by Teumariki, his father-in-law who was also Naiti's maternal grandfather. All were of Taku village. Some of Teumariki's secret knowledge about eel traps had come in a dream when a spirit Ten Tekaba'o (Sir Large Adze) had taken him into the ocean to an assembly house called Teniraki, "The Whirling, or Giddiness," where he was told about the eel trap. From there they had gone farther on to a second *maneaba* Touakatea, meaning "Hurry up," or more literally, "Lean toward the Outrigger." In part of his dream Teumariki had learned about the Taku eel trap Temakoro, "The Cutting," and two of the ritual measurements to make before cutting off the *Pemphis* sticks (Luomala 1981:233–234).

Although eel-trapping is the province of men, exceptions apparently occur, at least as far as building a trap properly is concerned. According to Baram, an Eita villager formerly of Aiwa village and recommended to me by many as a specialist on fishtraps, Taku village men know about the eel trap because of an Aiwa woman who married a Taku man and taught it there. Baram added that the first eel trap was built at Auenene, a Tabiteuean islet, and then spread to nearby Aiwa and Barebatu islets, and from Aiwa to the rest of the island. This was "a long, long time ago." Where Auenene got its knowledge was not stated.

The effectiveness of the Gilbertese eel traps may be judged from Reao islanders of the Tuamotus imitating them after having seen them in Tahiti (Emory 1975:188). In the late nineteenth century many Gilbertese worked on Tahitian plantations, and one finds not only their eel traps but other fishing gear imitated. Eel traps called *ū* and looking something like the Gilbertese are also present in other parts of Micronesia besides the Gilberts but they are outside the scope of my study.

Other methods of catching eels. Other fish beside eels are caught by hook and line by day or night out on the ocean. Young men shoot fish, mostly smaller varieties including eels, with a metal spear from a rubber sling, *bana* or *katebe*. Wearing goggles, they dive down looking for fish to shoot. The older spearing method by which large eels and other fish were caught required a spear, *kani*, made of seasoned coconut wood or *Pemphis*, shaped and sharpened to a deadly point. Now that metal is available, most fishermen prefer a round metal spear or an eight-foot coconut-wood shaft fitted with a metal point two or three feet long. The *baenata* is a method for trapping many different kinds of fish, among them eels. Members of a family, but not children, pile up coral rocks to form an enclosure, a form of weir, that is a foot high, two yards wide, and three yards long. It is like a very bumpy pavement. It is always on the ocean side of the island, either parallel or perpendicular to the shore. After a week or so, family members return to collect the fish. They surround the weir with half mats, a leaf sweep, or a net, but leave one side open toward which the fish will be driven and caught in a large basket. The family begins picking up the rocks from the opposite side, frightening the fish toward the rocks ahead, and finally into the basket. The rocks that have been taken out are arranged to form a new weir. (Luomala 1980:239; Koch 1965:24.)

Conclusion. As must be evident, there is much more to be learned about the highly specialized knowledge and experience of Gilbertese eel-catchers. Perhaps what has been written here may provide a starting point for someone else to correct and supplement.

Acknowledgments. I am grateful for financial and other assistance from the Wenner-Gren Foundation for Anthropological Research, 1948–1949; the John Simon Guggenheim Foundation, 1956, 1960; the National Science Foundation and Smithsonian Institution, 1966–1967; and the University of Hawaii since 1946. Special thanks go to museums in the United States, Europe, and New Zealand for letting me study their collections. And I owe much to Naiti, Tebina, Baram, and others of the Gilbert Islands for their attempts to teach me something about their islands.

REFERENCES

Anell, Bengt
    1955 *Contribution to the History of Fishing in the Southern Seas.* Studia Ethnographica Upsaliensis, 9. Uppsala. Almqvist & Wiksells.

Banner, A. H. and J. E. Randall
    1952 *Preliminary Report on Marine Biology Study of Onotoa Atoll, Gilbert Islands.* Atoll Research Bull. 13. Washington, D.C. The Pacific Science Board.

Baraka, Tiona
    1947 "Aia Bai n Akawa Ara Bakatibu" (Our Ancestors' Fishing Devices). *Tero* 17. Tarawa, Gilbert Islands.

Buck, Peter H. (Te Rangi Hiroa)
    1930 *Samoan Material Culture.* B. P. Bishop Mus. Bull. 75. Honolulu.

Catala, René L. A.
    1957 *Report on the Gilbert Islands: Some Aspects of Human Ecology.* Atoll Research Bull. 59. Washington, D.C. The Pacific Science Board.

Cooper, M. J.
    1964 "Ciguatera and Other Marine Poisoning in the Gilbert Islands." *Pacific Science* 18:411–440.

Emory, Kenneth P.
    1975 *Material Culture of the Tuamotu Archipelago.* Pacific Anthropological Records 23. B. P. Bishop Museum. Honolulu.

Finsch, Otto
    1893 *Ethnologische Erfahrungen und Belegstücke aus der Südsee.* K. K. Naturhistorisches Hofmuseum in Wien, Annales 8. Wien.

Grimble, Arthur
    1933 "The Migrations of a Pandanus People." *Journal of the Polynesian Society* 42. Memoir Supplement pp. 1–50.

Groves, Kenneth E.
    1951 *Report of an Expedition to Polynesia for the Purpose of Collecting Fishes, Epidemiological and Ecological Data Relative to the Problem of Ichthyotoxism.* Office of Naval Research, Biological Division. Washington, D.C.

Hale, Horatio
    1846 *Ethnography and Philology.* Vol. 6, U.S. Exploring Expedition, 1838–1842. Philadelphia. Lea and Blanchard.

Hambruch, Paul
    1914– *Nauru.* 2 vols. Ergebnisse der Südsee-Expedition, 1908–1910. II. Eth-
    1915 nographie. B. Mikronesien, Vol. 1, Pt. 2, 1915. Hamburg. L. Friederichsen & Co.

Handy, E. S. Craighill
    1923 *The Native Culture in the Marquesas.* B. P. Bishop Mus. Bull. 9. Honolulu.

Kayser, A.
    1936 "Die Fischerei auf Nauru (Pleasant Island)." *Mitteilungen Anthropologische Gesellschaft* 66:92–131, 149–204. Wien.

Koch, Gerd
    1965 *Materielle Kultur der Gilbert-Inseln. Nonouti, Tabiteuea, Onotoa.* Museum für Völkerkunde. Berlin.

1969 *Kultur der Gilbert-Inseln*. Institut für den Wissenschaftlichen Film. Göttingen.

Krämer, Augustin
1906 *Hawaii, Ostmikronesien und Samoa*. Stuttgart. Strecker & Schröder.

Lobel, Phil S.
1979 "Folk Remedies for Tropical Fish Poisoning in the Pacific." *Sea Frontiers* 25:239–245.

Luomala, Katharine
1980 "Some Fishing Customs and Beliefs in Tabiteuea (Gilbert Islands, Micronesia," *Anthropos* 75:523–558.
1981 "Eels in Gilbert Islands Culture: Traditional Beliefs, Rituals and Narratives." *Journal de la Société des Océanistes* 37:227–237.
1983 "Sharks and Shark Fishing in the Gilbert Islands, Micronesia." In *The Fishing Culture of the World*, Bela Gunda ed. Pp. 1203–1250. Akadémiai Kiadó. Budapest.
(1985) "Vernacular Names of Marine Eels in the Gilbert Islands." Ms. to appear in *Proceedings*, Fifth International Coral Reef Congress, Reef and Man, Tahiti, May 27–June 1, 1985.

Randall, John E.
1955 *Fishes of the Gilbert Islands*. Atoll Research Bull. 47. Washington, D.C. The Pacific Science Board.

Sabatier, E.
1939 *Sous L'Équateur du Pacifique. Les Iles Gilberts et La Mission Catholique*. Paris. Editions Dillen.
1954 *Dictionnaire Gilbertin-Francais*. Tabuiroa, Gilbert Islands. Mission Catholique.

Schmeltz, J. D. E. and R. Krause
1881 *Die Ethnographisch-anthropologische Abtheilung des Museum Godeffroy in Hamburg. Ein Beitrag zur Kunde der Südseevölker*. Hamburg. L. Friederiksen & Co.

Takaria, Tekautu
1953–1954 "Matan te Rabono." *Tero* 88:4; 96:7. Tarawa, Gilbert Islands.

ANY OLD PORT IN A STORM: SEA WORDS GONE AGROUND

W. Edson Richmond
Indiana University

THE ENGLISH LANGUAGE EVOLVED in maritime nations. Its progenitors—the Angles, Saxons, Jutes and their Scandinavian cousins—were dependent upon the sea for their livelihood whether it consisted of fishing, raiding foreign shores, or voyages of exploration with possible emigration in mind. As a result, the language of the sea has permeated the English language itself and has become a part of every-day vocabulary even among those who live as far from the sea as Albuquerque, New Mexico, Colby, Kansas, or Des Moines, Iowa. Such people may not know bow from stern, port from starboard, or a sheet from a halyard and may never have any need for using such words, but they will understand and employ such words as *skipper* and *filibuster* and even such phrases as "three sheets to the wind" and "to be taken aback" although they may be all at sea if queried about the origins of such words and phrases.

For many reasons, the language of the sea is not supposed to be variable. As Horace Beck, or any other skipper, will tell you, survival, life itself, may well depend upon one's understanding of terminology. When one is told to "let go the mainsheet" or to "fend off on the port bow," life, or at least the safety of the ship and all on board, may well depend upon knowing the terms and recognizing what to do. One must, in other words, "know the ropes" (about which phrase, more later) when he goes down to the sea in ships. Often, however, such terminology suffers a change—it would be illogical, perhaps, but not inappropriate, to say "a sea change"—when it goes ashore. Nautical language has in fact become a part of standard English and is used for purposes far broader than its original functions. It has, in effect, become metaphorical, and one needs know nothing about the sea or ships to understand its present meaning.

As a matter of fact, and in spite of what has been said above, even aboard a ship the terminology is sometimes ambiguous. In rare instances, words originally used primarily ashore, have developed multiple meanings when used aboard ship. For example, the word *tack* may refer (1) to a line leading from the lower, windward corner of a square sail to some point forward of the sail, (2) to the point at which the lowest forward corner of a triangular sail may be fastened to the deck or the juncture of mast and boom, (3) to a course which one may be sailing, or, in its verb form, (4) to the process of changing from one course to another if the wind is coming over the forward portion of the boat. And, as another example, the word *devil* may refer (1) to a plank which, roughly speaking, lies just outside the edge of a deck or (2) to a plank which lies just above the keel.

Ambiguity is also compounded by the use of general purpose words for specific nautical purposes. Sailors insist that aboard ship there are no ropes unless they are unattached, even though a landsman is overwhelmed by what he sees as a maze of ropes. There are sheets, shrouds, stays, braces, clews, buntlines, tacks, mooring lines, rodes, painters, and the like; only spares, however, are called ropes. Yet even seamen agree that one of the principal duties of a mate, usually the third, or a bos'n, is to teach a neophyte the ropes.

Moreover, there is confusion at least twice if not thrice compounded with other words borrowed by sailors from the general vocabulary and given very particular, technical meanings when used afloat. In many instances such words are pronounced differently by sailors from the way they are pronounced by landsmen. There are, for example, the words *boatswain*, *forecastle*, *gunwale*, *leeward*, and the shipwright's term *treenails*. With the possible exception of the last which went out-of-fashion among land-based carpenters with the introduction of iron nails, not one of these words is mystifying to the non-sailor; that is, each element of the compound word is recognizable and none is confusing until a sailor pronounces the compound, for the sailor says *bo's'n*, *fo'c'sle*, *gun'l*, *loo'rd*, and *trunnel*.

The *boatswain*, once simply a "boat boy" (the word *swain* originally meant "boy, servant to a knight" and did not pick up the meaning of "one who courts" until the 17th century) came to refer to a petty officer with considerable responsibility which included the maintenance of the ship's boats. The *forecastle* was once just what its compounding suggests, a tower-like, castellated structure at the foremost part of a ship intended to protect archers and gunners, and later the portion of a ship immediately below where such a structure once stood, now the living quarters for the hands. A *wale* once referred to any strengthening plank on a ship; later on, the form *gunwale* referred to the plank that ran below, then above, the guns, and finally it came to mean the topmost rail above the topmost deck. *Leeward* refers to the side of a ship away from the direction of the wind. And *treenail* (*i.e.*, wooden nail) refers to a wooden peg used for fastening side and deck planks to the ribs of a ship, a kind of dowel.

The sailor's pronunciation of each of these words represents a normal phonological development, but landlubbers who seldom used the words reverted to a spelling pronunciation; the words were introduced to their vocabulary by visual rather than oral means. *Leeward*, however, is a little more complex, even though still normal. No one, landsman or sailor, ever pronounces *lee* as "loo," but the word *lee* evolved from Old English *hleo*, and the diphthong *eo* in final position normally developed in Modern English to rhyme with *see* and in internal position to rhyme with *so*. Thus, while both landsmen and sailors will speak of being on the lee side of something (sailors, for example, "sit in the lee of the longboat") only those acquainted with the sea would speak of anything as being to loo'rd, though this is how the word would have been pronounced by everybody, landsman as well as sailor, were it not for the power of conservative spelling.

It is now time, however, to "trim our sails," for we have been "sailing too close to the wind" and in danger of writing more about the adoption of general vocabulary by sailors than about nautical terms ashore. There is nothing strange, of course, about any single word in the two phrases that introduce this paragraph, but to the sailor the phrases are specific and to the landsman, metaphors. A sailor knows that if his ship (boat) is to be sailed efficiently, he must "trim" (adjust) his sails to get the most efficient effect of the wind and that if he is "sailing too close" he will not be sailing as effectively as possible. Landsmen extend such phrases, however, to mean that one should become more careful (one should trim his sails) and to suggest that someone is approaching the outer limits of legality or acceptability (sailing too close to the wind). A legion of landsmen who neither know nor care about the difference between the leech and the luff of a sail use such phrases daily and effectively without understanding their true significance. Indeed, they might well be "taken aback," another phrase borrowed from sailors, were they to realize that they were speaking or writing metaphorically. (For a sailor, "to be taken aback" is to have the wind blow on the wrong side, *i.e.*, the forward side, of a sail and thus to stop the forward motion of his ship.)

Many such words and phrases which come ashore become so common, even if not completely understood, that they easily adapt to lexical variation. Take the word *grog*, for example. The word has come to mean any sort of alcoholic beverage and so thoroughly accepted into everyday language as to develop the adjectival forms "groggy, groggier, groggiest," the extended nominal form "grogginess," and the compound "grog-shop." Originally, however, the word had nothing to do with liquor. It derives from the French word *grosgrain* which became *grogram* in late Middle English and this denoted a coarse, handwoven fabric. In 1770, however, Admiral Sir Edward Vernon, who affected a grogram cloak as part of his seagoing attire and was thus nicknamed "Old Grog," decided in a fit of penury to cut the regulation rum ration aboard his ships with water. To the disgust of the entire British navy, watered rum became the standard ration and was derisively called "grog" in memory of the miserly admiral.

Not everyone, of course, frequents grog shops, and many there are who would let neither the word nor the spirits pass their lips. Everyone, however, makes frequent use of the word *anchor*. Like *grog*, the word has been completely absorbed into the living language. One finds it not only in its original nominal form *anchor*, but also in such verbal forms as "to anchor, anchoring," and the adjectival-participial form "anchored," and the derivative nominal form "anchorage," as well as a recent compound "anchor-man, anchor-woman." (One expects to see "anchor-person" soon!) As everyone knows, an anchor is a device, sometimes as simple as a rock or a discarded engine-block and sometimes a scientifically complicated instrument, which is attached to a boat or ship by a rope (a rode) and when dropped to the bottom of the sea is intended to keep a boat from drifting. As a metaphor, however, it is more complex. Even a non-native speaker of English would have no problems with a sentence such as "the ship of state is firmly anchored in the muck of Reagan's ideology," but what about "anchor-man, anchor-woman"? So much a part of everyday vocabulary have these words become that newspapers no longer hyphenate them, and few sportswriters (for whom the anchorman is the final member of a relay team) or newscasters (for whom the anchorman is the principal member of a news team) are aware that they are using a metaphor.

Indeed, when nautical terms go aground, they often reveal ignorance of their origins. In a novel which he published in 1966 (*The Zinzin Road*), Fletcher Knebel wrote on page 179 "He came here early this morning and shanghaied the whole bunch to work on his farm," and on the immediately preceding page one finds "There's the devil to pay . . . , but I guess ol' Ghenghis Khan already paid him." The novel, which deals with the Peace Corps in Africa, has nothing to do with the sea, and both of these sentences show that the author is completely unaware of the origin of the phrases "the devil to pay" and "to shanghai." "To shanghai" derives ultimately from the place named Shanghai (China), which, incidentally, is a Mandarin word meaning "above" or "at the sea." It has become so much a part of the English language, however, that it can be written without capitalization and can adopt a past-tense form. Legend has it among sailors that a crimp known as Shanghai Bill in San Francisco was so adept at getting men, sailors and landlubbers alike, drunk and delivering them aboard ship to serve as deck hands, willy-nilly, that his eponym became a word for the process. Ashore, the word *shanghai* is now roughly equivalent to the word *kidnap*. The phrase "the devil to pay" is, however, more complicated.

As was noted earlier, the nautical word *devil* refers to a plank either directly above the keel or at the outermost edge of the main deck of a ship. Just how this plank got the name is unclear, but it is logical to assume that it did so because of its Satanic or Mephistophelian qualities: it was "the devil of a job" to work on them because it put the sailor in mortal danger. Yet to the 18th century sailor, the devil was a strake, not a fallen angel. When a ship began to leak at the devil strake, a sailor had to descend on a bos'n's chair and was literally between "the devil and the deep blue sea," and he could well complain that there was "the devil to pay (calk) and no pitch hot" if his work were delayed and he left hanging over the side because his calking compound, usually pitch, was not yet hot enough to work with.

He might, in fact, be literally "at loggerheads" with those responsible. A loggerhead is an iron bar terminating in a bulb. In the days of wooden ships and iron men, these bars were heated white hot and immersed in the already heated, bubbling pitch to keep it hot when sailors were engaged in tarring stays and shrouds and calking seams. Both their length and shape made loggerheads lethal weapons second only to belaying pins for convenience. Thus when two seamen were at loggerheads in the 18th and 19th centuries the result was often fatal. Today, and ashore, the phrase has been modified, and those who are "at loggerheads" are merely argumentative.

Both at sea and on shore, those who are at loggerheads are apt also to be "three sheets to the wind," in other words to be tipsy or drunk. If so, they may be told to "pipe down." Sheets, as has been noted above, are lines (ropes) used to control the angle presented by a sail to the wind and thus to affect both the speed and direction taken by boats. Obviously, when a sheet gets loose, control is lost and the boat wallows like a drunken sailor. Few are the landsmen who know the source of the phrase, but there is hardly one to whom it is foreign. Even more common is the phrase "to pipe down." Commands have been passed from time immemorial aboard ship by means of a whistle called a bos'n's pipe, a whistle easily audible above the clatter of blocks and the rattle of halyards. A system of rising, falling, and trilling tones, as systematic as standardized bugle calls, was developed in both the navy and the merchant marine during the 18th and 19th centuries. One such call (tune) demanded all to be quiet in anticipation of further commands—"a clean sweepdown fore and aft," "abandon ship," "man the yards," *etc.*—and the order passed to the bos'n became a part of everyday speech, even though the verb *pipe* remains a mystery to non-sailors.

Perhaps even more ubiquitous is the use of the word *bells* to indicate time, the use of the word *scuttlebutt* for "gossip," and the exclamation "son-of-a-gun," which is not simply a euphemism but truly an explicit reference though its origin is long-forgotten by both landlubbers and sailors. Traditionally, work aboard ships has been organized into four-hour shifts known as watches, a tradition which has been maintained aboard pleasure-craft and is still maintained verbally though no longer for actual working hours by navies and the merchant marine. For each four hour watch, bells are rung to indicate the passage of each half-hour. The bell is struck once at 12:30 a.m., twice at 1:00 a.m., and so on until the bell is struck eight times at 4:00 a.m. The sequence is then repeated with one stroke at 4:30 a.m., two at 5:00 a.m., *etc.* until eight strokes occur at 8:00 a.m. It is not uncommon ashore, however, to have someone reply, if asked what time it is, at say, 3:00 p.m., "it's three bells." Aboard ship, however, three bells occurs at 1:30, 5:30, and 9:30, both a.m. and p.m. Never does it occur at 3:00 o-clock, either a.m. or p.m. The only times that the number of bell strokes aboard ship happen to agree with conventional clock-time are at 8:00 a.m. and 8:00 p.m.

In view of the fact that Seth Thomas, Westclock and other mantle clocks often strike the appropriate number of times for a given hour, conventional perversions of ship's time in terms of bells is not to be wondered at. But what about "scuttlebutt" as a synonym for gossip and uninformed information? A "butt" is a cask (note the two *t*s), and, especially during the 18th and 19th centuries, the "scuttlebutt" was the cask with a trapdoor in its top (a scuttle) in which the day's drinking water was stored, the mariner's equivalent of a twentieth-century office drinking fountain. Here information—often misinformation—was exchanged, just as it is today, and, having been grounded, the word *scuttlebutt* became synonymous with "gossip" or "what's going on" and "what do you know" even though landsmen know little or nothing about either scuttles or butts.

Similarly, ignorance has contributed to the frequent use of the phrase "son of a gun." Rather than allow "enlisted" (often impressed) sailors ashore when they might more often than not disappear, both the British and American navies not only allowed but in home ports enthusiastically invited ladies aboard ship. It is difficult to conceive of the crowded conditions and lack of privacy aboard ship at this time, but conception was possible in the shadows of a gun which afforded all the shelter needed. Since wives came aboard as well as less well-connected consorts, to be a son-of-a-gun was not necessarily disreputable. Only when the phrase came ashore, only when the phrase went aground, did it become equivalent to, or substituted for, the landlubber's SOB.

"Son-of-a-gun" is used often not only as an expletive and not only as derogatory, but sometimes as mildly approving. Thus when one exclaims "he's a real son-of-a-gun," one may be expressing a kind of amused approval of someone who is lively and mischievous, a far cry from the implications of SOB; indeed, both landsmen and sailors alike may go on to say that they "like the cut of his jib." The jib is a triangular foresail, and especially during the 18th and 19th centuries, the cut—that is, the shape—of jib sails varied and particular cuts were characteristic of the sails of ships of particular nations; the nationality of a ship could be recognized by the shape of its jib, and some were more attractive than others. Thus, after the middle of the 18th century, one might hear a sailor exclaim "She's a limey, I know by the cut of her jib." The word *limey* as a slang reference to Englishmen is not uncommon in North-American English. It came about because British ships served lime juice to their crews in an attempt to eliminate scurvy. Both "the cut of his/her jib" and *limey* are frequently used ashore in spite of the fact that few non-sailors are aware of their origins.

Perhaps even more common than any word or phrase mentioned above is the word *blazer* referring to a sport jacket, especially a navy-blue jacket, though today's mens-outfitters offer blazers in a rainbow of colors. Originally, however, a blazer was a vertically-striped, blue and white jacket prescribed as a uniform—perhaps the first official uniform for ratings in the British navy—by the master of *H.M.S. Blaze* in 1845. Later, dark blue became the official color and it became a sort of uniform for youngsters in British public schools as well.

Other nautical names, too, have become a part of everyday English. Though *Fiddler's Green*, an eternal resting place for sailors, has not entered common speech, *Davy Jones's Locker* has become a familiar euphemism used both at sea and shore. Its origin is obscure, though its nautical beginnings are certain. Etymology has always been an imaginative science, but the best it has come up with for *Davy Jones* is that he, a kind of nautical Mephistopheles, was a Welshman who became quartermaster for Poseidon or, alternately, that his name was a corruption of "Duffy Jonah." *Jonah* was a symbol for bad luck even in biblical times, and *duffy* is said to be a phonetic spelling for a word borrowed from a sub-Saharan, African language; the word meant "ghost," and was changed to "Davy" because of phonological similarity. The argument is not persuasive, but the phrase has certainly entered the vocabulary of all English speakers. On the other hand, the common noun *doldrums* meaning "to feel ill at ease, uncomfortable, getting nowhere," certainly derives from the proper noun *Doldrums*, the part of the ocean near the equator characterized by squalls and shifting winds. And then, of course, there are the phrases "ship-shape and Bristol fashion" and "to run to gravesend for news." The former is used ashore primarily in an abbreviated form, "ship-shape," and it means, of course, that everything is well-organized. In days of yore, however, ships whose home port was Bristol, England, were reputed to be especially well-organized and neat; thus the expression. The phrase "to run to gravesend for news" is not common outside the British Isles, though it was recorded in central Ohio in the 1940s, and it is not generally recognized as a nautical term except in the offices of Lloyds of London. The phrase has nothing to do with death and burial. Gravesend is a village at the mouth of the Thames near the English Channel, the spot at which ships from the continent of Europe made their first landfall. Thus those in urgent need for news "ran" or "sailed to Gravesend" for it.

Just as *Gravesend* has been misinterpreted because of confusion with the common English words *grave* and *end*, so has the phrase "not enough room to swing a cat" been confused because of the usual denotation of the word *cat*. The "cat" here referred to, however, is not the feline animal but a whip consisting of a stout handle and a number of leather thongs—often tipped with brass knobs—used for disciplining sailors and called a "cat-o-nine-tails." Since it was often five or six feet long, it required considerable space to swing. Similarly, the phrase "cold enough to freeze the balls off a brass monkey" has in the 20th century become taboo, something not to be mentioned in mixed company, because of a misunderstanding. The brass monkeys here referred to are not statues of animals nor are the balls mentioned testicles. On 18th-century ships, the racks on which cannon balls were stored beside the guns were often made of brass and called monkeys. Cannon balls were usually made of iron. When it became bitterly cold, because of the different contraction and expansion rate of the two metals, the iron balls were often popped off the racks. Thus linguistic confusion has turned a once forceful and accurate but certainly innocuous phrase into what is today understood as an obscene expression.

Less obscure and certainly more pervasive in the language are, of course, such phrases and words as "a clean slate," *figurehead*, *filibuster*, *flagship*, *galley*, *head(s)*, *landmark*, and *skipper*. All of these originated aboard ship, and all, with the possible exception of *head(s)*, broadened their meaning ashore.

During the 18th and 19th centuries, the watch-officer going off duty copied the happenings of his watch into the logbook and erased the slate on which he had jotted down such things as course changes, squalls, and the like. Thus the oncoming watch officer started out with a clean slate, just as the new president or chairman of the board of a company may today be said to be beginning with a clean slate. From time immemorial, the foremost portion of a boat has been decorated, sometimes with simply painted-on eyes—oculi—which were presumed to see ahead and avoid danger, to ferocious figures—such as dragon and serpent heads on Viking longships—to merely symbolic figures such as the mini-skirted, bare-breasted wench who graced the bows of the clipper *Cutty Sark*. Because of the dangers inherent in repairing and restoring such ornaments, sailors were never fond of them, but it is interesting to note that when the word ran aground, it was often incorporated in the phrase "a mere figurehead," that is, one who was awarded the perquisites of a leader but didn't really lead.

The word *filibuster* was originally a noun, an Anglicization of the Spanish *filibustero*, in turn possibly a phonological corruption of the English word *freebooter*, a synonym for *buccaneer*. When the word came ashore, it became primarily a verb and its connection with pirates was forgotten. The word *flagship*, on the other hand, underwent no phonetic shift and only a mild semantic modification. Originally it referred principally to the ship which carried the flag of an admiral or a commodore, a "flag" officer. Today, and ashore, the word has been stretched to mean the principal office, the headquarters, of any institution.

Like *flagship*, the words *galley* and *head(s)* have simply been adopted into standard English. Borrowed into Middle English from French which originally got the word from Greek, *galley* first referred to a long, narrow vessel propelled by sails and oars. Later, in the 18th century, the word narrowed to mean simply the "kitchen" of a ship, and then expanded, once ashore, to refer to any kitchen and even to accept such compounds as "galley-slave." Less omnipresent, perhaps is the word *head(s)*. In Great Britain, the word is always plural; in the United States, it is most often singular. In one sense, it is a euphemism, a synonym for other euphemisms such as *toilet, privy, outhouse, loo, john, bathroom,*

W.C., etc. In the 18th and 19th centuries, however, "seats of convenience" (almost always two, sometimes four, thus the British *heads*) were placed on a grating protected by highly ornamented railings immediately below the bowsprit at the foremost part, the head, of a ship. Today, no matter where the toilet is located aboard a ship, it is called a head. Even in midwestern America, far from the sea, one must be aware of this, for the word *head* is often used in lieu of the words "john" or "toilet" in bars avoiding such terms as "His'n" and "Her'n," "Pointers" and "Setters," or simply "Men" and "Women."

Penultimately we may look at the words *skipper* and *landmark*. The former was introduced into the English language during the 14th century, probably borrowed from Middle Dutch *schipper*. It is obviously akin to Old English *scip*, "ship," with the agentive suffix "-er" as in "farm, farmer," "drive, driver," *etc*. The Dutch word, however, even in the 13th century, meant the captain or master of a ship, and the initial "sk" pronunciation as in "skip" and "scud" suggests a direct borrowing from Dutch rather than the evolution of an Old English word. At any rate, the word is no longer limited to nautical language. Today the word *skipper* can be used to refer to the head of any organization. The word *landmark*, on the other hand, is basically English. It was originally used in coastal navigation to refer to especially noticeable objects ashore which allowed a skipper to determine his exact position. When the word itself was taken into non-nautical language it became a metaphor for anything outstanding ("the signing of the Declaration of Independence is a landmark in the history of the United States").

The list of words and phrases which sailors have contributed to standard speech is virtually endless and would require a volume were they to be thoroughly and scientifically discussed. Since neither time nor space allow, it might be well to conclude with a phrase dear to the heart of Horace Beck and all other sailors: "the sun is over the yardarm." There is no one, temperate or intemperate, whether he lives in Portsmouth, New Hampshire, Peoria, Illinois, Phoenix, Arizona, or Portland, Oregon, who does not recognize this expression as an indication that the time that drinking is permissible has arrived. Contrary to popular opinion, some sailors have been known to refuse a drink, even of Myers rum, because the offer was made too early in the day. During the 18th century, the appropriate time for a first drink in the British navy was when the sun had risen so far that it was visible above the lowermost (main) yard on the foremast—conservative captains required that it be above the lowermost yard on the mainmast which was a little higher. Yards are spars which run at right angles to masts from which sails are hung. Thus when the sun was above either the fore- or mainyard, the sun was reasonably high in the heavens and time was approaching noon. Fortunately for the sobriety of the British navy, the position of the main foreyard and the mainyard were fixed, they could be neither raised nor lowered.

Words common to sailors which go ashore are not choosy. They find any old port in a storm and they are often changed as a result as drastically as are sailors who retire to farms in Missouri.

BELIEF PERFORMANCES ALONG THE PACIFIC NORTHWEST COAST

Barre Toelken
University of Oregon

SOME YEARS AGO AT A SYMPOSIUM on western folklore held at Lewis and Clark College, I listened to Horace Beck as he spoke on "Folklore of the Sea."[1] Grasping the podium with gnarled hands, Beck swayed slowly back and forth (the floor creaked obligingly from time to time) looking very much like a stern captain dressing down a new crew for being caught whistling on board. When the hour was over, the audience—a bit seasick—were convinced of the practicality of some (and the psychological necessity of other) beliefs of sailing people, felt as though they had been on a voyage with Captain Beck, and were very relieved indeed that they had not brought their black umbrellas on board with them.

I was impressed by his talk, not because of its unsettling effects on my stomach but because of its reformative impact on my way of thinking about popular belief, "superstition." The few sailors' beliefs I knew of were clearly holdovers from a now-vanished past, maintained, perhaps, out of nostalgia for a way of life now mostly outmoded by new machinery and methods. Fishermen and sailors generally are a close-knit and culturally conservative people, so it only stood to reason that they would hang onto old notions (or at least say they did) out of respect for their heritage. But while Beck did not rule such possibilities out, he had also shown that beliefs and customs are passed along because they continue to play an important role in the lives of those who use them. By accepting the whole set of beliefs, Beck suggested, a seaman has access to perhaps a couple thousand years of experience and judgment to help him out of trouble. Disaster strikes fast at sea, and a sailor does not have time to learn everything by personal experience before he is in a situation which requires a quick, automatic response. I have come to believe that this can be said of all occupational folklore, but especially of those trades and occupations that are particularly dangerous or unpredictable.

Robert McCarl has made the same point more recently in his several excellent pieces on the folklore of urban firefighters in particular, and others over the past fifteen or so years have commented more fully on the functional aspect of folklore; indeed, the point is a fairly common one in current folklore studies.[2] But at the time I heard it from Beck, it gave me a perspective I needed in order to approach and study the beliefs of the Northwest Coast fishermen, for I wanted to do more than simply collect their folklore: I wanted to understand it. And I wanted to come at the subject as someone who had sympathy for the validity of traditional belief, not as a scholar-outsider collecting odd seashells from exotics along the shore. I was considerably disappointed, then, when I later discovered, by asking fishermen themselves, that western fishermen do not have any superstitions and popular beliefs.

There had been a time, of course, when fishermen had superstitions, but those times are long gone now, I was assured. Modern fishermen are businessmen running modern business machines, and superstition—or any uncritically accepted notion—is likely to be more harm to the business than good for the fisherman. Fishermen study their radar and the value of the dollar on foreign markets, and only dusty university professors believe you can still find someone still believing and following the old ways. So I was told by those fishermen along the Oregon coast who were garrulous enough to be willing to talk at all.

On one occasion, when I pursued the question with one young and very successful fisherman, he responded with some heat: "What the hell do you want to know for, anyway? Want to prove to the government that we're a bunch of dumb codgers smoking our pipes and carving scrimshaw? They'd absolutely love to hear that: they'd send us a few more 'experts' to tell us what to do!" Somewhat at a loss, and not wanting to take the hint, I said "Well, for example, I noticed that most of you guys don't leave port on Friday. That some kind of a federal regulation, or just a coincidence?" Several pairs of astonished eyes swung in my direction, and Terry Thompson blurted, "Christ, that's not superstition! *Nobody* leaves port on Friday! Do you, Al?" Al shook his head, as did two others who had gathered to hear the conversation on the Newport docks. "*I* don't leave port on a Friday," Terry went on, "I've got my reputation to think of, you know!" (the reader will want to recall this conversation later in this essay where I describe how Thompson assured a group of foreign visitors that he leaves port on any day the fish are biting).

Of course, what I was experiencing is something that nearly every field collector must live through: the sudden recognition that not only do specialists use terms in ways different from those in everyday usage, not only do people misunderstand words like "folklore" because of their redundantly negative use in journalistic writing, not only do superstitions have the connotation of ignorance about them, but that all of these are concepts used by outsiders, not insiders: fishermen do not need to define themselves as a folk group, and they have no reason to regard their own beliefs and customs as anything other than standard, everyday ways of doing things properly. They do not need to know that the ancient disinclination to fish on Friday may go back to some primitive fertility rituals centered on fish-loving goddesses (some do know it because they have read about the matter, but it does not explain their own reasons for following the custom). They may cite other, more recent reasons (see below), but their basis of action will usually be their connection with their peers and their ability to articulate that connection in recognizable ways. A belief, along with its related customary actions, becomes so to speak a part of the cultural language: the belief may or may not be actually believed, but its performance says something that cannot be said in any other acceptable way.

A widespread concept among fishermen and loggers in the Northwest could be stated as follows: "cold extremities (hands or feet) at night are a sign of impending death or injury on the job; persons heeding the omen will withdraw from planned activity." Stories are often heard about people who felt the sign but paid no attention to it, and were injured or killed on the job next day. One hears these anecdotes, but would seldom if ever hear the text of the belief recited as I have quoted it above. Rather, in its proper context a man would say to his wife some morning, "Boy! I just couldn't sleep last night. Hands and feet got so cold I just couldn't get any rest." His wife will respond that he probably has the flu, and should stay home from work. He calls in sick. His buddies, knowing he was healthy yesterday and almost never catches cold, will say, "Probably got cold feet," and they may chuckle about it, but not with derision, for they will use the same device when they have the same foreboding of disaster. Off the job, when an acquaintance backs out of something which would clearly *not* have been life-threatening, they may use the phrase figuratively (thus hyperbolically) for its derisive effect: "Decided not to get married, eh? Did you get cold feet?" In an occupational culture where one seldom admits to being afraid, but where lives are threatened every day, the strains build up and must be dealt with in a way that satisfies the value system of the group. A belief like this one functions far below the surface, but finds expression in a euphemistic performance. This leaves out a consideration of the question: do the loggers and fishermen actually believe this omen, or is it only a figure of speech? In view of the function I am describing here, it almost does not matter. And of course, as with almost all beliefs, one can find some who do "believe" and some who do not. Many of the beliefs which I will discuss in this paper will not provide us with clear evidence on this matter; others, on the other hand, will be evident as expressions of real belief from the way in which they are practiced. Still others, such as the following, will depend for their meaning on knowing that they are *not* believed.

On the boats of Yugoslav-American fishermen in Washington State, one will hear the skipper say during an unusually heavy downpour "Aha—it's raining real nice. Salmon really like fresh water; the fishing's going to start getting better now." On another occasion, after a good squall when the weather starts to clear and the sun begins to come out, the skipper will say "Aha! The sun's coming out. Salmon love warm weather; the fishing's going to start getting better now." If one were to hear these from two different skippers, or if one were out only during a rainstorm and heard the one, and then read the other one somewhere, one could conclude without difficulty that these represent a couple of interesting beliefs connecting weather phenomena with observed (or desired) fish behavior. But if one heard the same skipper use them both during the same trip, one would sense a discrepancy and wonder if these really were beliefs after all. One could conclude that, as with proverbs, there is a belief to cover any situation, and therefore—since they exist in opposition and disagreement, they cannot really reflect observable phenomena. One could, of course, ask the skipper if he actually believes them, and might hear to his surprise that, yes, the skipper believes them *both* without question. But in fact, neither one is actually believed as stated; rather, both together are performative expressions of an unmentioned belief that one must always speak positively about the fishing. There is a belief, but it does not achieve articulated form in the "texts." The situation in this example is actually rather complex, for the beliefs as stated are not believed in, but the area of concern they refer to, covered in fishermen's language broadly by the term "Lady Luck," is very much a matter of serious belief. Typical dialog: "Do you know of any beliefs or customs practiced mostly or only by fishermen?" "No." "Do you believe in Lady Luck?" "Who doesn't?"

In this paper I would like to discuss a few of the beliefs of Northwest fishermen that seem to me to fall into a few important categories: those that are practical ways of doing things, or that simply cut down on confusion or danger under the stressful situation of working under dangerous conditions; those that are practiced mainly as a way of showing that one knows the ropes well enough to be considered an insider (and thus worth hiring, working with, working for, or paying attention to); those that have to do with personal or group psychology; and those that have to do with "Lady Luck." Many of these overlap, of course, and nearly anything one does on board a ship has something to do with "Lady Luck." But some of the beliefs and customs are probably used for special reasons as well, and a discussion of their expressive complexity may lead to a better understanding of why they continue to survive strongly in the modern fishing business.

Survival on board a fishing ship (as well as success at fishing) is seen by the fishermen as a highly practical affair, but one recognizably beset by change, circumstance, unpredictability. Many if not most of the ideas which would be classified by folklorists as popular beliefs deal with both of these elements at once, but some are phrased as ways of interpreting signs or performing tasks on the practical level, while others relate to gestures made and not made in order to better one's chances with Lady Luck. Practical interpretations include weather signs such as the almost universal ("red sky in the morning, sailor's warning; red sky at night, sailor's delight") and the observation that finding stones in cod stomachs foretells stormy weather ("They eat stones for ballast"). Whether these signs are usually reliable or not, they must represent the evidence of accumulated experience, and must have been accurate at least often enough to have ensured their continued use. Of course, since the northwest coastal weather patterns feature change and storminess, it may be difficult to test the cod theory fairly, but suffice it to say that such beliefs are not considered magical, but natural and practical.

As well, leaving hatch-covers right-side-up when open, storing canned foods right-side-up on the shelves, and hanging coffee cups so that they open toward the stern, are all described as purely practical matters of order and reduction of confusion: the fewer decisions that need to be made by men working together, the more orderly things are, the more predictable the patterns of work can become, the easier the physical action is for everyone, so much the better, for it allows the men to keep their minds on the work and open to the hazards around them. But these customs also overlap with ideas about luck, for they represent potential erroneous actions, which, if performed, will bring bad luck down on the boat: bad weather, a poor catch, death. In the abstract, then, such beliefs as these are phrased as practical considerations for the workplace; once they are "performed" in error, they are not simply signs but actual symptoms of disaster forming, for everyone's attention should be on keeping everything on the boat right-side-up. Another way to describe this is to say that under normal circumstances, with everyone on board knowledgeable and alert, proper performance of these beliefs consists in placing things appropriately; it is when they are "mis-performed" that they are perceived to have symbolic meaning.

Other beliefs are more obviously symbolic, both in their descriptions and in their usage. One does not whistle on board most boats worldwide, small or large. Here the issue is not practical (although I have heard it argued that whistling gets on others' nerves and can have psychological and practical effects), but magical: in discussion one hears simply that someone who whistles might whistle up a storm. In performance, things may actually get rough: the whistler may find himself slammed up against the wall of the pilot house by furious shipmates. Nonperformance is the ideal, and thus the full emotional charge of the belief is seldom seen unless a mistake is made and an inadvertent performance takes place. Although responses may not be so violent, the serving of pea soup or bringing of peas on board (because of "pea-soup" fog? because the good split peas sink?) is considered by many northwestern fishermen to be a mistake which can *presage* (but as far as I can tell, not *cause*) bad luck for the boat.

As Beck and others have pointed out, much of shipboard lore and belief acknowledges the psychological stresses of the hard life in restricted space. Thus the belief about whistling may owe its continued existence as much to psychological factors as to any ongoing fervent belief about imitative magic (but in any case, don't tempt Lady Luck). Loss of work gloves, hat, or knife overboard is seen as symptomatic of a psychological slip which can lead to bad luck, for losing anything overboard is a sign that the person is not being careful, not paying attention, or has lost his grip or dexterity. Such an action, though entirely accidental, endangers the person (if he grabs for the item) and puts the crew on alert for his safety. Loss of an important item like a hat, knife, or glove is especially significant because these items relate directly to the work and safety of the men on board—so of course there are practical ramifications. Symbolically, anything overboard brings up the idea of crew overboard, and that thought takes men's minds off the fishing. People begin to watch each other carefully, wondering if they will have to watch out for the others' safety, and, finally, in an atmosphere of increased tension, someone slips or trips, and the foreboding is fulfilled. On the positive side, one can not overlook the solid and confident feeling engendered by seeing everything in its place, everything right-side-up, tools and gear all in place: accidents are rare on such a boat, and the men can concentrate on fishing. Many seasickness preventatives may also fall into the psychological category. Several fishermen I have talked to along the Oregon coast have told me that in bad weather they tie a brown paper bag over their stomachs against the skin; others report using a dab of mentholatum in the navel, and all claim the method works.

Fishermen along the northwest coast recall when women were seldom allowed on board a working fishing vessel. Though the belief is an ancient one, the modern explanations I have heard are both practical and psychological: a woman takes the men's minds off their work and thus creates a dangerous working situation; men eventually vie for her attention and begin competing with each other, sometimes losing their tempers. One solution to the problem is said to have been "the skipper's prerogative"—the absolute right of the captain to claim as his own consort any woman who sailed with the vessel. Today the situation has changed considerably: many fishing boats are operated by a family or by a married couple, and women are now a common sight on the docks and on the boats. Single women now hire out as deck hands, and are said to work as well as anyone. The skipper's prerogative still remains in usage, but now only as a rhetorical probe, or as a joke: "I don't know if you really want to make a trip with us; are you willing to follow the skipper's prerogative?" The woman so asked then inquires as to its meaning, and can show by her response whether she thinks the offer is an interesting one. As long as she works as hard as anyone else, she may go to sea without acquiescing. Also psychological may be the connotations of some items avoided by the fishermen here. As in the east coast fishery, fishermen avoid having umbrellas and black suitcases on board. Proper performance would mean that the subject would seldom if ever come up, for no knowledgeable person would try to bring one on board. When asked about the custom, fishermen are likely to reply not with an articulated explanation but with an expression indicating that everyone already knows why: "What? A black suitcase? Never! Doctors and lawyers carry the damn things." Or "Farmers carry 'em; fishermen don't." Or, "Umbrellas? Now, come on: just think about it for a minute. *Who* would carry an umbrella?" Unstated but intended are the obvious dangers for fishermen symbolized by some other professions: sickness or death, litigation, and people who don't know how to tie knots properly (one term for ignorantly-tied lines is "Valley rigging," in reference to the Willamette Valley, inland). And who *would* carry an umbrella, after all? Well, certainly not a fisherman, who is accustomed to rain and whose both hands are supposed to be busy. People who do not know what should be happening on board, people who symbolize ideas the fishermen would rather not think about, are considered dangerous to the mental stability of skipper and crew.

In terms of performance/non-performance, there is an important dimension to be noticed here. These beliefs come up for discussion and response chiefly when an outsider who does not know the ropes makes a mistake. His clothes may be dumped out onto the dock and his suitcase thrown into the bay, or his umbrella may suddenly get bent over a knee or thrown javelin-style back toward land. These beliefs, whatever their background, continue to mark the distinction between insider and outsider, between those who know the ropes and those who don't; and it's a delicate line, for on the one hand, the fishermen want to call attention to the difference, but if the outsider is coming to work on the boat, they want to impress on him immediately the absolute necessity of picking up the customs so that he will not be a danger to everyone on board, including himself. Thus, knowing the ropes is not only a practical matter of learning about the details of the job, but a way of demonstrating with distinctive performances that one knows and respects the system of conventions that mold fishermen into a working unit.

In this category, then, go nearly all of the beliefs and customs of the sea. The more one knows, the more appropriately one performs the customs and avoidances, the more proficient one is thought to be in the nature of the work (this does not guarantee, however, that one will catch fish), then the more likely it is that one will find a good job on a good boat. One skipper said, "It's really simple: I don't hire greenhorns. Don't have time to train 'em. No point in wasting their time or mine. They'd just get washed over the side anyhow, first trip."

Some of the beliefs and customs have directly to do with luck, or at least with putting oneself into position to receive good luck (it's unlucky to *assume* anything). North coast fishermen still throw change overboard when passing the whistler buoy, outward bound; some say it's to insure a good catch, others want good weather, others simply say it's for luck. Many do not observe the custom at all, but it still remains in practice widely enough to be known by everyone, as is the custom of having a coin (the favorite here is a gold $20 piece) under the mast, or, for some, under the radar housing. In older times it might have bought a favorable wind, but today it shows up in conversation partly as a way of demonstrating that a fisherman has been in the business for a long time. Is there a residual belief that the coin itself brings luck? I think so, although most fishermen have avoided a straight answer on the subject. Since wind is not the issue these days, and since gold coins are hard to find and expensive, it would seem to represent a bit more than a mere survival.

Changing the name of a boat will bring almost certain disaster, although sometimes a new owner, in order to change the luck of a boat that "won't fish" or one that is already thought to be a bad luck boat, will try a new name. Most people avoid it, even when they detest the name of a boat they have purchased. The names themselves would be worthy of a special study; many are clever plays on words or letters which often express a wish for good weather or good catches (example: E Z C—"easy sea").

Gooney birds (albatrosses) are thought (by some) to be the spirits of departed fishermen who will try to signal to a perceptive fisherman when to pull the nets or will show where the fish are. Even those who do not subscribe to the spirit theory will admit that the "gooneys know sometimes better than the fishermen when to pull the nets; they'll just start flying around and clacking their bills together and that's how you'll know the time is right." Gooney birds are not to be killed, of course, even Coleridge knew that—for killing one can bring about terrible consequences for the whole boat. Recently a skipper out of Newport, Oregon, interrupted a fishing tour to bring in a wounded albatross that had gotten caught in his propeller, hoping that scientists at the Marine Science Center could save its life.

There are still other forms of folk "performance" which help to solidify the relationships among fishermen; although they do not fall into the category of belief, they nonetheless function to provide codes of information and communication among closely associated workers, and to suggest within the occupational community still other constellations of identity—regional and ethnic.

For example, fishermen use a system of signals to indicate what operation they are engaged in and what their intentions about direction and speed may be. Nowadays, most fishermen are in touch with each other by Citizen's Band radio, and many of the visual signals have been replaced by slang phrases which are mostly understood by the daily participants in the conversation. One visual signal remains in general use along the coast, however: when a trawler is "dragging" or trawling (pulling nets along the bottom or just above the ocean floor), a basket is displayed on the mast. It has nothing to do with luck, but probably continues to function because it warns other nearby boats that dragging is in process and the skipper may be too busy or too concentrated on the operation to be able to talk on the radio.

Fishermen signing on to work on a Northwest coast boat will usually work on the "share," or "lay" system. Each person on the boat gets a certain percentage of the profit, agreed upon beforehand. When a catch is brought in and sold, after the boat's operating expenses are paid (fuel, net repairs, and the like), the remaining money is paid out in shares. The skipper may get two or three shares (depending on whether he is the boat's owner, who also, of course, gets a share), and each crewman gets a share. For the boats which "fish well" (some boats are believed to have their own properties of sound, shape, color, etc. which either attract or repel fish) and which have experienced and skillful crews (and this would include their command of the proprieties and attitudes suggested by the beliefs discussed above), the income can be quite attractive. In a good year, a good crewman can bring in more than $40,000 in share payments. But not all years are good, and the resultant unpredictability of the business, in addition to the unpredictability of the sea and weather, function to promote both the beliefs about luck and the various systems of communication which provide close ties among the fishing people.

One of these important performative elements is of course their occupational language. Terms range from those which describe the gear to those which denote the distinctive fishing methods. Trawlers use "doors," and the nets are referred to as "trawls"; the end of a trawl, where the fish are collected, is narrower than the rest and is called the "cod end." Steel "bobbins" help to guide the net over obstacles on the ocean floor. If the catch is too large to be dumped on deck all at once, it may be emptied in "splits" before being put into deck bins called "checkers." Shrimp trawlers use "tickler chains" to stir up the shrimp from the bottom.

Trollers, instead of dragging nets behind them, draw separate lines through the water. Typical terms are "trolling pole," "flopper stopper," "crosstree," "spreads," "cannonballs," "hoochies," and "jigs." Gillnetters (allowed only in the rivers) and crabbers also have their specific terms, all of which not only describe the items and their usage, but which also suggest attitudes about the work.

When ocean-going boats leave Newport harbor, they pass a promontory called "Chicken Point" by the fishermen. This is the last chance to read weather signs and decide whether to try crossing the bar or not. Especially in bad weather, when waves on the bar can easily swamp a boat, this is the "fail-safe" point at which a clear decision must be made. "I couldn't get out past Chicken Point" refers more to a shrewd reading of all the signs than it does directly to the weather, or to ineptness; but it does simultaneously admit to fear in a socially-sanctioned way.

The gillnetters in the Columbia River fishery once used a very gracefully-shaped, wind-driven boat reminiscent of Scandinavian boat types. These eventually were converted to motor power in the 1930s, and since they were designed primarily for a one-man operation, they have now almost disappeared in favor of the larger boats which use a bow reel. The local "feel" of the boat style, along with its ethnic connections, seems to have disappeared, but the old Columbia River gillnetter is still seen on the most modern gravestones as a distinctive occupational marker. And, in the families who still fish, there are other important traditional elements which still determine the nature of the fishing culture. For one thing, many of the net designs and the methods by which they are repaired are family or ethnic "secrets"; some fishermen will have their nets repaired or even stored only by someone of their own national background. Family traditions dictate the shape of nets, their size, and the subtle way in which they are weighted in order to fish a certain way in the water.

In some ports, the Scandinavian fishermen prefer boats built by other Scandinavians according to older procedures and beliefs. One custom which was still observed a few years ago in Astoria was that of having a virgin girl urinate in the hold at a certain point in the construction process. Boatbuilders have been reluctant to discuss it, but I have had several students who, when they were younger, were paid $10 for the job, which was done in total privacy. Georgia Maki, a fishnetmender of Finnish extraction, remains busy in Astoria, repairing mostly the nets of Finnish fishermen. Families in this area fish both the river and the ocean, and the range of nets and gear is stunning in its complexity. Gillnets are usually made of nylon monofilament these days, but the netmender's shuttle is still carved out of wood, following family designs centuries old.

Families who have specialized in so-called "drift fishing" on the Columbia have inherited drift areas along the river, places where they normally fish, and which are considered their legitimate first choices. In these drifts, they have been accustomed to keeping the river clean of snags, the shore cleared of driftwood, and have exercised "salvage rights" to any large logs or objects found floating in their domain. These rights are inheritable, although, since they are not supported by state law or federal regulation, they cannot be sold. Nonetheless, bargains are made between old friends and families, and the drift rights are carried on—even though they are now constantly under challenge by shoreside landowners (land developers, mostly) and by lumber companies, who now cannot afford to lose a choice log that happens to float away downstream. At the same time, lawyers and judges trying to decide how other fishing issues may be dealt with have found that fishing customs are often of longer standing than state or federal laws, and thus they have often been used in court as a kind of common law which helps decide matters which are not covered in any other way.

I hope it is clear by this time that the traditions of the fishing people in the Northwest share much with those that have been studied and discussed by folklorists elsewhere in the country, that there may be some distinctive Northwest particulars which will be well worth following further, and that—even though fishing itself remains unpredictable in this part of the country—fishermen's traditions remain a solid part of their self-definition and expressive system, regardless of how much or how deeply a particular fisherman "believes in" the old ways. The functions of these customs and beliefs, as I hope I have shown, are far more complex than the single concern with Lady Luck would require, although that remains a strong force. Larger than that is the esoteric/exoteric dimension, that line between insider and outsider that not only helps to distinguish who the "summer people" are, but that signals who the respected and trustworthy fishermen are: the people who are safe to work with or profitable to work for. This was demonstrated to me most eloquently not long ago when I took a small group of foreign visitors to visit Dock 5 in Newport, Oregon, where most of the bigger boats tie up when they are in port. I wanted to introduce the visitors to Terry Thompson, one of the best younger fishermen in the area. Thompson is articulate and loves to talk about the limitations placed on modern fishermen by a government that sees everything from a desk in Washington. He is one of the most successful fishermen in Newport, and is respected as one of the toughest skippers to work for. He showed the visitors his boat, with all its electronic gear, and stunned them with his knowledge of international exchange rates and their impact on the fishery. In answer to the questions about fishermen's traditions, he laughed, and assured them that the old beliefs were mostly found today among folklorists, not among fishermen, who after all had their work to do, and who could not be held back in their businesses by quaint beliefs which no longer had validity. He assured them that women were welcome on board his boat (two of our group were women and toured the boat with interest), and that he even employed them on occasion. His current crew (all of them skippers of other boats) stood by and nodded assent as he "punctured" all the old beliefs: *he* leaves port anytime the fish are running, and all this nonsense about Friday just isn't in the fishermen's vocabulary any more; he does not care what his men bring their clothes on board in because it isn't any of his business—as long as they know how to fish, and so on. Fishing is high-tech on the open seas, and folklore represents a quaint but useless voice from a previous life.

As we left the dock to look for shelter from the drizzle, Terry Thompson in tow, we met by chance another fisherman, Barry Fisher, formerly of Gloucester, Mass., who had relocated to the Northwest years ago and had originated the "joint-venture" fishing operation with the Russians and the Poles. Fisher is a prosperous fisherman and the owner of two boats. He spotted me (having seen me give a lecture on sea songs some time previously), and shouted "Say, I've been meaning to tell you something, something about the so-called *folklore* of fishermen!" The group halted around us, and we stood in the rain while Fisher poked me reprovingly in the chest and held forth with a long monolog that went something like this: "Those customs aren't folklore; they're based on real elements of the life at sea. You know why nobody leaves port on Friday? Because Christ was killed on a Friday, that's why. You won't find anybody around here going out on a Friday. You know why no-one lets women on board? Too much trouble and jealousy; you just can't have it; it'll cause so much trouble you won't be able to fish. You know why the hatch-covers always stay right-side-up? Because they're easier to get hold of and close, especially when you need to do it in a hurry." "Do you allow your hands to bring their clothes on board in a black suitcase?" I asked. "Hell no! Lawyers carry black suitcases. That's just common sense, not folklore." The interesting aspect of this conversation for me was not simply that Barry Fisher was repudiating almost point by point the comments made a half-hour earlier by Terry Thompson, but that Thompson was standing there with us, smiling and nodding his head in agreement with everything Fisher was saying. In fact, Thompson usually does not leave port on Friday, and is said by his acquaintances to wear a brown paper bag tied over his stomach to prevent seasickness (a performance not easily seen by a visitor or open to verification by a professor), while Fisher does not himself in fact follow all the beliefs he claims *all* fishermen honor. The performance we saw was a demonstration of esoteric/exoteric identity, not a declaration of belief. What this means, of course, is that here, as elsewhere, the "text" of a belief or a custom is only a small part of a larger network of meaning, usage, inference, and shared values.

Although this brief essay has provided only an overview of the matter, its insistence on the importance of shared value and context over manifest textual content would seem to raise serious questions about the large collections of superstitions which have become representative of the pioneering work in this area of folklore: are these compendia—existing as they do without extensive contextual description and connotative reference—in the final analysis useless or pointless? No more than a dictionary is pointless only because it provides a visible listing of items which are similarly most meaningful in the living context of usage. Just as a dictionary or a thesaurus can be superficially used or thoughtlessly employed, just as it is possible for someone to believe that words in a dictionary are "real" while sentences in living language are some kind of tarnished vernacular, so it is possible for the student of superstition to see the list as more important than the live cultural language from which it has been obtained. Our obligation as folklorists and students of culture is to utilize the massive contributions of such scholars as Wayland D. Hand deeply, not superficially, as catalogs of live values, not lists of droll survivals from the untalented past. Nowhere is this task more approachable than through the close study of the ancient and still ongoing codes and performances passed traditionally among those who share the sea.[3]

NOTES

[1] This speech was later published as "Sea Lore" in *Northwest Folklore*, 2 (1967), 1-13.

[2] See Robert S. McCarl, Jr., "Smokejumper Initiation: Ritualized Communication in a Modern Occupation," *Journal of American Folklore*, 89 (1976), 49-66; also McCarl's *Good Fire/Bad Night: A Cultural Sketch of the District of Columbia Fire Fighters as Seen Through their Occupational Folklife* (Washington, D.C.: District of Columbia Fire Fighters Assn., 1980); also Robert H. Byington, ed., *Working Americans: Contemporary Approaches to Occupational Folklife*, a special issue of *Western Folklore* (37, 1978), reprinted as Smithsonian Folklife Studies #3 (1978).

[3] The examples used in this essay were taken for the most part from larger collections in the Randall V. Mills Archives of Northwest Folklore at the University of Oregon, and are augmented by materials collected and recollected by the author. In particular, I wish to thank Patricia McLaughlin, Archivist of the Mills Collection, for her unfailing help and support in maintaining and refining the holdings of this Archives and making them available in sensible and efficient ways for projects such as this. As well, I would like to thank Barry Fisher and Terry Thompson for their candid remarks, and Don Giles of the Mark Hatfield Marine Science Center at Newport, Oregon, for his unflagging interest and encouragement for the study of sea lore.

THE GALLOPING GOURMET, OR
THE CHUCK WAGON COOK AND HIS CRAFT

John O. West
University of Texas at El Paso

THE TRAIL DRIVE OF THE AMERICAN COWBOY is well known to the reading and viewing public of the entire world, thanks to the influence of television and movies and their enormous capacity for education. As is also well known, unfortunately Hollywood is not always careful with its facts—indeed, a new folklore might well be said to have developed because of the public media's part in the passing on of information and mis-information. Such is the nature of oral transmission itself, one might recall: one old cowpoke remembers singing to the cattle to keep them calm; another points out that the average cowboy's voice was far from soothing, and his songs might well have precipitated (rather than averted) a stampede. Of course, with the dulcet tones of Gene Autry and the Sons of the Pioneers as evidence, the popular view is of the romantic persuasion, as is much of the lore of the American cowboy.

Usually overlooked are the factual matters of the cowboy cook and his rolling kitchen. Of course, "everybody" knows that chuck wagon cooks are genially irascible—"as techy as a wagon cook" goes the old saying.[1] George "Gabby" Hayes of the Western movies of the 40s is an excellent model; and all Western movie buffs know that a chuck wagon looks pretty much like an ordinary covered wagon with a pregnant tailgate. But that's about as much as most folks know. The day-to-day routine of the cook gets him up hours before breakfast to rustle grub for a bunch of unruly, and often unappreciative, cowpokes. Then there is the day-long battle to keep ahead of the herd, arriving at pre-designated meal-stops with enough time to spare to put together a meal that would stick to the ribs. But all that is a largely unsung epic!

The portions that have been sung are all part of the past, recorded reminiscences of cowboys and bean-artists that have long since gone up the Long Trail. Still, from those memories a pretty clear picture can be drawn of the lore of the chuck wagon cook. Frank S. Hastings, veteran manager of the SMS ranch, wrote that "a Ranch in its entirety is known as an 'Outfit,' and yet in a general way the word 'Outfit' suggests the wagon outfit, which does the cow-work and lives in the open from April 15th when work begins, to December 1st, when it ends."[2] Thus for three-quarters of a year the chuck wagon was home for a dozen or so cow punchers, and the cook was the center thereof. The cowhands stuck pretty close to camp: "They rarely leave the wagon at night," says Hastings, "and as the result of close association an interchange of wit or 'josh,' as it is called, has sprung up. There is nothing like the chuck wagon josh in any other phase of life, and it is almost impossible to describe. . . . It is very funny, very keen and very direct."[3]

"Jack" Thorp, Easterner-turned-cowboy who wrote *Songs of the Cowboys*,[4] among other works, described "A Chuck Wagon Supper" for the New Mexico Federal Writers Project of WPA days. Apparently never before published, it gives a clear picture of a bygone scene:

"A chuck wagon arrives at Milagro Springs. The cook, who has been driving, hollers 'Whoa, mule,' to the team of four which has been pulling the load. Getting off the seat he throws down the lines, and calls to the horse wrangler, who is with the *remuda* of saddle horses following the wagon, to 'gobble them up,' meaning to unhitch the team and turn them into the *remuda*.

"The cook now digs a pit behind the chuck wagon, so when a fire is built, wind will not blow sparks over the camp and the punchers surrounding it. The chuck wagon is always stopped with the wagon tongue facing the wind; this is done so that the fire will be protected by wagon and chuck box. The horse wrangler, with rope down, drags wood for the fire. The many rolls of bedding are thrown off the wagon, and the cook brings forth his irons. Two of them are some four feet long, sharpened at one end, and with an eye in the other end. The third is a half-inch bar of iron some six feet long. Once he has driven the two sharpened irons into the ground above the pit, the long iron is slipped through the eyes of the two iron uprights; this completes the pot-rack, or stove. Cosi, as the cook is usually called—which is an abbreviation of the Spanish word *cocinero*—hangs a half dozen or so S hooks of iron, some six inches long, on the suspended bar, and to these are hooked coffeepot, stew pots, and kettles for hot water.

"The rear end of the wagon contains the chuck box, which is securely fastened to the wagon box proper. The chuck box cover, or lid, swings down on hinges, making a table for Cosi to mix his bread and cut his meat upon, and make anything which may suit his fancy. (There are several dishes whose names cannot be found in any dictionary, so consequently not knowing how to spell them, I omit.) There is an unwritten law that no cow puncher may ride his horse on the windward side of the chuck box or fire, or Cosi is liable to run him off with pot-hook or axe. This breach of manners would be committed only by some green hand, or 'cotton-picker,' as Cosi would probably call him. This rule is made so no trash or dirt will be stirred up and blown into the skillets.

"The *cocinero*, now having his fire built, with a pot-hook in hand—an iron rod some three feet long with a hook bent in its end—lifts the heavy Dutch bake oven lid by its loop and places it on the fire, then the oven itself, and places it on top of the lid to heat. These ovens are skillets about eight inches in depth and some two feet across, generally, but they come in all sizes, being used for baking bread and cooking meat, stew, potatoes, and so forth. The coffee pot is of galvanized iron, holding from three to five gallons, and hanging on the pot-rack full of hot coffee for whoever may pass. Then Cosi, in a huge bread pan, begins to mix his dough. After filling the pan about half-full with flour, he adds sour dough, poured out of a jar or tin bucket which is always carried along, adds salt, soda, and lard or warm grease, working all together into a dough, which presently will become second-story biscuits. After the dough has been kneaded, he covers it over, and for a few minutes lets it 'raise.' A quarter of beef is taken from the wagon, where it has been wrapped in canvas to keep it cool. Slices are cut off and placed in one of the Dutch ovens, into which grease—preferably tallow—has been put. The lid is laid on, and with a shovel red hot coals are placed on top. While this is cooking, another skillet is filled with sliced potatoes, and given the same treatment as the meat. Now the bread is molded into biscuits, and put into another Dutch oven. These biscuits are softer than those made with baking powder, and as each is patted out, it is dropped into hot grease and turned over. These biscuits are then put in the bake-oven, tight together until the bottom of the container is full. Now comes the success or failure of the operation. The secret is to keep the Dutch oven at just the right heat, adding or taking off the right amount of hot coals, from underneath the oven or on top of the lid. If everything goes right, you may be assured of the best hot biscuits in the world. Sometimes a pudding is made of dried bread, raisins, sugar, water, and a little grease, also nutmeg and spices; this is placed in a Dutch oven, and cooked until the top is brown. This is the usual cow-camp meal, but if there is no beef in the wagon, beans and chili are substituted.

"Along in the evening, as the men are through with the day's roundup or drive, tired horses are turned into the *remuda*, and Cosi hollers 'Come and get it or I'll throw it out.' The punchers in their chaps, boots, and spurs flock to the chuck wagon, and out of the drawer get knives, forks, and spoons, and off the lid of the chuck box take plates and cups that Cosi has laid out. They then go to the different bake ovens and fill their plates, which like the cups are made of tin; the knives, spoons, and forks are of iron or composition. Lots of banter usually passes between the punchers and Cosi, though he generally gives as good as he receives. Plates filled, the boys sit around on the different rolls of bedding, the wagon tongue, or with crossed legs either squatting on the ground or with their backs against a wagon wheel. Of course, there is no tablecloth on the chuck-box lid, but it is usually scrubbed clean enough for the purpose of eating—though no one uses it.

"As the boys finish their meal, plates, cups, knives, forks, and spoons are thrown into a large dishpan placed on the ground underneath the chuck-box lid. If some luckless puncher should place his 'eating tools' on top of the lid, he would be sure to be bawled out by Cosi. All the eating tools, when washed, are put on shelves or in drawers of the chuck-box, while the heavy Dutch ovens and such are put into a box bolted underneath the wagon bed at its rear end.

"This is the real chuck wagon and way of eating as found in New Mexico, though some Northern outfits have a different lay. From the Cimarron River north, as far as grass grows, many outfits have quite elaborate lays. Those that have a large tent or tarp spread over the wagon and extending out on both sides are generally called by real punchers 'Pullman outfits,' and old hands will tell you that they use them so that the punchers won't get sunburned, and usually add 'bless their little hearts,' also explaining, with very straight faces, that these Pullman boys usually wear white shirts, and are obliged to shave and shine their boots every morning before starting work."[5]

A photograph in *From the Pecos to the Powder* shows a chuck wagon with an iron cook-stove plus a tarpaulin shelter[6]—obviously a Pullman outfit—and a description in the same work tells how the stove is chained on behind, with poles extending behind and rawhide thongs holding the whole thing secure.[7] The famous chuck wagon races engaged in annually at the Calgary and other Canadian rodeos began, says Cliff Claggett, in cooperative roundups when cooks actually raced to get the best locations to set up their campsites; further, in the present-day races, an outrider has to hoist a stove onto the rear of the wagon to start the race.[8] But in chuck wagon races filmed at the Calgary Stampede for the Academy Award-winning Disney movie *Hacksaw*, the outrider loaded a trunk onto the back of the wagon, rather than a stove.[9]

The original chuck wagon, according to tradition, was created by pioneer cowman Charles Goodnight, who took a "government wagon" and had it altered, replacing the wooden axles with iron ones, and adding the chuck box at the rear.[10] The chuck box was widely copied, says Ramon Adams: two to three feet deep and four feet high, it had shelves and drawers covered by the hinged lid. The inside thus resembled a kitchen cabinet, holding some supplies, pots, and simple medical nostrums —including horse liniment for man or beast. With sideboards added to the wagon bed, there was room for sacks of beans and flour, and canned goods.[11]

Not to be forgotten is the "possum belly" or "cooney" (from Spanish *cuna*, cradle), where firewood was carried, or, in treeless areas, "prairie coal"—cow or buffalo chips.[12] It was simply a cowhide stretched beneath the wagon while still green, and filled with rocks to stretch it.

Of course, there was no such thing as a school for cooking for cowboys nor soldiers nor lumberjacks—they just grew. Jack Flynt remembers how his dad, Holbert W. Flynt, back about the turn of the century, got "elevated" to such a position: "They were building the old Orient railroad, down near Alpine, Texas, and Dad was a teamster, running a six-mule scraper. One day the assistant cook didn't show, and somebody had heard Dad tell about how he had learned to barbecue goats from *his* dad—so they put Dad to work as assistant cook. Later, when the cook quit, Dad got the job. Wasn't but about nineteen, but he handled the job for quite a while. He'd boil a hundred pound sack of potatoes at a time, in a 55 gallon drum!"[13]

That railroad crew was lucky, judging by the oft-told tale of the amateur cowboy cook. A version I picked up from a contestant at a rodeo in Odessa, Texas, in 1960 tells of the outfit whose cook had been run off by the sheriff, and no replacement was at hand. So the foreman had the hands draw straws, and the short straw-drawer was elected cook, to serve 'til somebody complained. Well, nobody complained for a good while, and Cosi wasn't too happy in his job—so he started getting careless; but nobody dared complain, since whoever complained had to take the job himself. Finally he got desperate, and dumped a double handful of salt into the beans and served 'em up. One of the boys took a mouthful and nearly strangled. "By God," he hollered, "them's the saltiest beans I ever et!" About then he noticed the cook starting to take off his apron. "But that's jest the way I like 'em!" he concluded. Both the tradition of using substitute cooks and a host of stories arising out of it, "all of them almost too old to bear repeating," are mentioned in *Come and Get It*.[14] I have often been told the same tale—except that the extra ingredient is usually cow manure—a detail that links it with the lumberjack's story found by Barre Toelken in Maine in 1954—both as an oral tale and in the form of a ballad, where the cook-against-his-will served up what *should* have gotten him fired:

> One by one the boys turned green,
> Their eyeballs rolled to and fro;
> Then one guy hollered as he sank to the floor
> "My God, that's moose-turd pie!
> [Shouted] Good, though!'"[15]

Frequently the chuck wagon cook was a stove-up cowboy who could no longer handle regular range chores, but he soon became master of his small, vital kingdom, guarding it jealously from any encroachments. Even the owner of the cattle was expected to stay out of a sixty-foot circle surrounding the wagon.[16] Range etiquette required that a horseman slow his steed when nearing the cook wagon, to avoid stirring up dust—or the cook's temper. The body of the wagon, as Jack Thorp noted, usually carried bedrolls for the hands, but the rest of the rig was the cook's domain. One old timer recalled a double killing that arose out of a cowboy's brashness:

"French and a fellow named Hinton got into it over Hinton digging into the chuck box, which was against Frenchy's rule, as it was with any good cooky. They did not want the waddies messing up the chuck box. Hinton seemed to get a kick out of seeing French get riled. . . . Frenchy never refused to give anyone a handout, but Hinton insisted upon helping himself. The evening that the fight took place, Hinton walked past Frenchy and dove into the chuck box. Frenchy went after Hinton with a carving-knife and Hinton drew his gun. The cooky kept going into Hinton slashing with his knife and Hinton kept backing away shooting all the while, trying to get away from the knife, but French never hesitated . . . ; finally he drove the knife into Hinton's breast and they both went to the ground and died a few minutes after."[17]

The huge coffeepot was the first item to go on the cook's fire when it was built, and generally the last to come off when breaking camp. "Around chuck wagons," says Francis Fugate, "early Westerners renewed their energies with coffee, the aromatic brew that 'quickens the spirit, and makes the heart lightsome.' Chances are that Arbuckles' was the brand in all those coffeepots. In fact, the use of Arbuckle Bros. coffee was so widespread that its brand name came to be synonymous with the word 'coffee'. . . ."[18] The cook (strongly supported by the cowhands) believed in making it stout: "A recipe went the rounds from ranch to ranch, confided by cooks to greenhorn hands: 'You take two pounds of Arbuckles', put in enough water to wet it down, then you boil it for two hours. After that, you throw in a horseshoe. If the shoe sinks, the coffee ain't ready.' "[19] One of the reasons the brand was so popular was the premiums used by John Arbuckle to stimulate sales—and thereby hangs a chuck cook trick: a stick of sugar candy included in each bag lightened the cook's load. "If a cook wanted the next day's supply of coffee ground, he would call out 'Who wants the candy?' and get a rash of volunteers to turn the crank on the coffee grinder, which was inevitably fastened to the side of the chuck wagon."[20]

One of the proofs of the existence of a folk group is a shared language—and the chuck wagon scene had its share of useful terms, far beyond those already cited herein. Jack Thorp, in a list he termed "not finished," recorded a number of these for the New Mexico Federal Writers Project:

```
Air tights..........canned goods
Biscuit-shooter.....a waitress
Chuck..............food of any kind
Dough-gods.........biscuits
Dough-wrangler.....cook
Feed-trough........to eat at a table
Fluff-duffs........fancy food
Frijoles...........beans
Gouch hooks........irons to lift the heavy lids of cooking vessels
Lick...............syrup (or a salt lick)[21]
```

Salt pork went by "'sow belly,' 'hog side,' 'sow bosom,' and 'pig's vest with buttons.' Bacon was often sarcastically referred to as 'fried chicken,' 'chuck wagon chicken,' and 'Kansas City fish.' It was not used to a great extent, because it became rancid in the heat and anyway the cowman preferred fresh meat."[22] Of course there were names for particular dishes, son-of-a-gun stew, for example, which was also called by its more natural, less polite name. Ramon Adams says it was made of practically everything the cook had at hand, excepting "horns, hoof, and hide." And perhaps the name came from the first cowboy who tasted it, and hollered "Sonofabitch, but that's good." But Adams also notes the tendency for an outfit to call the dish by the name of some enemy—"a subtle way of calling him names which one dared not do to his face."[23] The good chuck wagon cook learned to make do with whatever he had. A mixture of sorghum and bacon grease was a substitute for butter, for example,[24] and it was a mighty poor cook who couldn't spice up the usual menu, which was always strong on "meat and whistle-berries [beans]."[25] Dried apples and raisins were staples on many wagons, and they served to make pies—one item cowboys dearly loved. Cosi would roll out his dough with a beer bottle, put it in a greased pie pan and add the previously stewed fruit, then cover it with another layer of dough—with the steam escaping through the outfit's brand cut in the crust.[26] "Spotted pup"—raisin and rice pudding—did pretty well, especially with sugar and cream (when it was available), but as a steady diet it could produce mutiny![27] "Some cooks were expert at making vinegar pies," reports Ramon Adams, concocted of a combination of vinegar, water, fat, and flour, all turned onto a layer of dough in a pie pan, and then covered, cobbler style, with criss-crossed strips of dough and baked.[28] And then there was "pooch"—tomatoes, stewed with left-over biscuits and a little sugar—that cowboys enjoyed as much as dessert.[29] Rather than pack a lunch, a hand would carry a can or two of tomatoes to tide him over if he was going to be gone over the meal hour; they served as both food and drink.[30]

Another side of the grouchy cook—the very one who died defending his turf in the story above—is presented by John Baker:

"The belly-cheater on the Holt outfit was a fellow called Frenchy, a top cooky. He was one of them fellows that took enjoyment out of satisfying the waddies' tapeworm. Frenchy was always pulling some tricks on us waddies and we enjoyed his tricks, because he always made up for the tricks by extra efforts in cooking some dish we hankered after. He could make some of the best puddings I ever shoved into my mouth. One day at supper we were all about done eating and French said: 'If you dam skunks wait a second I'll give you some pudding. It is a little late getting done.' Of course we all waited and he pulled a beauty out of the oven. We all dived into it and took big gobs into our mouths. We then started to make funny faces. What he had done was to use salt instead of sugar when he made it and that pudding tasted like hell. We all began to sputter and spit to clean our mouths. He then pulled a good pudding on us and that sure was a peach. We had forgot that the day was April 1. He would use red pepper on us in some dishes we hankered after, also cotton in biscuits, but we knew something extra was coming up to follow."[31]

The cowboys often cussed the chuck and the cook, and called him names like Vinegar Jim, and Bilious Bill, and Dirty Dave—not to mention some less polite handles.[32] But on a dry drive, when the cowboys were working the clock around to keep the steers moving north, the cook kept open house all night long, with food and Arbuckles' to keep the waddies going; he knew that hardship is easier to bear if the hands are well fed.[33] And on more normal nights, when the cook had put a lighted lantern on the tip of the wagon tongue to guide the night crews back to the outfit, and pointed it towards the North Star to provide bearings for the next day's drive,[34] it was easy to remember that the wagon was home, and the chuck wagon cook—ugly and irascible though he might be—was in some ways the heart and soul of the outfit. Jack Thorp said a bunch when he wrote "when it came to serving up ample and good-tasting food under unfavorable conditions, I never saw anybody to beat the average cow-camp cook."[35] Without him the roundup, the trail drive, and the cattle industry could never have been—and even with the distortions of fact that Hollywood provides, his lore lingers on, relic of a bygone day.

NOTES

[1] Ramon F. Adams, *Come and Get It: The Story of the Old Cowboy Cook* (Norman: University of Oklahoma Press, 1952), 5.
[2] Frank S. Hastings, "Some Glimpses into Ranch Life," History of Grazing in Texas, Division VI, Part A, Steps Toward Stability and Conservation, Texas Writers Project, Barker History Center, The University of Texas at Austin. Unpaginated.
[3] Hastings.
[4] N. Howard Thorp, *Songs of the Cowboys* (Estancia, New Mexico: News Print Shop, 1908).
[5] N. Howard Thorp, "A Chuck Wagon Supper," File 5, Division 4, Folio 3, Folder 5, New Mexico Writers Project, History Library, Museum of New Mexico, Santa Fe, New Mexico. The bread, raisin, and sugar pudding is essentially *capirotada*, a traditional Mexican delicacy served during Lent; Lucina L. Fischer, interview with the author, El Paso, Texas, 12 December 1984.
[6] Bob Kennon as told to Ramon W. Adams, *From the Pecos to the Powder: A Cowboy's Autobiography* (Norman: University of Oklahoma Press, 1965), 36.
[7] Kennon/Adams, 82-83.
[8] Glen Ohrlin, *The Hell-Bound Train: A Cowboy Songbook* (Urbana: University of Illinois Press, 1973), 213.
[9] Larry Lansburgh, Producer/Director, *Hacksaw*, Walt Disney Productions, 1971.
[10] J. Evetts Haley, *Charles Goodnight: Cowman and Plainsman* (Boston: Houghton Mifflin, 1936), 121, qtd. in Adams, 11.
[11] Adams, 12-13.
[12] Adams, 14-15.
[13] Jack Flynt, interview with the author, El Paso, Texas, 23 November, 1984.
[14] Adams, 155-156.
[15] J. Barre Toelken, *The Dynamics of Folklore* (Boston: Houghton Mifflin, 1979), 66-67, 179-180.
[16] Adams, 5-6.
[17] John J. Baker, "Ft. Worth Texas Narrative," Fort Worth History Notes, Folder 68: Interviews, Texas Writers Project, Barker History Center, The University of Texas at Austin, 26856-26857.
[18] Francis L. Fugate, "Arbuckles': The Coffee That Won the West,"*American West* 21, No. 1 (January-February 1984):61.
[19] Fugate, 62.
[20] Fugate, 63.
[21] N. Howard Thorp, "Cowland Glossary," File 5, Division 4, Folio 3, Folder 6, New Mexico Writers Project, History Library, Museum of New Mexico, Santa Fe, New Mexico.
[22] Adams, 111.

[23] Adams, 91-92.
[24] Adams, 116.
[25] Baker, 26830.
[26] Adams, 103-104.
[27] Kennon/Adams, 87.
[28] Adams, 105.
[29] Adams, 111.
[30] Adams, 110.
[31] Baker, 26855.
[32] Kennon/Adams, 82-87.
[33] Andy Adams, *The Log of a Cowboy: A Narrative of the Old Trail Days* (Boston: Houghton Mifflin, 1903, 1931), 60.
[34] Ramon Adams, 154.
[35] N. Howard Thorp in collaboration with Neil M. Clark, *Pardner of the Wind* (Caldwell, Idaho: Caxton Printers, 1945), 270.

REFERENCES

Adams, Andy.
   1903   *The Log of a Cowboy: A Narrative of the Old Trail Days.* Boston:
   1931   Houghton Mifflin.
Adams, Ramon F.
   1952   *Come and Get It: The Story of the Old Cowboy Cook.* Norman: University of Oklahoma Press.
Baker, John J.
   "Ft. Worth Texas Narrative." Fort Worth History Notes. Texas Writers Project. Barker History Center, The University of Texas at Austin, Austin, Texas.
Fugate, Francis L.
   1984   "Arbuckles': The Coffee That Won the West." *American West* 21, No. 1 (January/February 1984), 61-68.
Haley, J. Evetts.
   1936   *Charles Goodnight: Cowman and Plainsman.* Boston: Houghton Mifflin.
Hastings, Frank S.
   "Some Glimpses into Ranch Life." History of Grazing in Texas. Texas Writers Project. Barker History Center. The University of Texas at Austin, Austin, Texas.
Kennon, Bob, as told to Ramon W. Adams.
   1965   *From the Pecos to the Powder: A Cowboy's Autobiography.* Norman: University of Oklahoma Press.
Lansburgh, Larry, Producer/Director.
   1971   *Hacksaw.* Tab Hunter, Susan Bracken, George Barrows, and Russ McCubbin. Walt Disney Productions.
Ohrlin, Glenn.
   1973   *The Hell-Bound Train: A Cowboy Songbook.* Urbana: University of Illinois Press.

Thorp, N. Howard.
    "Cowland Glossary." New Mexico Writers Project. History Library, Museum of New Mexico, Santa Fe, New Mexico.
    "A Chuck Wagon Supper," New Mexico Writers Project, History Library, Museum of New Mexico, Santa Fe, New Mexico.
  1908 *Songs of the Cowboys*. Estancia, New Mexico: News Print Shop.
Thorp, N. Howard, in collaboration with Neil M. Clark.
  1945 *Pardner of the Wind*. Caldwell, Idaho: Caxton Printers.
Toelken, J. Barre.
  1979 *The Dynamics of Folklore*. Boston: Houghton Mifflin.